D0983724

FREEDOM OF THE PRESS FOR WHOM?

THE RIGHT OF ACCESS TO MASS MEDIA

FREEDOM OF THE

THE RIGHT OF

PRESS FOR WHOM?

ACCESS TO MASS MEDIA

JEROME A. BARRON

Indiana University Press / *Bloomington* / *London*

Published in Canada by Fitzhenry & Whiteside Limited,
Don Mills, Ontario

Library of Congress catalog card number: 72–75387

ISBN: 0–253–12840–4

Manufactured in the United States of America

TO MY PARENTS

CONTENTS

Contents

PREFACE

In the middle sixties, after a period of teaching and study-ing problems of free expression and communications, I became increasingly dissatisfied with the failure of our law to provide any right of public access for ideas. It struck me that our law was backwards. It was designed to protect speakers and writers from the fury of either the mob or the state—those who somehow had managed to express themselves.

But in the era of mass communication, the words of the soli-tary speaker or the lonely writer, however brave or imaginative, have little impact unless they are broadcast through the great en-gines of public opinion—radio, television, and the press.

The major obstacle to freedom of expression in America is the difficulty of penetrating the media in a serious rather than a bizarre way. In the May 1967 *Harvard Law Review*, I advocated a positive interpretation of the First Amendment which would provide and require access to the media.

The legal and social climate was readier to respond than I had dreamed. The suggestion that the law permitted, even re-quired, imposing affirmative obligations on the mass media ran against the grain of traditional constitutional theory, which held that the government is the only censor to be feared. The role of private censorship was not considered. Support for opening up the media came from unexpected sources. In 1968, the Ameri-can Civil Liberties Union, a bastion of the traditional approach to First Amendment problems, devoted part of its biennial ses-sion to considering the affirmative obligations of government in the First Amendment field.

A breakthrough came first in the broadcast rather than the print media. In 1969, the Supreme Court held that freedom of expression in broadcasting had to mean something other than the right of broadcasters to broadcast whatever they pleased and exclude whomever they wished. In choosing between the proprietorship rights of the media owners and the participation and information rights of the public, the Court chose the latter. The access resolution was given judicial recognition in a single sentence which inaugurates a new right: "It is the right of the public to receive suitable access to social, political, esthetic, moral, and other ideas and experience which is crucial here."

Two years later, in June 1971, a Supreme Court opinion supported by three justices acknowledged for the first time the need for access to the print media. "Constitutional adjudication," said Justice Brennan for the Court, "must take into account the individual's interest in access to the press."

This book chronicles the struggle to open the media. It states the case for access. The basic premise is that our communications policy is presently in the grip of a romantic conception of free individual expression, an assumption that the marketplace of ideas is freely accessible. But "laissez faire" economic theory is inadequate and unsuitable to govern the interplay of ideas in American life. Private censorship characterizes both the print and the broadcast media. Dissatisfaction with the performance of the media spans the political spectrum, from Herbert Marcuse to Spiro Agnew. Efforts of dissenting groups on both the left and the right to secure something as fundamental and simple as advertising space in their community newspapers are often futile. Similar problems exist in securing broadcast time. This book's basic argument is that the First Amendment should be restored to its true proprietors—the reader, the viewer, the listener. Freedom of the press must be something more than a guarantee of the property rights of media owners.

The rise in court decisions and FCC proceedings supporting access to the media is set forth; a core idea is that the privately-controlled media have a responsibility to provide opportunity for expression. Also portrayed are new ways of broadening public participation in the media through law and technology; citizen groups are now regularly challenging renewals of existing television station licensees across the country, and some, like Nicholas Johnson of the FCC, are working to change the regulatory process from within.

The cost and complication of communications technology, combined with the concentration of ownership, increasingly limits the marketplace of ideas. A new theory of freedom of the press is essential to restore public dialogue, especially for those large segments of the people who are now distrustful of and alienated by the media.

I use the idea, *opening up*, in two senses. First, I probe American mass communication in a critical analysis of how the media presently function. Second, I show the new public pressures for greater participation in the media and describe the means by which greater public access to the media can be achieved.

I would like to thank my friend Professor Arthur Miller for encouraging me in this project as in many others. A note of thanks is due to Dean Edward Potts of the National Law Center, George Washington University, for his help in this as in so much else. Finally, many thanks are owed to Mrs. Linda Frank for the patience, skill, and care with which she typed the manuscript.

To my wife, Myra, and my children, Jonathan, David, and Jennifer—my thanks for the love that made the writing go faster.

JEROME A. BARRON
Washington, D.C.

FREEDOM OF THE PRESS FOR WHOM?

THE RIGHT OF ACCESS TO MASS MEDIA

1 /

Access to the Press

Introduction

THE FALL OF 1971 SAW A MAYORALTY ELECTION CONTEST IN Daytona Beach, Florida, between incumbent Richard Kane and challenger James Huger, a City Commissioner. The city's only daily newspapers, the Daytona Beach *News Journal* (morning and evening edition), endorsed Huger against Mayor Kane. The *News Journal*'s political editor, Ray Ruester, wrote a column entitled "Kane City Hall Power Grab," which Mayor Kane felt attacked his personal character as well as his record. He asked for space to reply. The *News Journal* refused.[1]

The events recorded above are not unusual. Dailies in communities without newspaper competition often support one political candidate and ignore his opponents. Neither is it unusual for a newspaper to assume unlimited discretion over what it chooses to print. In fact, the *News Journal*'s behavior was not completely unfair to Kane: it had printed Kane's response to an earlier editorial attacking him. Further, the reply which Kane wanted published had appeared earlier in a biweekly shoppers' guide.

3

The unusual thing about the Daytona Beach situation is that the *News Journal's* editor, Herbert R. Davidson, was arrested for failure to publish Kane's reply. Refusal to publish a reply under such circumstances is a misdemeanor under the Florida law.[2]

Editor Herbert Davidson refused to comply with the law because he contends that Kane's reply was not a true reply and that the Florida law violates freedom of the press. Questions about the Florida right of reply law have been raised, but its constitutionality had never been squarely tested.

In the early part of 1972, a county judge in Daytona Beach dismissed the complaint against editor Davidson on the ground that the Florida right of reply statute was unconstitutional. To the regret of both the Daytona Beach *News Journal* and the parties seeking reply, the county prosecutor did not appeal the decision and thus robbed American law and journalism of a full-dress consideration of the constitutionality of a state right of reply statute by a state supreme court.

Though the Florida statute is unusual among state laws, it raises a problem which is far from unique. Does forcing a newspaper to print a reply from a victim of one of its own attacks implement or violate freedom of the press?

In the contemporary life of ideas, the victories and defeats of politics and the fortunes of intensely important social issues are resolved in the mass media—the daily press and the television networks. Our constitutional guarantee of freedom of press is equipped to deal with direct and crude governmental assaults on freedom of expression, but is incapable of responding to the more subtle challenge of securing admission for ideas to the dominant media. In general, it seems that ideas are denied media space and time unless they come in the carnival attire of the violent or the bizarre. Conventional free press theory is a barrier to the admission of ideas to the media. The media owners and managers have astutely identified the constitutional guarantee of freedom of the press with themselves. They read freedom of the press as an immunity from accountability and any kind of legal responsibility.

The consequences of this interpretation must be seen against the background of two communications revolutions within a century. One is the revolution of technology which has brought the television screen, the radio voice, and the magazine and newspaper page within the reach of every person. Accompanying the rise of media saturation has been the concentration of control in ever fewer hands. Not surprisingly, another revolution has followed, an economic revolution that has placed with fewer and fewer persons the power to decide whatever larger and larger numbers shall see, hear, and read. The two revolutions together have bred a new class—the media managers.

The rise of the media managers has until recently gone unnoticed. One reason for the lack of public interest has been the myth of the free press which has lumped together the fighting colonial printer-editor John Peter Zenger and the modern newspaper chains and media conglomerates. The myth says that if the press is kept "free," liberty of discussion is assured. But, in how few hands is left the exercise of "freedom"!

Another reason for the lack of public interest has been that the media managers have not tried to put over any disturbing ideas. The media exist to sell commodities. Their sustenance is advertising and advertising is by and large their ideology. Indifference to politics has contributed to the stability of media power; determined blandness has given no occasion for governmental or public scrutiny. But blandness as operating editorial policy fails in a time dominated by social problems that are not bland. Reporting of the nation's torment over bitterly contested social, national, and international issues revives interest in the media and the way that admission to them is obtained.

The relentless effort by the disaffected and the disadvan-

5

taged to find ever more unsettling forms of protest is an attempt to obtain by drama that free entry into the media which is denied to polite or conventional requests.

The German theologian Paul Tillich said that when he first came to this country, he frequently encountered a question never asked in Europe. After discussing the human situation the American students would ask: what shall we do? Access to the press as a legal right suggested one practical answer, as well as a positive counter to the problem of concentration of ownership and control in the media. This chapter chronicles the development of access to the media as a theme in American communications policy, one which I first set out in 1967.[3]

Newspapers and other media now enjoy a larger freedom from libel judgments than they have in the past. In the Warren Court's view of the First Amendment, the law of libel was a barrier to the robust and vigorous social and public criticism which the First Amendment existed to assure. Curtailing that law began slowly in 1964 with a case that made it very difficult for an elected public official to recover against a newspaper for libel.[4] By 1971, the Supreme Court precluded even a private plaintiff from recovery in libel against the media if the controversy involved a public issue.[5] The only small area where the libel law yet lived was in those cases where the media deliberately misrepresented the public issue in controversy. If the newspaper story was published in good faith and involved a public issue, the newspaper was home free. Thus the media are freer to criticize and less obligated to be fair than ever before.

At the very minimum, the creation of two remedies is essential—(1) a nondiscriminatory right to purchase editorial advertisements in daily newspapers, and (2) a right of reply for public figures and public officers defamed in newspapers. These remedies could be instituted by either judicial or legislative action.

6

They represent the very least of what ought to be done to broaden public participation in the press.

"Heed Their Rising Voices"—
The Rise of the Editorial Advertisement

To explain what an editorial advertisement is and to indicate the intensity of the need for a right of reply in American journalism, let us consider one of the most famous recent cases in the American law of freedom of expression.

On March 29, 1960, a full page editorial advertisement appeared in the *New York Times* under the headline "Heed Their Rising Voices." The ad supported the southern Negro use of nonviolent demonstrations to affirm constitutional rights and recounted the campaign of terror against participating southern Negro college students. The ad was signed by sixty-four persons, including Harry Belafonte, Marlon Brando, Sidney Poitier, A. Philip Randolph, and Mrs. Eleanor Roosevelt.

An elected official, L. B. Sullivan, one of three elected commissioners of the city of Montgomery, Alabama, contended that two paragraphs in the advertisement libeled him. One stated that after the students had sung "My Country, 'tis of Thee" at the State Capitol, student leaders were expelled from school and "truckloads of police armed with shotguns and tear-gas ringed the Alabama State College campus." The ad went on to say that the entire student body at Alabama State College protested by refusing to reregister at the college and that state authorities then locked the college dining room to starve the students into submission.

The other offending paragraph said that "Southern violators" had intimidated Dr. Martin Luther King:

They have bombed his home almost killing his wife and child. They have assaulted his person. They have arrested him

7

seven times—for "speeding," "loitering" and similar "of-
fences." And now they have charged him with perjury, a *fel-
ony* under which they would imprison him for *ten* years.

Before suing the *Times*, Commissioner Sullivan wrote to demand a public retraction. The *Times* reasonably asked, How are
you libeled? Conceding that the ad did not mention him by
name, Sullivan noted that among his duties was supervision of
the Montgomery police so that anything that reflected adversely
on the police reflected on him. Charges that students had been
beaten into submission, that the Alabama State College campus
had been ringed with police, and that Dr. King's home had been
bombed and his person assaulted, all reflected adversely on him,
yet many of the events had occurred before he was elected.

Other statements in the ad, he said, were simply inaccurate.
The students had not refused to register, the college dining
room had never been padlocked, and the police had never
"ringed" the campus. The intimidation of Dr. King occurred before Commissioner Sullivan's tenure.

The ad in the *Times* cost the group which had purchased it
$4,800. The *Times'* Advertising Acceptability Department had
not attempted to verify the facts in the ad, because, the manager
said, the ad carried the names of well-known people whose reputation he "had no reason to question."

Sullivan filed suit in the Alabama trial court, which awarded
$500,000 in damages to him. Sullivan's suit against the *Times*
was not the only libel suit generated by the editorial advertisement. Another $500,000 verdict had been awarded against the
Times. Damages sought in three other Alabama cases were
$2,000,000.

As a matter of law, Sullivan's libel case was conventional
enough. Newspapers should respond in damages when they assert charges against someone which contain false and defama-

tory statements. Conventional law was that a public official could recover damages for libel if a jury thought a publication tended to injure his reputation or brought him into contempt as a public official. A newspaper could survive a libel judgment only if what it had published was true and if it was published with good or justifiable motives. Under these facts and under this law, the *New York Times* was in trouble, particularly since its own files would have disproved some of the allegations of the advertisement.

But the *New York Times* responded novelly, arguing that awarding a libel judgment under these facts was a violation of the constitutional guarantee of freedom of the press. Why? Libel judgments had been obtained by public officials before and after the enactment of the First Amendment. But the *Times* contended that the central meaning of the First Amendment's guarantee of freedom of the press was to permit criticism of government. The old common law crime of seditious libel, designed to punish criticism of existing government, had been hateful to the draftsmen of the Constitution.

If the *Times* couldn't inferentially criticize a government official like Sullivan without risking $500,000 in damages, free press and free debate would be the sure losers. After all, the *Times*' only gain from publishing "Heed Their Rising Voices" was $4,800 for the ad and the subscription fees of the something more than 300 papers that it sold in the state of Alabama. The risk to which it was exposed as a result, on the other hand, was in the millions. The Supreme Court of the United States accepted the *Times*' argument and held that in the case of a public official suing a newspaper for libel, it would henceforth be more difficult to obtain a libel judgment—not impossible but more difficult. The libel plaintiff would have to show that what was printed by the offending newspaper was printed with malice. By malice, the Court meant that which was printed with reckless disregard of the truth or falsity of what was said. The Court believed that the interest of an informed public demanded that newspapers should not have to live in fear of oppressive libel judgments. Newspapers should not hesitate to publish matters of vital interest to the public because sufficient time to secure verification was lacking. Fundamentally, the Court held that unless it could be shown that a newspaper either deliberately lied or did not care whether it was deliberately lying, public officials could no longer recover damages for press criticism.

The lawyers for Sullivan argued that freedom of the press was not really involved in the case, since commercial advertising did not warrant constitutional protection. The Supreme Court had held in 1942 that regulation of the distribution of commercial advertising on the streets of New York was permissible.[6] The Court responded that "Heed Their Rising Voices" was not a commercial advertisement but an editorial advertisement, a distinction of great importance:

> Any other conclusion would discourage newspapers from carrying "editorial advertisements" of this type, and so might shut off an important outlet for the promulgation of information and ideas by persons who do not themselves have access to publishing facilities—who wish to exercise their freedom of speech even though they are not members of the press.

These remarks on the importance of editorial advertisements are intriguing. They suggest some sensitivity to the access problems of the public. Of course, the use of the editorial advertisement as an outlet for dissent and protest is more common today than in 1964 when "Heed Their Rising Voices" was published by the *Times*.[7]

In some respects the *Times* case is helpful in the effort to build at least one truly open section in newspapers—the advertising pages. The case can be read as saying that responsibility for the content of the editorial advertisement is with the ad's sponsors and authors rather than with the paper. In broadcasting, if a broadcaster once permits a political candidate to use his facilities, there is a duty to allow other legally qualified political candidates for that office equal opportunities if they so request.[8] If, after having requested time, such a candidate libels someone, the station has no legal responsibility.[9] That seems eminently just. If a paper or a station must give time, it would hardly be equitable if it was subject to libel suits because of irresponsible statements then made. But notice the difference in the case of newspapers. The *Times* is not instructed that it has a duty to take an editorial advertisement. The *Times* is told only that if it does take an editorial advertisement to serve the interests of public debate and criticism of government, the newspaper may not be sued for libel so easily as in the past. Newspapers are thus given an inducement to be hospitable to dissent and controversy, but are placed under no obligation to print dissent or to voice any opinion whatever.

The *New York Times* case is bewildering. It is an example of judicial law making; but it is incomplete law making. On the surface, the decision appears quite attractive. Freeing newspapers from libel suits brought by public men enables people in a state like Alabama, where the press was generally segregationist, to see another point of view. Similarly, the general cause of public scrutiny of officialdom seems to have been advanced. But unfortunately, the Supreme Court opinion interpreted problems of freedom of the press only as a need for new newspaper immunities. Nothing is said about new newspaper responsibilities.

Justice Brennan's words in *New York Times v. Sullivan* are now famous in the literature of free expression:

Thus we consider this case against the background of profound national commitment to the principle that debate on public issues, should be uninhibited, robust and wide-open, and that it may well include vehement, caustic and sometimes unpleasantly sharp attacks on government and public officials.[10]

But has the national commitment to debate been advanced? What about the elected public official? Is he to be permitted to enter the debate? How does he secure access? The assumption is that newspaper freedom from libel will encourage debate. Newspaper publishers' interests and the public interest are held to be identical. But until publication of editorial advertisement is a legal right and until a right of reply to those whom newspapers attack is also legally required, the assumptions of *New York Times* will appear romantic and lopsidedly pro-publisher.

The signatories of "Heed Their Rising Voices" decided to bring pressure on a local injustice through publication of an editorial advertisement in a national newspaper. But surely a most important factor in all this is that local access to local media to reach the local population is a very difficult and presently unresolved problem in the United States. In the next chapter, we will discuss an example of access to the *local* press.

2 /

Freedom of the Press,

Chicago Style

A STRIKING EFFORT TO CREATE A LEGAL RIGHT OF PUBLIC access to the press occurred recently in Chicago involving a labor union's attempt to buy an ad.

Chicago has four daily newspapers today but only two owners. Field Enterprises owns both the Chicago *Sun-Times* and the Chicago *Daily News*. The Chicago Tribune Company owns the *Chicago Tribune* as well as *Chicago Today*. In 1946 there were five independently-owned daily newspapers in Chicago. The four survivors have a total circulation of 2,220,000.

The Amalgamated Clothing Workers of America wanted to persuade the people of Chicago that the retail sale of imported men's and boys' clothing jeopardized the job security of American workers. To focus attention on the most important and prestigious offender, the union picketed the Marshall Field department store in downtown Chicago. The union was promoting an idea as well as the usual bread and butter issue of higher wages or shorter hours; it sought public support for the principle that countries exporting to the United States should observe voluntary quotas. The union contended that as long as large department stores like Marshall Field bought and sold imported clothing without restriction, foreign nations are not likely to limit their exports voluntarily.

The union prepared an advertisement for submission to the four Chicago dailies. It was entitled, "You bet we're picketing Marshall Field & Co.," and said in part:

> Marshall Field & Company and other retailers insist on carrying, in ever-increasing amounts, foreign made clothing, produced overseas (in some cases by 14 and 15 year old girls) and produced by those being paid as little as 8 cents an hour in Hong Kong to as low as 50 cents an hour in Europe. Our people have fought for decent wages and a decent standard of living.
>
> We've been called the largest employer of minority groups in the nation. If it were not for the hundreds of thousands of jobs in the apparel field, where would our people go for jobs?

All four Chicago dailies rejected the ad. To justify its action, the *Chicago Tribune* referred to a sentence in its "Advertising Acceptability Guide":

> The *Tribune* does not accept advertising which, in its judgment, contains attacks of a personal, racial or religious nature, or which reflects unfavorably on competitive organizations, institutions, or merchandise.

In an affidavit, the advertising manager said that "unfavorable treatment of a retailer was unfair and would be misleading to readers of the *Chicago Tribune* and *Chicago Today*."

Field Enterprises rejected the advertisement on the ground that their papers did not print statements naming others unless those others consented to their names being used. Shortly afterward, the same Chicago dailies printed a full page advertisement by the Building Construction Employees' Association which accused by name the Coalition for United Community Action, a black organization, of turning down an industry offer to open up four thousand construction industry jobs to blacks. Lawyers for the coalition contended that no one had asked it for consent to use its name.

The advertising directors of American newspapers thus exercise a powerful private censorship. Traditionally we associate censorship with government: we call the decision of private individuals to publish or not to publish an exercise of freedom of choice, freedom of expression, editorial discretion, or other attractive phrases. This position assumes that there are enough publishers so that any idea can get published somewhere. But two corporations have the power to shut off access to the daily press of Chicago.

The Amalgamated Clothing Workers Chicago local decided to challenge this interpretation of freedom of the press and filed a suit in federal court asking that the four Chicago dailies be permanently enjoined from refusing to publish the union ad. The federal district judge in Chicago, Abraham Marovitz, ruled for the newspapers and against the union.[1] The constitutional guarantee of freedom of the press, he ruled, is directed to governmental restraints on the press and does not apply to publishers and private censorship.

Judge Marovitz conceded that the constitutional obligation to permit freedom of expression had been applied in recent years to privately owned facilities. The Supreme Court, for example, has said that pickets cannot be banished from suburban shopping centers merely because the shopping centers are privately owned. But, the judge argued, newspapers in the Chicago case were different because "no other private industry or organization has been afforded any protection similar to that granted under the First Amendment." The judge went on to say, with unintended humor, that the only other industry ever given specific and special treatment in the Constitution was the liquor industry, through the Eighteenth Amendment which introduced prohibition—but fourteen years later that had been repealed by the Twenty-first Amendment.

The implication appears to be that before the newspapers could be made more open, the First Amendment would have to be repealed. Judge Marovitz said that there is no interdependence between government and newspapers and that the press is not inherently governmental. There is, he said, "no American equivalent to Izvestia and Pravda." That is true. But the press does not have to be a department of the state to perform a governmental function.

Freedom to publish, not freedom to censor, is guaranteed by the First Amendment. Freedom of the press exists, as Justice Louis Brandeis put it more than forty years ago, to aid in the "discovery and spread of political truth." Freedom of the press is guaranteed in order that the people may have sufficient information to participate intelligently as self-governing members in a democratic order.

Perhaps, with the current deluge of facts and propaganda, an informed public opinion is no longer possible. If so, democracy is not possible either. I prefer to think that it is possible, but it certainly requires that the public, through newspapers and broadcasts, have access to all shades of opinion.

In refusing to recognize a right of access in the Chicago newspaper cases, Judge Marovitz did not argue that the remedy as applied to the press was inflexible. Indeed, he said that access was easier to achieve in the press than in broadcasting:

> If a right of access existed with regard to newspapers, compliance with the rule would be simpler than it is for broadcasters, for a newspaper is relatively flexible and expandable. The defect in [the union's case] is that no such rule exists.

So, by failing to give an affirmative reading to the guarantee of freedom of the press, the Federal District Court in Chicago refused to create a right of access by judicial means. But the judge seemed to hint that if the legislature were to pass a right of access statute, he might view the question more sympathetically. If concentration of private media power is in fact "stultifying," the proper mode of relief, said Judge Marovitz (using the language of my Harvard paper), is "experimental, innovative legislation." But, in fact, my argument is that relief can and should be sought through the courts as well.

The labor union appealed to the Federal Court of Appeals, which affirmed the district court decision.[2] The union counsel argued valiantly that monopoly power in an area of immense social concern should be considered the equivalent of government action. Judge Castle, who wrote the federal opinion, seemed baffled by the union's argument that the Chicago daily newspaper market was a monopoly. Were there not four daily newspapers? But the power of the two corporate ownerships was enough to keep the union's case from the public. Monopoly power was in fact at work.

The Supreme Court declined to review the Chicago newspaper case,[3] and so has not yet directly passed on whether the courts can command access to the press. (But in a later opinion, the Supreme Court suggests that both the legislatures and the courts may ultimately be able to do just that.[4])

Journalist and access critic, Gilbert Cranberg, writing on the Chicago newspaper case in the *Saturday Review*, concluded, "The weakest link in the right of access argument is the lack of state action in the operation of newspapers." [5] He was critical of the argument that the newspapers' special mailing privileges amounted to a subsidy by taxpayers. Cranberg asked whether the taxpayers, by bearing the excess cost over the amount actually paid by newspapers, were acting to benefit newspapers or acting to benefit themselves as newspaper subscribers? A better example of governmental involvement with the press, sufficient in Cranberg's opinion to indicate state action, was demonstrated by the passage by Congress of the Newspaper Preservation Act in the summer of 1970.[6] In it Congress specifically exempted joint operating agreements among newspapers from the anti-trust laws. The Act made it possible for two newspapers in a community to share facilities and to establish joint advertising rates. This made it even harder financially for any new entrant to enter a community where such an agreement was in force. Should this kind of extraordinary governmental aid impose new responsibilities? If government can legislate to benefit the press, can it not also legislate to benefit the readership?

Cranberg showed more intellectual integrity than has the American Newspaper Publishers Association, which backed the Newspaper Preservation Act but hardly supports a right of access to the press. Cranberg's position was admirably simple: the press should not expect to receive special immunities from government without expecting to bear new responsibilities.

Berkeley law professor Stephen Barnett had testified to the same effect at the Senate hearings on the failing newspaper act. Barnett warned that by insisting on legislative aid in the matter of antitrust relief, publishers might well provide a legal basis for the enactment of right of access legislation.[7]

Antiestablishment journalist Nicholas von Hoffman turned his vitriolic pen on the Newspaper Preservation Act.[8] He pointed out that the Agnew anxieties about concentration of ownership in broadcasting were not reflected in the Nixon administration's support for a law which allowed over forty newspapers in more than a score of cities legally "to rig prices, divide markets and pool profits in the grand tradition of John D. Rockefeller." [9] He justly ridiculed the justification offered for the bill that without it the financially weaker newspapers in applicable cities would fail. He pointed out that the beneficiaries of the legislation included such "failing" journalistic enterprises as the Scripps-Howard, Knight, Hearst, and Newhouse communications chains.

Most relevant to our purposes, however, is the argument offered by supporters of the Newspaper Preservation Act, that if two newspapers in the same city were not permitted to pool facilities, rising costs would cause the smaller paper to die with the loss to the public of a competing editorial page. In the context of the Chicago newspaper decision, this argument boomerangs on the publishers. If passage of the failing newspaper act was rooted in a concern that as many communities as possible should continue to have two editorial pages to read, then the Newspaper Preservation Act is federal legislation designed to provide for diversity of opinion. But if Congress has constitutional power to enact legislation to encourage diversity of viewpoint in the press, then Congress can enact legislation to give readers rights of access to the press. The scope of legislation to assure diversity of expression cannot fairly or logically be limited to serving the interests of publishers to the exclusion of the interests of the newspaper public.

It remains to be seen whether an access argument can be successful against a newspaper benefiting from the Newspaper Preservation Act because such a paper has sufficient governmental aid to be obligated not to restrain opinion. What is clear is that federal legislation with regard to the press is not so unheard of as publishers sometimes forgetfully suggest.

Judge Castle included in his Federal Court of Appeals opinion in the Chicago newspaper case a familiar litany: "Newspaper publishers clearly are not engaged in the exercise of any governmental function, nor do they process or exercise any delegated power of a governmental nature." Judge Castle delivered his opinion on December 17, 1970. The Newspaper Preservation Act had become law on July 24, 1970.

Despite the glowing respect paid to freedom of the press and its public benefits in judicial reports, a hard-boiled view of the decision in the Chicago newspaper case is that property is the indispensable prerequisite to the exercise of that great freedom: those who do not own the press have no rights to it. Judge Castle stated the case with harsh honesty: "The Union's right to free speech does not give it the right to make use of the defendants' printing presses and distribution systems without the defendants' consent." In a society which otherwise is a blend of the private and public, is this degree of press absolutism acceptable or tolerable?

The new pressure for access to the press revealed by the union effort in Chicago has been duplicated elsewhere in the country. At Wisconsin State University, Whitewater, a valiant effort by a small group of faculty and students to establish a right to buy an ad to protest the Vietnam War was finally successful in the federal courts in Wisconsin.[10] What is the reaction of the newspaper industry to these developments?

The February 3, 1970, issue of the *Bulletin* of the Minnesota Newspaper Association is instructive on this point. Discussing the Chicago and Wisconsin access cases, the *Bulletin* reminds its publisher members that they still have an absolute right to refuse advertising:

> (The only postscript we have added to this is a warning never to be drawn into discussions why—such as you want to protect your local merchants—you're turning down an ad.) The right was again affirmed December 19 in Chicago when a judge there dismissed a suit against several Chicago dailies by a clothing workers' union. The four newspapers had refused an ad advising people not to buy imported clothing at Marshall Field & Co.

Why does a state publishers' association urge that the basis for publishing decisions not be articulated? Presumably because if the publisher makes it clear that he does not like the political or social philosophy expressed, the decision not to publish begins to look like what in fact it is—censorship.

The contemporary passion of the daily press is not with ideas but with profits. Desire to protect local merchants is often a desire to protect newspaper advertising revenue. The fact that the local merchant may be involved in a controversy suffused with social and political issues seems irrelevant against profit-loss considerations. If government acts to someone's disadvantage, it is a basic principle of due process that the standards by which the government acts should be articulated. When newspapers act to someone's disadvantage, there are presently no clear standards for appeal or restitution, at least none generally publicized or consistently followed.

There is a contradiction in the press position that as a private body it is incapable of censorship, or immune from the imposition of constitutional duties. We have seen that the press is not nearly so inviolately private as it pretends. Newspapers have been granted tax exemptions and mailing privileges not enjoyed by other individuals, organizations, or businesses. The newspapers argue on the one hand that if one doesn't like newspaper editorial or publishing practices, the dissenter should go elsewhere. But the law makes that rather difficult to do, at least in Chicago where the Municipal Code has a very interesting provision: "Nothing shall be exhibited, offered or sold from newspaper stands except daily newspapers printed and published in the city." Even if one managed to place an ad in a suburban daily, that paper could not by law be purchased in the streets of Chicago. The media lords often reply to their critics: "Well, if the audience doesn't like it, it can always go someplace else." —Not if the media lords can help it.

Freedom of the Press for Whom?

A Judicial Solution for Access to the Press?

As indicated by the foregoing account of the struggle for access to the press by the Amalgamated Clothing Workers Union, one way to bring diversity into the American daily press would be through judicial creation of a right of access. Advertising space, a traditionally "open" section of the newspaper, would appear to be the most logical place to start.

The present law on the matter is clear. Except for legal notices, newspaper publishers are under no duty to publish anything. They are under no duty to accept advertisements. Yet the courts can be useful in this area and in fact have been. Over fifty years ago, an Ohio lower court held that community dependence on the only local newspaper placed on such a paper a duty to permit the purchase of nondiscriminatory advertising by members of the public.[11]

In that case, a merchant contended that some competitors had influenced the newspaper to refuse to accept his advertisements, and that the Crescent Publishing Company, which published the paper, was a quasi-public corporation and as such it must treat its customers in a nondiscriminatory fashion. Private persons and companies have absolute power to accept or reject the offer made by the other. Not so businesses which are quasi-public; they are affected with a public interest and have a duty to deal with the public on a nondiscriminatory basis. Examples of such quasi-public concerns, said the court, were railroads, street railways, gas and water companies, and telephone companies. Usually they hold a monopoly in a community. It is that position which has caused the law to place a greater obligation on them to provide service than is expected of less essential enterprises. Quasi-public concerns are not free to pick and choose among their customers. This does not mean that they have to deal with everyone. It does mean that they have to apply the same standards to everyone. The court granted the merchant a mandatory injunction requiring the newspaper to publish his ads.

The foregoing case compared a monopoly newspaper with a common carrier or a public utility. It is not an analogy which has met with much favor in succeeding battles for access. In Battle Creek, Michigan, the Eastown movie theatre's advertising was refused by the only daily newspaper in that community of 125,000, the *Enquirer and News*. The movie theatre owner said he had complied with all the rules of the paper with regard to advertising, including the usual fee. The Michigan Supreme Court held that the newspaper business was a "strictly private enterprise" and that the newspaper publisher "is under no legal obligation to sell advertising to all who would buy it." [12]

The owner of the Eastown theatre emphasized his dependence for advertising in the only newspaper in his community, arguing that because of the paper's monopoly in the community it was clothed with a public interest. The paper was the chief source in Battle Creek and vicinity for local and national news, weather reports, news of government proceedings, notices of bids for public contracts, rates of taxation, and many other legal and public notices, some required to be published by Michigan law. Finally, the *Enquirer and News* was the sole outlet for commercial advertising for many business houses in the area.

The most serious objection of the theatre owner was that the advertising of all the other local movie theatres was accepted but not his. The Battle Creek decision did show some judicial disapproval of the "public be damned" philosophy of many newspaper publishers. A dissenting judge on the Michigan Supreme Court, Justice Adams, sharply disagreed with the proposition that newspaper publishers have an absolute right to contract or refuse to contract with anyone as they see fit. Such a ruling could be used, he said, to deny political candidates and local governmental units a "right to insist upon access to newspaper coverage when a newspaper controls the sole means of daily paid printed communication within a given area." Justice Adams preferred to base a right of access not on the First Amendment but rather on an advertiser's right to nondiscriminatory treatment by the only newspaper in town.

The *Enquirer and News* accepted advertisements for adult movies being shown in Battle Creek. Before the suit, the complaining Eastown theatre's advertisements had been published for a while. But then the Eastown Theatre was told that no more of its ads would be accepted, ostensibly on the ground that they contained suggestive or prurient material. The paper claimed that the theatre's advertising required too much editorial work by its staff. This action by the paper provoked the suit by Eastown Theatre. The real meaning of this theatre's attempt to secure access is thus clouded by the newspaper's argument that the ads were rejected because the material submitted had prurient and suggestive appeal. (Both the Michigan Supreme Court and the Michigan Court of Appeals emphasized this factor.)

The Eastown theatre responded that at all times its ads had conformed to the paper's published standards. Further, it had submitted advertisements mentioning only the name, address, and telephone number of the theatre. The *Enquirer and News* refused to accept even those innocuous ads.

On close examination of the Battle Creek access case, newspaper immunity from legal obligation to publish appears much less firm than the broad language about newspapers being a private business might suggest. All the judges in the case appeared to agree that *if* the advertiser can show discrimination, a right of access should be recognized. The judges could not agree on whether there was a rational basis for the exclusion of Eastown theatre's advertising.

In both the Ohio and Michigan access cases, commercial advertising was involved. There is a First Amendment interest in political advertising not present in commercial advertising, since the central meaning of the First Amendment is to encourage political expression, particularly criticism of government.

The Ohio trial judge who refused in 1919 to allow the only newspaper in a town to banish a businessman from its advertising page was very much ahead of his time. He recognized that a monopoly press, like other monopoly public services, should have some compulsory obligations. Indeed, this concept is already recognized by the federal courts with regard to state-owned bus terminals and subways. The theory is that public facilities are dedicated to public use and that the state, of all power entities, cannot prohibit political communication in buildings and areas which have invited the public. Surely, this analysis is even more applicable to a community's only daily newspaper. When First Amendment objectives are combined with the quasi-public role of the monopoly newspaper, the legal case for access to the press becomes very strong.

Nevertheless, the reality is that the struggle for access to the press has now foundered on the courts' unwillingness to engage in judicial law-making. The general attitude of the courts seems to be that the first move should come from the legislature.

Access to the Campus Press

The Royal Purple *Caper*

IN ONE AREA, MEDIA CENSORSHIP HAS BEEN SUCCESSFULLY challenged entirely through judicial efforts. A beachhead for entry to the media has been established in the campus press in the state universities and public high schools, whether the administration in question is actively hostile to those ideas for which a hearing is demanded or merely concerned to maintain campus tranquility at all costs.

One of the earliest struggles to open up the publicly-owned press began in 1967 at Wisconsin State University, Whitewater. The campus daily, the *Royal Purple*, suddenly closed its advertising pages to advertisements against the Vietnam war. In doing so, the paper reckoned without a political science professor, Miss Ruth Miner. Using access to the press theory, she and others took the *Royal Purple* to court.

The *Royal Purple*'s case shows the strange uses to which the conventional approach to freedom of the press can be put. Said the paper on October 26, 1967:

The First Amendment to the U.S. Constitution guarantees freedom of the press to the press not advertisers.

So, where there is only one newspaper in a community, as is the
usual case on a campus, the First Amendment is offered as au-
thorization not for maximum freedom of expression but for
shutting out disturbing viewpoints. As we have noted, the fram-
ers of the Constitution were concerned to protect the writer or
the speaker from an enraged majority. Here again we see that
the contemporary free expression problem is how to reach the
majority by conventional means.

An editorial advertisement concerning a university employees' union was twice submitted to the *Royal Purple* and twice
rejected in October 1967. In the same month an advertisement
entitled "An Appeal in Conscience," dealing with racial discrimination, was refused. In November 1967 an advertisement was
submitted to the *Royal Purple* covering both race relations and
the Vietnam war. The paper refused to accept the ad, in line
with its recently-formed policy of not accepting "editorial advertisements."

A recurring access problem in the campus press, and the
press generally, is the hunt for the hidden censor. In the *Royal
Purple* case, the students whose ads were rejected charged that
the policy had been set by the Student Publications Board. The
Board of Regents of the State University contended that it had
never authorized a Student Publications Board. There actually
was a Board, composed of both faculty and students and chaired
by a faculty member (who incidentally had responsibility for deciding the promotion of the Board's other faculty members), but
it said that it had no knowledge of the *Royal Purple*'s advertising policies and had heard no complaints about them.

The *Royal Purple*'s ad policy of not accepting editorial advertisements was formally published in 1968–1969. A hint of the

new policy first came on March 9, 1967, when the paper announced in an editorial:

IMPENDING WAR REQUIRES RETREAT

The *Royal Purple* has decided not to accept advertisements on political philosophies. This decision was made in view of an impending war of ideas in advertising.

Many features of the *Royal Purple* case are typical. The censor is often in control of a higher authority, which sometimes finds it convenient to disavow responsibility or knowledge. The Whitewater Board of Regents professed ignorance of the censorship activities of the Student Publications Board, just as the Chicago newspaper publishers and editors passed the buck to their advertising managers.

Similarly, advertising standards announced by newspapers often seem to have been improvised and implementation of them is erratic. Some controversial ideas manage to see the light of day and others do not. For example, the *Royal Purple* published one ad, evidently not deemed to espouse a political philosophy, which urged young men at Whitewater State to join the Air Force. But when a professor at the college, Mrs. Elsie B. Adams, prepared a response entitled "We Don't Want to Waste Your Bachelor of Science Degree Any More Than the Air Force Does," urging that college men choose nonmilitary careers such as teaching and social work, it was rejected as a political attack. Mrs. Adams complained in the letter column of the *Royal Purple*:

In short, your policy seems inconsistent and unfair. You accepted an ad saying in effect "Go to the Air Force"; but you rejected an ad saying "Go into medicine, social work, or education instead." I would suggest that you re-evaluate your policy and the principles upon which it is based.

28

Immediately following Mrs. Adams' letter there was a note from the business manager:

> The advertisement submitted by the writer fell under section five of the *Royal Purple*'s policy statements concerning types of advertising accepted, which states "Advertising of a public service nature will be accepted if . . . it does not attack specific groups, institutions, products or persons."
>
> It is the opinion of the business manager that the ad in question represented a direct attack upon the Air Force and military service while the Air Force ad was not a direct attack upon the industry AS A WHOLE.
>
> The policy referred [to] was formalized this fall and was recently approved by the Student Publications Board, composed of students and faculty. It was formalized prior to receipt of both the Air Force ad and that of the writer.

An interesting feature of the *Royal Purple* fracas is that the paper was apparently willing to publish the disputed editorial advertisements as letters to the editor. Nevertheless, the court ruled that this did not affect plaintiff's right to have the material published as advertisements, since an advertisement can get more attention than a letter to the editor. Economically and technologically the paper had no reason to turn down an ad. In broadcasting there are simply so many hours to the broadcast day, but the pages of a newspaper are expandable. Why then did the newspaper prefer that protests appear as letters to the editor rather than as ads? Probably because in advertisements, the purchaser and not the editor is in control. A purchaser can use large type, photographs, and fill pages of space. He can specify timing and content. In a letters to the editor column, the timing of publication cannot be controlled and the effect of the letter can be dissipated by editor's notes before or after a communication. Moreover, the letter to the editor that is finally published may be a much edited version of what was submitted.

Some students and faculty took the Board of Regents at Wisconsin State University to court. The demand for access prevailed.[1] Said Wisconsin federal judge James E. Doyle:

> As a campus newspaper the *Royal Purple* constitutes an important forum for the dissemination of news and opinion. As such a forum, it should be open to anyone who is willing to pay to have his views published therein—not just to commercial advertisers.

Is a student publication a newspaper? The school position was essentially that the school paper shouldn't be taken too seriously. But unless a principle of free access and free communication is followed, school papers can serve neither journalistic nor educational ends. The judge, using the dictionary definition, had no difficulty in finding the *Royal Purple* to be a "campus newspaper." A newspaper was a paper distributed at regular intervals "to convey news, advocate opinions, now usually containing also advertisements and other matters of public interest."

The *Royal Purple* accepted commercial advertisements and public service ads that did not "attack an institution, group, person or product." But rejecting editorial advertisements, said the Wisconsin federal court, constituted an impermissible form of censorship. The restrictive advertising policy was a denial of free speech and expression.

Judge Doyle recalled the importance ascribed to the editorial advertisement by the Supreme Court in the famous libel case discussed above, *New York Times v. Sullivan*: the editorial advertisement provided an outlet for information and ideas by those who themselves had no access to publishing facilities. Justice Brennan's opinion was cited: the function of editorial advertisements was to provide the exercise of freedom of speech to those who are not "members of the press." The court criticized the fact that "anyone wishing to sell a product or a service" can advertise it in the *Royal Purple,* yet those who want to "sell their ideas" may not do so. This, said the court, was a violation of freedom of speech.

The Board of Regents appealed the district court's decision, unwilling to accept the limitation to its authority.

The Board of Regents lost again. The Federal Court of Appeals affirmed the lower court's decision in favor of a right of access to the press.[2] As the Federal Court of Appeals saw it, the issues were simple. Could state college newspapers reject advertisements protesting racial discrimination or the Vietnam war in light of the fact that the paper was open to commercial and other types of ads? The courts answered that rejection of advertising on the basis that it was editorial was in itself discriminatory. Whether or not editorial advertisements could be prohibited altogether was an issue the court ducked. However, other federal courts have concluded that in such situations the affirmative duty imposed by the First Amendment to provide access for controversial ideas might come into play.[3]

In the end the decision produced an anomaly. The Federal Court of Appeals that considered the *Royal Purple* case involved the same issue that had previously been confronted with the Chicago newspaper case. In the *Royal Purple* case access to the campus press was declared a constitutional right. In the Chicago newspaper case the union was told that there was no right of access to the privately-owned Chicago daily press. An observer might conclude that the two decisions were in conflict.

Determined to distinguish the two cases, the court pointed out that everyone conceded that the campus newspaper in Whitewater was a state facility. The Whitewater appeal did not present the question of whether there was "a constitutional right of access to the press under private ownership." The court's logic was that the *Royal Purple* could not discriminate for ideological reasons in its advertising columns because it was a state facility.

The *Chicago Tribune* or *Sun-Times,* on the other hand, as private papers are free to discriminate for whatever reason they choose. There seem to be many difficulties with this logic.

If the argument had never been made that access to the media is a First Amendment value which can or should be legally enforceable, entry to the state college press would not now be required. Until recently, it was not contemplated that a state-financed newspaper owed any rights of access to the community which it served. But now that a right of access exists to the relatively insignificant state college press, it is startling by contrast that no such right exists for the enormous populations served by the great metropolitan dailies. It is hard to see why the right of access to the campus press now available to every beginning freshman student at the Whitewater campus of Wisconsin State University should not be available to the readership of any newspaper of general circulation serving any American community.

In another access case, the Fitchburg, Massachusetts, State College administration objected to the content of the college paper and set up a board of faculty as censors to approve each issue before publication.[4] Perhaps such efforts can be defended as attempts to depoliticize the university, but the depoliticization accomplished by such measures is really illusory. A requirement of access to the campus press is a more sensible and less prejudiced solution. A right of access can be used on behalf of any group or issue. For on many a campus the interchange of opinion is now threatened in another way. Some college newspapers have lent their facilities entirely to the point of view of the New Left. Opportunity for entry into such campus papers by students who disagree with that position is far better assured by a legal obligation of access than by appointment of a board of censors or by avoidance of controversy altogether.

When a movie censor says that a distributor may not show a movie, the theatre owner can bring a suit to protect his financial investment. When a point of view is denied access to the campus newspaper, the entire student audience is often deprived of considering it, because those who hold it lack the financial backing needed to support a suit to protect their right of free expression.

Recognition of a right of access to college and even high school newspapers for political expression provides some odd contrasts. For example, the definition of obscenity is much broader when children are the primary audience of printed material than when adults are the intended readership on the theory that children are more susceptible to obscene material than adults are. Yet now high school children and college students are able to avail themselves of a right to be confronted with a wider range of opinion in the newspapers of public educational institutions than that enjoyed by the adult population, which must depend on its daily newspaper, where the daily strife of political ideas may be presented unfairly or not at all.

Why the new concern that students should have access to political ideas in campus newspapers? There are at least two reasons. One is that the campus newspaper cases have arisen thus far in state institutions where the free expression argument is easy to make: state action has caused a restraint on free expression. Another is that the courts apparently are able to discern the relationship of access to the college newspaper to stability and a sense of justice in the college community. If the campus newspaper is freely accessible to the intense political viewpoints which now abound on the campus, the legitimacy of violence as a tool to reach the community with controversial ideas is sharply reduced. The choice between requiring dialogue in the state college press or encouraging violence on the campus is not a difficult one, even for the least socially perceptive observer.

Storming the Huguenot Herald

A new pressure for students to participate in basic institutional decision-making is found not only on the college campus but in the high school as well. One of the reasons that people are increasingly receptive to the idea of access to the media is that it offers them an opportunity to escape from the passive role of listener or viewer or reader. In New Rochelle, New York, a group of high school students, the Ad Hoc Student Committee Against the War in Vietnam, decided to publish an advertisement opposing the war in Vietnam in the high school newspaper, the *Huguenot Herald*. The students offered to pay the *Herald* the usual student rate.

The ad stated:

> The United States government is pursuing a policy in Viet Nam which is both repugnant to moral and international law and dangerous to the future of humanity. We can stop it. We must stop it.

What was stopped was the ad. The principal and the school authorities contended that the paper had a long-standing policy of publishing only matters relating to the high school and its activities.

The students brought the school authorities to court and won. The students had no difficulty in showing that the claim that the paper had long been limited to school-related matters and commercial advertising was simply not true. Issues such as Biafra, racial problems, drug abuse, and the basis for graduate deferment and the draft had all been reported.

On the commercial advertising point, the school authorities were on firmer ground. The paper had in fact never carried political advertising. But just here, the difference between nondiscriminatory treatment by a newspaper and a right of access becomes both visible and crucial.

34

The federal court held in the New Rochelle case that when a facility has made itself available for commercial advertising, it cannot refuse to accept political advertisements.[5] To favor commercialism over political expression would be to invert, if not to parody, the reason for freedom of the press. Freedom of the press exists to aid political freedom. This ruling by the federal court in New York in the New Rochelle case followed an earlier and similar conclusion reached by a California state court[6] in a case where a publicly-owned bus company attempted to accept only commercial advertising.

Commercial advertising is often preferred because it is unlikely to ruffle many feathers. But an approach which sees access to the media as the positive side of the First Amendment is not satisfied by an argument that so long as *all* public or political expression is excluded there is no constitutional violation. Requiring access so that there may be vigorous and robust debate prevents an approach to press liberty which merely gives a bonus to the bland.

The so-called alternative forum argument is frequently encountered when access to any of the media is sought. For example, the school authorities in New Rochelle argued that as long as the group seeking access had some other forum in which to voice its position, no First Amendment right is infringed. In this as in much else, the shut out group is in a better position to gauge what is the most effective forum than are those who are doing the shutting out. The "effective forum" is the important forum.

An ironic aspect of the *Huguenot Herald* affair was that the school authorities insisted that New Rochelle school children should be in no better position than citizens in general who have no right of access to the private press. The federal court, of course, held that the school children *were* in a better position.

Different policy considerations govern whether a privately owned newspaper has an affirmative duty to grant access to its pages, and whether a school newspaper has such a duty. For instance, there would be involved the thorny issue of finding state action, a problem which does not exist regarding a school newspaper.[7]

The fortuitous fact that a school newspaper is published with public funds gives a school community larger rights than can now be claimed by the readership of a daily newspaper, despite the community's dependence on the latter and despite the governmentally conferred advantages such as mailing rates. A simplistic dichotomy between private and public is seriously affecting the exercise of First Amendment rights. The serious and ludicrous results of this distinction can be appreciated when it is realized that what a labor union was unable to gain from four Chicago newspapers—recognition of a duty to publish—was in fact obtained by a small group of school children from a high school newspaper.

Contrary to what the school authorities argued in New Rochelle, the anomaly is not that school children have succeeded in exercising a right which the ordinary citizen does not possess. The anomaly is that the ordinary citizen does not enjoy a general right of access to the press.

4 /

The Campus Press—

Underground or

Aboveground?

THE FERMENT IN THE CAMPUS PRESS IS A MICROCOSM OF THE struggle for access to the press generally. The new developments in the college and high school press have not met with approval in all courts. Near the Jamaica, New York, High School, a student distributed an issue of the underground newspaper, *High School Free Press*, in which the school principal was criticized. According to the principal, the story contained "four-letter words, filthy references, abusive and disgusting language, and nihilistic propaganda." The student distributing the paper was suspended. He went to court. The court refused its aid. High school students, unlike college students, said the court, were "in a much more adolescent and immature stage of life and less able to screen fact from propaganda." [1]

At Warren High School in Beverly Hills, California, a group

of students gave up on the school paper, *Justice*, saying that criticism of the high school administration and student ideas generally would not be welcomed there. In November 1968, some students formed their own paper, called *Oink*, and distributed it just outside the main gate of the school. After about a year, two student editors of *Oink*—the president of the student body and the president of the senior class—were suspended for ten days for using "profanity or vulgarity" in the paper. Their parents sued for a declaration that their children's constitutional rights had been infringed by the school authorities.

The California federal court was not persuaded. It argued that espousing a political cause in a way that did not disrupt the school's educational program was a separate issue from using profane or obscene expressions. (That raises the question, are moral heresies less tolerable than political ones?) The court suggested that the rights of high school students to criticize may be curtailed to a greater degree than can those of college students,[2] noting that the Supreme Court has concluded that the state has greater latitude of control of obscenity in connection with children than with adults. Yet it is very clear, as we have seen, that the access rights of students are now greater than those of adults. Had the material in *Oink* which provoked disciplinary proceedings been presented to the official school newspaper for publication and been rejected, would the students have succeeded in an access case? Probably. It is unlikely that a rigid distinction between political expression and obscene expression would survive in the courts. In the politics of the militant young, obscene expression has become a vehicle for political protest. President Nixon in the midterm campaign of 1970 recognized that fact when he asked his supporters to respond to the profane protests of his youthful detractors with a four-letter word, *v-o-t-e*.

The special relationship between access and campus stability is revealed by the different results in a campus press incident that did not involve access.

In New Rochelle, some of the students had considered forming an antiestablishment paper, but they then gained access to the school paper. No profanity or vulgarity had been involved.

In 1969, in an important school case which dealt with the limits of political communication in the schools, the Supreme Court gave political communication great latitude. Some school children in Des Moines, Iowa, decided to wear black armbands to school to protest the Vietnam war. School authorities prohibited their act. In a very significant ruling the Supreme Court held that political communication and expression *per se* could not be barred from the school house.[3] Protest and political ideas could be barred only if they disrupted normal school activities. Since only seven of eighteen thousand school children in Des Moines had worn armbands, the public school system had not been threatened with disruption. Under those circumstances, the wearing of the armbands was a "symbolic act" protected under the free speech provision of the First Amendment.

The Des Moines incident illustrates that students below the college level have a great interest in politics. In high school newspapers across the country during the 1970 election campaign, it was not unusual to find political editorials favoring the election of particular candidates. Sharp political discussion in the usually bland and silly high school publications is a novel development.

Certainly what happened in Jamaica and Beverly Hills suggests that the courts are considering legitimate access to the established media in an educational community to be a better alternative than an underground campus press. The courts seem to be gambling that giving access to a school's institutionalized media will encourage the exchange of ideas and contribute at the same time to the maintenance of an orderly educational program.

An overview of the struggle for access to the campus press does indeed reveal the emergence among the young of what sociologist Theodore Roszak called a counterculture. The courts have supported the concept that the counterculture should be free to operate aboveground if at all possible. The campus press should be open, with free access as its operating principle, not cynically to co-opt the counterculture but to recognize it and give it equal voice.

It is a reasonable idea that a university newspaper, although authorized and supported by the state, belongs to the student community it is intended to serve. Nevertheless, it is a new concept. In the fall of 1969, the editor of *The Cycle*, the campus paper at Fitchburg, Massachusetts, State College decided to reprint "Black Moochie," an article written by Eldridge Cleaver for *Ramparts* magazine. The local printer was horrified, stopped his presses, and called the college president to say that he thought the Cleaver article was obscene. The president responded by appointing a faculty advisory board to approve each issue of the paper before the college would release funds to have it printed.

Under the same law used by those trying to break into the *Huguenot Herald* and the *Royal Purple*, Fitchburg State College students sought relief in the local federal court. Astonishingly enough, they got it. Establishment of a faculty advisory board, consisting of persons unfamiliar with the complex constitutional tests for obscenity, was held an unconstitutional exercise of state power. The fact that the state authorizes creation of a newspaper does not make the state its master. Federal district Judge Garrity conceded that a state could legitimately restrict the college newspaper to student writers. Beyond that, the power of the state to control the paper apparently was minimal:

But to tell a student what thoughts he may communicate is another matter. Having fostered a campus newspaper, the state may not impose arbitrary restrictions on the matter to be communicated.[4]

The Fitchburg State College brouhaha was not strictly an access problem. But the conflict resulted in a conclusion that a state college campus paper should be much freer from the control of the state officials who authorized it than any private paper is from its owners. Any daily newspaper serving hundreds of thousands of readers is free to impose all the "arbitrary restrictions" on the "matter to be communicated" which it pleases. The language of the federal judge in the Fitchburg State College case, on the other hand, is fairly representative of the school cases:

> Because of the potentially great social value of a free student voice in an age of student awareness and unrest, it would be inconsistent with basic assumptions of First Amendment freedoms to permit a campus newspaper to be simply a vehicle for ideas the state or the college administration deems appropriate. Power to prescribe classroom curricula in state universities may not be transferred to areas not designed to be part of the curriculum.

The high school newspaper fracas in New Rochelle and the college paper battle in Whitewater have some common themes. Both courts rejected the argument that the papers were educational exercises and therefore not really newspapers. Both courts agreed that a practice paper that wasn't really hospitable to ideas or controversy was a bogus laboratory. In both cases the courts demonstrated the new cutting edge of access. Refusal to publish editorial advertisements as an operating policy was a violation of the First Amendment. So Federal courts in both New York and Wisconsin refused to accept a policy of neglecting all controversy equally.

Events on the campus illustrate that the relationship between access problems and monopoly situations is no accident. On October 29, 1968, the *Royal Purple* boasted to advertisers that it was "the sole medium that communicates bi-weekly with 10,000 students." On November 19, 1968, the *Royal Purple* asserted in an advertisement, "10,302 students, faculty and staff at Whitewater read the paper twice a week. . . . Are we communicating? . . . The *Royal Purple* Sole Communicator." Access cases are litigated because the forum to which entrance is sought is the only effective forum for the message to be conveyed.

The practical and instrumental uses of access to the press are highlighted by these campus developments. In the vast literature on political freedom which has been created by the Justices of the Supreme Court in opinions interpreting the First Amendment, it is often said that among our constitutional freedoms, freedom of expression enjoys a preferred status. Legal insistence on open political expression in the media is a means of realizing in practice the high value our society professedly places on freedom of expression.

The advertising manager for a publicly-supported campus newspaper can no longer escape legal responsibility for rejecting advertisements by the defense that, after all, one political view has not been given preference over another. At least where state sponsored facilities are involved, the predilection for the profitable and the bland has at last encountered a constitutional obligation. The policy of excluding anything but commercial advertising has been shown up for what it is—an invidious choice between classes of ideas.

Judicial displeasure with newspapers for maximizing the commercial and banning all else has considerable relevance for contemporary television, which is now being affected by it. The protection of commercialism and the systematic rejection of the controversial is being recognized as an obstacle to effective free expression, and that is particularly relevant to the broadcast media.

The Campus Press—Underground or Aboveground?

Of great significance for the future of this right is how easily the courts found a way to implement it. In both New Rochelle, New York, and Whitewater, Wisconsin, effective use was made of a post-Civil War federal civil rights statute, which says that anyone who under color of state law deprives anyone of his constitutional rights shall be liable to the injured party.[5]

This law enabled the courts to conclude that public facilities which denied access to the press violate the First Amendment. But the statute requires the presence of state action and thus the private media are temporarily safe. The Chicago newspaper case is proof of that.

There is a new respect for the campus press, partly because it is felt that protest is better expressed in print than in the streets. But there is another reason for the development of a right of access to the state-sponsored press. Lack of access to dominant newspapers has transformed the off-beat media into more important vehicles for the communication of ideas. We are witnessing a kind of public compensation for the closed-column privileges of the great private media. The campus access cases are significant because they illustrate that it is practical for courts to implement and enforce a right of access to the press. In this one area, the law of access is already a reality.

5 /

A Letter to the Editor

THE LETTERS-TO-THE-EDITOR COLUMN, LIKE THE POLITICAL OR editorial advertisement, is a natural field for the development of a legal right of access. Recently, there has been an upsurge of interest in letters-to-the-editor, both among letter writers and newspaper readers. Such letters could provide a valuable counterbalance to the publisher's dominating voice, particularly in the one newspaper city.

Unfortunately, letters columns are much less open than they appear. The letters, chosen for publication in the first place by a highly subjective process, often are so severely edited that in the end they may tell more about the editors' biases than about the opinions of the general run of letter writers.

That is the conclusion of two journalism scholars at Stanford University, Donald Grey and Trevor Brown. They found the research into letters-to-the-editor columns done over the past thirty years to be largely useless for determining what newspaper readers in general were thinking and writing about. Their own research indicates that what sees print may be quite unrepresentative of both the social and political pulse of the community and even of the total letters submitted.

To gain a true spectrum of community opinion, say Brown and Grey, the researcher should be given "access to all letters received, not simply to those published." The crucial information, they believe, is what "the gatekeeper is doing, how and why he is selecting and rejecting letters." Indications are that a broad, "largely invisible cross-section of Americans may have been writing for some time; theirs may be inarticulate sometimes abusive letters screened from print." Data have been published on letters that make the pages of newspapers but "the substantially unknown activities of editorial gatekeepers" has gone apparently unexamined.[1]

Brown and Grey analyzed the letters-to-the-editor column of the daily newspapers of two California cities during the 1968 election year—the *Redwood City Tribune* and the *San Mateo Times*. They discovered that the editorial policy as uncovered by their study "challenged the whole concept of letters as valid indicators of political feeling." The *San Mateo Times* in an October 9, 1968, editorial headed "McCloskey for Congress" complained that it was receiving letters supporting or attacking political candidates and ballot propositions. It was not the paper's policy to publish them said the editorial. The volume of political letters was so great that it would be "unfair to other writers to select a few." In other words, faced with massive comment on a public issue, the newspaper was simply going to suppress it on the ground of fairness. Why couldn't a technique of representative publication be developed to indicate the variety and strength of feeling on issues and candidates?

Legal efforts to establish a right of access in letters-to-editor columns are not without precedent. In 1953, a daily newspaper, the *Tulsa World*, was sued by a reader, Baker Wall, after it refused to publish his letter.[2] Wall claimed that the *Tulsa World* had breached a contract it had made with him and its other readers. He relied on the following heading to the *World*'s letters-to-the-editor column:

> Please keep your letter as short as possible—due to limitations, it is impossible to publish lengthy communications. Letters sent to the *Tulsa World* "Voice of a Free People" column cannot be returned. All letters must be signed and the address of the writer given; initials will be used in publication, however, if the writer so requests.

In his suit, Wall made many arguments which bear on the question of a right of entry to the letters-to-the-editor column. He claimed that the *World* was a Republican newspaper and discriminated against Democrats. He asserted that the *World* accepted the benefit of a subsidy from the United States government: the second class mail rate that enabled the *World* to use the mails at a cost to the government "in excess of the amount paid" in postage. Wall said his taxes support this subsidy on the theory that the newspaper "would justly and fairly transmit information of every kind fairly and impartially to all its readers."

Basically, however, Wall argued that the *World*, by not publishing his letter, had breached a contract with him. The Oklahoma court decided the case on this last point, saying, "We cannot agree with plaintiff that there was a promise to publish all letters received by it in response to its invitation." The court reasoned that the *World* had three hundred thousand readers. If each reader accepted the invitation to write, the *World* would have to publish three hundred thousand letters. Since no express promise to publish each letter submitted had been made by the paper, the court said it would not read the *Tulsa World*'s "invitation to its readers" as "an implied promise to publish all such letters." Since the paper had not promised to publish Wall's letter there was, concluded the court "no contract, and therefore no breach." [3]

Wall had wanted the paper to compensate him for not publishing his letter by giving him damages. But encouraging the dissemination of information, which supposedly is the justification of the newspapers' lower mailing rates, would be better served by making the newspaper print the rejected letters. The idea is not to punish newspapers for suppressing opinions but to enrich both the variety and contrariety of views available to the community.

The contract theory of right of access has a certain attraction. It would permit use of one of the major weapons of the private law of contracts, the remedy of specific performance. Viewing each letter as unique, a court could order the letter in controversy to be published. Only publication of the letter, it could be argued, would satisfy the wrong alleged.

The difficulty with this approach is that it frustrates any relief at all. It is too easy to come back with the argument that surely not every newspaper reader can expect to place a letter in his paper's letters-to-the-editor column.

Clifton Daniel of the *New York Times*, opposing implementation of a right of access to the letters column, warned that, as an administrative or practical matter, recognition of such a right would be impossible. Daniel observed that in 1968 the *New York Times* received nearly 40,000 letters-to-the-editor. In his judgment, "85 to 90 percent of these letters, in the words of our slogan, were 'fit to print' "—but only 6 percent were actually admitted to the letters-to-the-editor column of the *New York Times*. Daniel declared that if all the letters had been published, "They would have filled up at least 135 complete weekday issues of the *New York Times*." [4]

Emphasis on the volume of letters submitted is a convenient way of avoiding the issue. It is pleasant and comforting to picture one's opponent as asking for too much in the hope that he will get nothing. But access as a First Amendment right will provide legal ammunition for publication, not for the general run of letters-to-the-editor, but just for those letters which express views on vital political and social issues in the community that would otherwise be suppressed by the local press.

In the case following the unsuccessful efforts of the Chicago Amalgamated Clothing Workers to publish an ad in the Chicago daily press, the union argued in part that the newspaper's own general bid for advertisements was an offer to accept all advertisements submitted. The Federal District Court referred to the Oklahoma letters-to-the-editor case in indicating that such an advertisement could not be construed as an offer to publish any particular advertisement: such advertisements, the court said, were merely invitations to negotiate.[5] The court seemed to attach more weight to the argument that there is a First Amendment-based right to have an advertisement published on political and social issues, since the whole opinion is devoted to it. It is clear that a right of access, if it is to prevail, must be rooted on the theory that the First Amendment commands affirmative access to the open sections of the daily press—the letters-to-the-editor columns and the advertising pages.

A First Amendment-based right to have a letter-to-the-editor published has not yet been given full dress consideration by a court. A constitutional rather than a contract approach would inquire whether the letter which is denied publication involved a public issue, and whether it concerned a core area of First Amendment protection, like criticism of government. If it did, and if the reason for its suppression was ideological, the restraint on expression would be manifest. Under such circumstances, it would not be beyond the scope of courts by constitutional adjudication to fashion a right of publication through the devices of mandamus or mandatory injunction. As the Supreme Court observed in a 1971 opinion, "Constitutional adjudication must take into account the individual's interest in access to the press. . . ."[6]

According to Kent McDougall, writing in *The Wall Street Journal*, editor Jack Spalding has claimed that 25 to 30 percent of letters submitted to the *Atlanta Journal* come from "obscene and evil minds," [7] and so are never published. Thirty percent of the total seems a very large number of obscene and evil minds. It makes one wonder whether some disinterested tribunal might be a better judge of what is evil or obscene than the local editor. Another McDougall finding meshes well with that of Grey and Brown: "The typical newspaper letter writer is more conservative, older and more affluent than the average American."

The over-all point, in McDougall's view, is that letters-to-the-editor are taking on a new significance "in these days of widespread disenchantment with the nation's newspapers." Says McDougall, the press is more thin-skinned than ever to charges of unfairness and is devoting more and more space to readers' letters. In 1970 the *New York Times*, for example, decided to give twice as much space to reader's views. (But of the almost 40,000 letters it received in 1969, the *Times* ran only 2,622.)

At the same time, *Times* announced a new Op-Ed page which would be a "daily forum" furnishing a medley of views in the form of original articles by experts. Special attention would be given to contemporary political and social issues. A particular welcome would be extended, said publisher Arthur Sulzburger, to those points of view opposed to the editorial stance of the *Times*.[8] But such isolated voluntary efforts do not appear to answer the problem since scores of newspapers around the country are rather less visible and public-spirited than the *Times*.

What place then does the letters-to-the-editor column occupy in the struggle for right of access to the press? How is it related to the question of public access to the other traditionally open section of the newspaper, the advertising pages? When Clifton Daniel happily emphasized the sheer mass of letters annually submitted to the *Times* by its readers, I responded that I was not optimistic about establishing a beachhead for access to the press in the letters-to-the-editor column.[9] Letters-to-the-editor traditionally have been edited. No attempt is made to publish all the letters received or even a representative selection. In fact, the letters-to-the-editor column in most newspapers is at present more a feature item, meant to entertain, than it is a formal attempt to provide a balanced presentation of opposing views in a community.

Any attempt to change this will be met with the argument that journalistic discretion is being impinged upon. Access to the advertising section of the paper, where the content is traditionally supplied by the advertiser, presents much less of a challenge to the journalist's editorial control—especially since the newspaper is being paid for the privilege.

It is at this point, however, that we come to the particular role that the letters-to-the-editor column can play in establishing a right of access. Suppose an individual who cannot afford the price of an ad wishes to reply to a position that a newspaper has taken on a particular public issue? In that case, a requirement that the letter be published as a First Amendment right would result in a vital contribution to the community's access to information.

A litigated case illustrates the actual context in which imposition of a duty to publish a letter-to-the-editor would be appropriate and just. The *Winchester Star*, the only paper in a Boston suburb, took an editorial position on a bond issue which was soon to come before the voters for approval. A citizen of Winchester, Boston attorney Herbert Lord, objected to the newspaper's stand. He submitted a letter which the *Star* refused to publish.

Herbert Lord asked the Massachusetts courts to issue a writ of mandamus to compel the *Star* to publish his letter. The courts refused, and the Supreme Court declined to review the case.[10] The argument that the First Amendment itself might compel the publisher to admit entry was not urged before the courts. Neither was the argument that a monopoly newspaper operates like a private government, whose restraints on expression ought to be judicially resolved as a First Amendment matter. The *Winchester Star* case illustrates the interrelationship of free access and meaningful freedom of the press, applying the term *freedom* in a sense transcending the property rights of publishers. A case brought today on similar facts but using the preceding arguments might well lead to a different result.

The *Winchester Star* case exemplifies the situation where a small town newspaper's refusal to publish seals off debate on a political issue that uniquely concerns the affected community. Alternative forums are extremely unhelpful in such situations. Neighboring print media, like the nearby Boston metropolitan dailies, are unlikely to be interested in so specialized a local community issue. The resulting denial of access is, therefore, of the most serious kind. Yet legislation which imposed a duty to publish political or editorial advertisements would not solve the problem of how to deal with the individuals or groups who cannot afford to buy an ad. There should be a clear obligation laid upon newspapers to publish as letters-to-the-editor the views of individuals or groups opposing newspaper positions.

An attorney such as Mr. Lord might be able to purchase an advertisement. Yet the letter-to-the-editor column probably carries more weight and prestige than does an advertisement. A strong case can also be made that in order to give some semblance to equality of opportunity before the bar of public opinion, a group or individual which seeks to *reply* to a newspaper editorial should be permitted access to the letter-to-the-editor column. Where a newspaper monopolizes the print medium in a community, the opposition should not be forced to enrich the monopolist in order to engage in public debate. When a group wishes to raise a matter for the first time, the right to publish an advertisement may suffice. But the letter-to-the-editor is an equitable means for countering a newspaper's editorial stands. Because of that, as well as because of the expense involved in buying an advertisement, a legal obligation for newspapers to publish a letter on a vital community public issue, would be an entirely suitable and salutary remedy.

6 /

Access Through Congress?

Judicial efforts to create a law of access have stopped just where a right of access is most important—in the pages of the privately-owned daily press. A law of access now exists within the campus press of public high schools and universities. But judges have been unwilling to go beyond that. Perhaps they feel that access is necessary to keep the campus pot from boiling over but that the need in the general community is not so intense. In addition, recognition of a right of access to the campus press was made easier because it is clear that a public facility may not censor or restrain expression under the Constitution. The case of the privately-owned media is not so clear. That is why the Federal District Court in the Chicago newspaper suit indicated it might be willing to honor a right of access statute but was unwilling to create a right of access on its own. Congress would have to pass a law first.

The summer of 1970 saw some attempts to do just that. The office of Congressman Michael Feighan of Ohio asked for my help in drafting a right of access statute. Feighan, the second ranking member of the House Judiciary Committee and a congressman for over twenty years, had been defeated in the Democratic primary in Cleveland. His defeat rankled. His staff laid at least part of the blame for his defeat on lack of coverage of his campaign in the two Cleveland daily newspapers. Meanwhile, the Newspaper Preservation Act was before the House of Representatives, proposing to exempt certain newspaper anticompetitive deals from the federal antitrust laws. Congressman Feighan, his son William, his staff member Austin Fragomen, and I decided to tack a right of access rider on the Newspaper Preservation Act as a means of exposing the newspaper industry's two-faced attitude toward federal intervention in press affairs.

There was a certain poetic justice in the proposal for a rider. Congress had been lobbied to permit two newspapers in a community to pool resources in order to provide two editorial viewpoints. Keeping alive diversity in a community is the avowed highminded purpose of the so-called Newspaper Preservation Act. Under such circumstances, it seems just to ask an exempted paper to provide reasonable space to conflicting views on issues of public importance. Unfortunately, our rider had too little time to muster support. The House was about to adjourn. However, we did prepare a right of access bill which was introduced in the Committee of Interstate and Foreign Commerce of the House of Representatives. As we worked, I heard Clifton Daniel's challenge ringing in my ears:

"I defy Professor Barron . . . to write an access statute that would not entail some measure of official control of the press."[1]

Daniel believes that it is impossible to have a right of access without government surveillance of the press. In my judgment it is possible. But it is most likely to be accomplished if the federal courts are the vehicle for enforcement. By using federal judges a

54

sensitive problem would be entrusted to a disinterested and relatively detached group of independent men. Impetus for bringing complaints would be the responsibility of the particular aggrieved groups and individuals within the community. Difficulties which arise in using agencies like the FCC which combine judicial, prosecutorial, and investigative functions will all be avoided.

My reaction to the problem of the rise of a monopoly press had been to say there-ought-to-be-a-law. Congressman Feighan and his staff gave me an opportunity actually to participate in writing that law. The finished product was introduced by Congressman Feighan in the House of Representatives on August 12, 1970. The bill was called, somewhat sardonically, the Truth Preservation Act, since it was introduced shortly after the passage of the Newspaper Preservation Act.[2] A Truth Preservation Act will probably not be passed within the near future. The powerful American Newspaper Publishers Association, which lobbied vigorously for federal aid exempting certain newspapers from compliance with the antitrust laws, opposes it, and that Association has no access problems.

Nevertheless, it is important to discuss the provisions of the bill. This model right of access law illustrates that access to the press can be accomplished by practical legislation which will mutually serve the interests of the press and the public.

The bill reads as follows:

91st CONGRESS   H. R. 18941
2d Session

IN THE HOUSE OF REPRESENTATIVES

August 12, 1970

55

Mr. Feighan (for himself, Mr. Carter, Mr. Cowger, Mr. Leggett, Mr. Nix, Mr. Powell, and Mr. Thompson of Georgia) introduced the following bill; which was referred to the Committee on Interstate and Foreign Commerce

---

A BILL

To impose on newspapers of general circulation an obligation to afford certain members of the public an opportunity to publish editorial advertisements and to reply to editorial comment.

Be it enacted by the Senate and House of Representatives of the United States of America in Congress assembled, That this Act may be cited as the "Truth Preservation Act".

Obligation to Provide Access

Section 1. Each newspaper of general circulation shall—

(1) publish, in accordance with section 2, all editorial advertisements submitted to such newspaper, and

(2) provide, in accordance with section 3, a right of reply to any organization or individual that is the subject of a comment of an editorial nature by such newspaper.

Requirements Respecting Editorial Advertising

Sec. 2. (a) A newspaper of general circulation in a community shall be required to publish an editorial advertisement—

(1) only after all newspapers of general circulation in such community have been requested to publish such advertisement and have refused to publish it, and

(2) only if the person requesting publication has tendered a sum sufficient to pay such newspaper's rate for

56

such advertisement (subject to subsection (b)), and the newspaper has the space necessary to carry the advertisement.

(b) No newspaper of general circulation may charge for publication of any editorial advertisement any charge—

(1) in excess of its charges for publication of comparable advertisements which are not editorial advertisements, or

(2) in excess of its charges for publication of other comparable editorial advertisement.

Requirements Respecting Right to Reply

Sec. 3. A newspaper of general circulation which is required under Section 1 (2) to provide a right of reply shall afford the individual (or in the case of a comment on an organization, the chief officer or a person delegated by him) a reasonable amount of space in a comparable place in the newspaper as soon as practicable after the newspaper's receipt of the reply.

Enforcement

Sec. 4. Any person aggrieved by the failure of a newspaper of general circulation to comply with any requirement of this Act may obtain a mandatory injunction requiring such newspaper to comply with such requirement. The district courts of the United States shall have jurisdiction of any action brought under this section.

Definitions

Sec. 5. For the purposes of this Act:

(1) The term "newspaper of general circulation" means a newspaper intended to be read by the general public of any geographic area.

(2) The term "editorial advertisement" means an ad-

57

vertisement which communicates information or expresses opinion on an issue of public importance or which seeks financial support for an individual or organization to enable such individual or organization to advocate or carry out a course of action respecting such an issue.

The title of the proposed law is itself a frank statement of purpose: "A bill to impose on newspapers of general circulation an obligation to afford certain members of the public an opportunity to publish editorial advertisements and to reply to editorial comment." The bill requires newspapers of general circulation in a community to publish editorial advertisements only after all the other papers in the community have been resorted to and all have refused to publish. This provision properly emphasizes that it is only when closed-mindedness of all papers in a community results in the banishment of an idea that a right of access should come into play. If there are two dailies in a community, and one daily will publish an editorial advertisement, the kind of total censorship which completely smothers an idea for an entire community is lacking.

Total denial of access by the community's press therefore is what the new law would require before relief under it would be granted. Making total exclusion a requirement is designed to emphasize the quasi-public role of the daily press. The theory is that the greater the extent of public dependence on the press, the greater the constitutional case for access. Just as a public utility must meet certain standards of service, serve all legitimate paying customers, and be accountable to public agencies because of its monopoly position, so public dependence on the daily press should impose standards of service on the daily press.

The theme of the model law then is simple. Legal obligation should be imposed on the press only when proven necessity (total denial of access) demands it. The social interest in free expression is obviously served by requiring access when all outlets of expression have otherwise been blocked. But an important feature of the proposed law is that it goes beyond merely imposing a duty to publish editorial advertisements. It would also impose on newspapers of general circulation a duty to grant a right of reply to any individual or organization which has been the subject of their editorial comment. The commonsense of this proposal is that if a newspaper invites controversy, elementary fair play demands real debate. Particularly is this so when one of the debaters owns the only print forum in town. A newspaper that evaded all controversy would, I suppose, escape from the confines of the law. But I think that few papers would want to pay such a high price to evade access responsibilities.

The proposed access law contains features designed to prevent the right of access from being frustrated too easily. The ideological lepers in a community may not be discriminated against through advertising rates. A newspaper may not charge any more for one editorial advertisement than it does for a comparable commercial or other editorial advertisement. But the new law does have a loophole. In order to preserve as much editorial control in the paper as possible, a newspaper is obliged to publish an editorial advertisement only if it has the space. Obviously, the possibility exists that some papers will cry "No space" when they mean "Bad idea." But deciding when a person is acting in good faith is not a new task for the law. The bill assumes that editors want to do the right thing. The purpose is to get them off the hook. The editors can say, we didn't want to publish the views of that awful group, but we had to—it's the law.

Finally, the proposed law has teeth. If a newspaper does not obey the new law, the aggrieved person or group may obtain an order, a mandatory injunction, requiring it to comply. The law gives the federal district courts power to enforce complaints under it.

The model access law clearly will not resolve every access

problem. One that would still be a problem under it was raised recently by Jack Valenti, president of the Motion Picture Association. Some thirty-two daily newspapers around the country, he complained, ban ads for "X" rated films and some for films rated "R" as well.[3] The ratings, declared Valenti, were a public service. Yet in a city with a monopoly newspaper situation (only one paper or both papers under the same ownership) the effect of such a ban on a movie theatre could be very damaging. The hostility to the more restrictive ratings is presumably occasioned by the pious fears of the censoring newspapers that movies rated "X" or "R" will be a magnet for the sensualist. Yet the ban on the ratings sometimes merely serves to prevent the public from learning about award-winning movies. Valente observed that since *Midnight Cowboy* had an "X" rating, some newspapers refused to advertise it.

Earlier the problems of a small movie theatre in Battle Creek, Michigan, were examined, where the owner was the victim of a total ad ban by the only local newspaper. The conclusion of the Michigan state courts was that the theatre had absolutely no rights of entry to the newspaper. Would the model access law put the Motion Picture Association in any different and better position than the theatre owner in Battle Creek?

The model access law requires only that *editorial* advertisements must be published. It defines an editorial advertisement as one "which communicates information or expresses opinion on an issue of public importance." Certainly, the movie rating system is the communication of information. Does advertising a movie and indicating its rating therefore make the whole ad publishable as of right under the model law? Or do such ads merely advertise a form of entertainment and so not merit consideration as editorial advertisements?

Defining editorial advertisements with the precision necessary to answer all such problems probably is not possible. It is not even clear that such precision is necessary. Creating a legal right of access in some circumstances should encourage greater publisher responsiveness to access problems in general. In my view, ads using the movie rating system should be considered the communication of information. But the decision in such matters can safely be left to the courts. The basic need is to establish the beginning of some responsibility to publish.

Even if the model law were enacted, its success would depend on the good faith and good will of the press. Newspapers would still be free to counteract a right of access. Leonard Iaquinta, now of the Communications Research Institute of New York City, has publicized his effort to gain access to his hometown daily. His experience in attempting to purchase a political advertisement in the July 3, 1970, issue of the *Kenosha News*, a Wisconsin daily newspaper, illustrates the weapons still available to a publisher even after publication is permitted. Iaquinta's ad variously criticized the school board, the city council, the mayor, the police department, and a local judge. The major but not the total thrust of the criticism was that many in the city government had obstructive and unsympathetic attitudes toward the local activities of citizens who opposed the war in Vietnam. The mayor, for example, was criticized for condemning two youths who flew a peace flag from a local beach house. The school board had refused to allow peace groups to meet in the public schools.

The publisher of the *Kenosha News* contended that statements concerning local issues in the ad were in error. The publisher said that if the ad were published the paper would probably be obliged to print an editorial refuting its points one by one.[4]

The whole incident raises some interesting questions. If there is a right of access, is it a right of unharassed access? Iaquinta was confronted with a tough choice. Either his ad would be edited to reflect the paper's view of the facts concerning the local issues in controversy, which differed sharply from his, or it would be subjected to a "massive and overwhelming official newspaper rebuttal," perhaps destroying its usefulness. Certainly the model access law has not resolved this problem. All it has resolved is that the publisher of the *Kenosha News* would be legally bound to publish the ad. The publisher would still be free to respond editorially and by a house ad. The publisher in a sense still has the last word. But the community would benefit from the model law because at least it would be advised of the existence in the community of a small voice in real disagreement with that of the community newspaper.

At about the same time the Feighan proposal was introduced, another congressman, Lester Farbstein of New York, introduced two bills to impose affirmative obligations on the press. One bill, designed to follow up the Newspaper Preservation Act, would have given the FCC power to revoke a paper's antitrust exemption if the newspaper failed to present divergent points of view.[5]

The other bill introduced by Congressman Farbstein would apply the fairness doctrine to daily newspapers which had a monopoly in towns of more than 25,000 people—the situation of the daily press in the great majority of American cities. Under the bill, if a town's daily press is entirely controlled by a single ownership, the FCC would be authorized to ask a court to prohibit such a newspaper from failing to provide its readership with reasonable opportunity for balanced presentation of conflicting views on issues of public importance.[6]

To provide some perspective on what changes are likely to yield the best results in imposing obligations on the press, it is useful to focus on the specific problems about which Congressman Farbstein was concerned. Farbstein mentioned in support of his bill that five California daily newspapers had felt supermarket pressure against printing news concerning the consumers' grape boycott in support of the grape workers' strike. Each newspaper involved, except for the Los Angeles *Herald-Examiner*, was the only newspaper in its community. Each buckled under the advertiser pressure, according to Congressman Farbstein.[7] The grapeworkers complained that the California papers refused to cover boycott activities. For example, picketing of Safeway Stores was not reported. This is a depressing story. The monopoly press should at least have the virtues of its vices. A monopolist is in theory independent. But despite the complete monopoly of four of the papers, all the papers capitulated to the advertisers.

Congressman Farbstein noted that two leading food chains in Miami, Florida, stopped advertising in the *Miami News* immediately after the paper ran a three-part series on local food coding practices in early July. The loss to the paper is $22,000 monthly. A third chain, A&P, reversed its decision to begin advertising in the paper, and a fourth indicated it would not cooperate with the paper's reporters.[8]

The question Farbstein has raised concerns the power of advertisers to suppress news which may be harmful to their economic interests. What technique is likely to counteract such suppression? The policing of the press by the FCC appears unlikely to yield easier entry to the press. The model access law provides a simple and unbureaucratic method of enforcement. Under the model statute the grape workers would have an absolute right to buy an ad in the California daily press. A consumer's group would have a right to buy an ad explaining to the public the need for a food coding scheme that was intelligible to shoppers.

A major defect of the Farbstein proposal is that it provides no specific rights of access, or of reply to any group or individual excluded or attacked. The FCC is told merely that if a person

6 3

has been denied a reasonable opportunity to present a conflict-ing view, it may ask the court to enjoin the newspaper from so acting. Similarly, an individual who does not believe that a news-paper is providing substantially complete coverage of issues of public importance may complain to the FCC. Finally, the FCC may move on its own to ask for court action on either of these bases. A much more sensible solution is the model access law, which would provide for both access and a right of reply. But the model law would leave the content of publications obtained by virtue of the law in the hands of the individuals or groups de-manding access.

There is another serious flaw in the Farbstein proposals: The proposal to apply the FCC's fairness doctrine to the press would saddle the press with supervision by government but still fail to provide direct entry or participation in the press by the public. Such use of the FCC is almost bound to be self-defeating. Many newspapers operate television stations which are already under FCC jurisdiction. To put the media, print and electronic, under a single federal agency is most undesirable. The FCC has too often been an industry hostage in the past. Moreover, if a repres-sive national administration were able to appoint the commis-sioners of a single federal agency which controlled the entire media of the nation, it would not be a very cheerful prospect.

A right of access law is far more likely to serve as an effective counterpoise to media power if administered in the courts. Fed-eral judges, unlike government administrators, have life tenure. Their independence after appointment far exceeds that of agency administrators, whose terms will soon be up and who often keep an eye out for employment opportunities in the in-dustry they are purportedly regulating. The present requirement of balanced presentation of controversial issues in broadcasts has the merit of long history and recent strengthening. But it is by no means a model to meet the access problems of newspapers.

Fairness and access are not interchangeable concepts. The great difference between the two is that access provides an opportunity for a group to write its own copy and present its own view.

Judges, particularly federal judges, are not recommended only by their independence for the task of enforcing access to the press. They also have the expertise of long exposure and experience with the basic challenges to freedom of the press which have been posed by politically repressive legislation or anti-obscenity laws.

Judges decide when a book or a movie merits protection under the First Amendment, even though a prosecutor claims that it is obscene. Justices of the Supreme Court have shown awareness of the sensitivity of freedom of the press in such questions. In 1957 Justice Harlan explained in the most important obscenity case ever decided why courts had to resolve free press questions of great significance:

> Every communication has an individuality and "value" of its own. The suppression of a particular writing or other tangible form of expression is, therefore, an individual matter, and in the nature of things every such suppression raises an individual constitutional problem, in which a reviewing court must determine for *itself* whether the attacked expression is suppressible within constitutional standards.[9]

If we rely on courts to consider when expression should be suppressed, is it really so radical a step to ask them occasionally to rule whether some particular group has been denied an opportunity to express its opinion? Surely this is a task which accommodates itself to the basic purposes of the First Amendment and for which the federal judiciary is uniquely equipped.

7 /

The Media—Within or

Beyond the First

Amendment?

IN A 1970 *SATURDAY REVIEW*, NEWSPAPERMAN GILBERT CRANBERG noted a number of signs that a right of public access to media was an idea whose time was coming. Among the harbingers: a conference on access conducted at the American Bar Association Convention in Dallas in 1969 by the A.B.A.'s Section of Individual Rights and Responsibilities; discussion of the issue at the American Civil Liberties Union conference in Ann Arbor in 1968; and part of a committee report on access efforts submitted to the 1970 annual meeting of the American Society of Newspaper Editors. Cranberg referred to my article in the *Harvard Law Review* and suggested that one day newspaper publishers might "wish that Mr. Barron had never studied law." [1]

Unfortunately, that day is not yet near enough to cause publishers much discomfort. As Cranberg points out, the difficulty is that constitutional freedoms such as freedom of the press go into operation only against repressive state action. But denial of access by newspapers is private action and it is difficult for a court to transcend traditional constitutional categories.

That is not to say that a way cannot be found. The Supreme Court has held that private ownership of a park in Georgia City did not provide an escape from requirements of a duty not to discriminate by which it would be bound if it were public.[2] I conceded in my original article that to apply such an approach to the press would require a "rabid theory of state action." Judge Marovitz picked up this phrase in his opinion in the Chicago newspaper case:

> However, this court does not sit as a creative legislative body, nor do we accept the admittedly "rather rabid conception of 'state action'", *Id.* at 1669, that would compel private newspapers to print political advertisements.[3]

What if the courts continue to refuse to act judicially to implement a right of access to the private commercial press? Suppose that they continue to keep hands off newspaper action which restrains free expression. Legislation, such as the model statute discussed in the last chapter, would then become the only way by which access to the press could be realized. But another issue then arises. Does Congress have the constitutional authority to enact right of access legislation?

Congress does have such power. There are at least three sources in the Constitution for right of access legislation. The first is the Fourteenth Amendment: The fifth section says, "The Congress shall have power to enforce, by appropriate legislation, the provisions of this article." Since 1925 the due process clause of the Fourteenth Amendment has been considered to make the constitutional guarantees of freedom of speech and press binding on the states.[4] The argument would be that to enforce freedom of the press, federal right of access legislation is necessary. Such a statute would be "appropriate legislation" enforcing the due process provision of the Fourteenth Amendment which includes freedom of the press.

A Supreme Court decision has given new strength to this use of the Fourteenth Amendment. The Federal Voting Rights Act of 1965 contained a provision designed to make anyone who had received at least a sixth grade education in private or public school in Puerto Rico eligible to vote. Previously, literacy in English had been the precondition for voting under New York state law. Now, a reasonable literacy in Spanish would be sufficient.

In the New York literacy case a specific provision of the Fourteenth Amendment—the equal protection clause—was being implemented. The argument was that New York's Puerto Rican inhabitants, literate in Spanish but illiterate in English, were being denied the equal protection of the law. The Supreme Court ruled that Congress had authority to enact the Voting Rights Act by virtue of the grant of legislative power to Congress in section five of the Fourteenth Amendment.[5]

Freedom of expression, unlike equal protection, is not specifically mentioned in the Fourteenth Amendment. But in 1880, only a short time after the adoption of the Fourteenth Amendment in 1868, the Supreme Court observed that section five of the Fourteenth Amendment was designed, among other things, to give Congress power to "secure to all persons the enjoyment of perfect equality of civil rights." [6] Under such an approach, freedom of expression is a civil right in behalf of which Congress has power to legislate. Federal right of access legislation would enforce the right to freedom of expression since it would distribute capacity for the enjoyment of freedom of expression more effectively and with greater equality.

A second theory, which has been endorsed by former Com-

68

missioner Kenneth Cox of the FCC, would use the federal jurisdiction over interstate commerce, given in Article 1, Section 8, of the Constitution, to authorize right of access legislation:

> As a matter of logic and law it has long seemed to me that Congress could *if it wished*—constitutionally apply counterparts of our equal time and right of reply obligations to most newspapers, since they move in, or clearly affect, interstate commerce and since the public interest in their providing their readers with both sides of important questions is clear.[7]

Surely newsprint, newspaper chains, and newspaper readerships cross state lines. It would not be difficult to establish a basis for legislation as a kind of federal regulation of interstate commerce.

The flaw in this use of the commerce clause is that it avoids the fundamental issue: Should freedom of the press be given a positive dimension? The difficulty with such constitutional arguments is that they prove everything and nothing. Certainly the drafters of the Fourteenth Amendment would have been surprised to know that they had given Congress power to enforce freedom of expression: The issue had not yet arisen at the federal constitutional level. The reach of the Fourteenth Amendment has by now extended far beyond its nineteenth century understanding. It is a poor constitutional lawyer who cannot find authority for federal legislation in some constitutional clause. The commerce clause will usually serve if all else fails.

But our basic freedoms should not depend on squeezing constitutional clauses to yield a desired result. Rather, we should recognize that the distinction between what is public and what is private is becoming increasingly unsatisfactory to mark where constitutional obligation should begin and end. Charles Reich of the Yale Law School has pointed out that perpetrating a distinction between the public and the private keeps us from seeing "the real monolith of power." [8] The corporate state, he writes, is without checks or responsibilities.

Reich believes that we have two governments in América—one subject to the Constitution and one that is not. An example of a government which is not subject to the Constitution is the media. Reich points out that the newspapers and television can refuse to carry "radical" opinion. It is worse than that. The great media, if they wish, can insist on carrying only opinion on whether one deodorant is better than another, or whether one soap powder washes whiter than the next. The result is a common fury. The rage of the Wallaceites and the Black Panthers is rivaled only by the worship that crowds give Agnew as he lectures the faithful on the biases of the media. Reich says the "inapplicability of the Bill of Rights is one of the crucial elements in American society today."

This is not a new idea, but it has not yet been grasped or comprehended. Writing in the early 1960s, the Harvard constitutional scholar Carl Friedrich wrote, "The American Bill of Rights is no longer adequate." [9] Why? Among the reasons was the "attenuation of older rights which need to be reaffirmed or strengthened." Where was the real danger? Friedrich saw that, too. It stemmed from the threat of "monopoly power" to individual freedom.

The great newspaper chains and broadcast networks are corporations and sometimes they are monopolies. As corporations, they may claim constitutional liberties but, unlike governments, which they so much resemble, they are constrained by no constitutional duties. In 1952, Adolph Berle wrote that he saw the development of an emerging principle that the corporation, a state creation, should be subject to constitutional limitation when it infringes a constitutional guarantee, just as government is. [10]

The inadequacy of the Bill of Rights, as presently interpreted, is particularly manifest in the case of freedom of the press. The constitutional doctrine of "state action," written into the law nearly a century ago, mocks the economic and social realities of power in contemporary America.[11]

Yet in the Chicago newspaper case, Federal Judge Marovitz spoke of the press as a check on government. That the press had great power and little accountability was something he refused to see. The press, he said, is nothing but a "private enterprise, free and independent of government control and supervision."

Particularly annoying in Judge Marovitz's opinion is his avowal that he is not "insensitive to the problems that have developed or may arise because of lack of access to the marketplace of ideas." It is true, he concedes, that private censorship may be as important as public censorship. Yet for him the dominant fact is that "the right of free speech was never intended to include the right to use the other fellow's presses, that the Constitution relates only to governmental and not private action."

But to individualize the problem in this way is to make the problem unreal. First of all, it is not the other fellow's presses. It is a corporation's presses that are involved. The reason the corporation's presses are important is that the other fellow has no press and cannot get one in any effective way.

Charles Reich has pointed out how the government and the private corporation have formed an alliance which outwits and is outwitting the Constitution. Women's liberation, the Black Panthers, student draft resisters—none is permitted to propose its own programs on television. Neither, I would add, may George Wallace, or Carl McIntire, or even Strom Thurmond, at least on network television.

For free discussion to live in the arena to which it is now confined—the corporate press of the corporate state—new constitutional duties must be imposed on the press. The essence of the idea of access is participation in the media for the authentic voice of each variety of opinion. It is exactly this idea which the

7 1

present legal approach to the press defies. As for broadcasting, Reich shows the consequence of a regulatory policy which makes broadcasters depend on a government license. It is a way of anointing one class of opinion—that which is commercial in spirit and in content—and of excluding, in any counterbalancing way, all else. Such delegation to ostensibly nongovernmental groups dodges governmental responsibility and accountability while it permits television monopolies to be granted to the dominant power groups in the corporate state and effectively silences all others.

The eighteenth century dread of the state as the primary power source has bred a myopia to private restraints on expression. Our society finds it difficult to challenge any restraint on expression, no matter how severe, unless it is a formal governmental one. The My Lai massacre story is a case in point. The great wire services refused to publish news accounts of the massacre. Publicity was only made possible because the small, radical Liberation News Service distributed the story to underground and other papers. Naturally, the conveniences of the eighteenth century conception of freedom of the press have not been lost on Madison Avenue. Broadcasters, a small group chosen by government, see no incongruity in insisting to this day that freedom of speech on television means that they can do what they please.

The British M.P. and writer R.H.S. Crossman has observed that a political revolution as important as the Industrial Revolution has occurred. The result has been to concentrate "coercive power and thought control in a few hands." [12] In countries with a private or mixed economy, control of the processes of opinion is ostensibly in private hands. In Marxist countries, the opinion process is in the hands of the state. But in both the power of a few can control the basic opinion process of a nation. Even in Marxist countries, where state control of the media is equated with proletarian control and so thought desirable, misgivings have emerged. In 1967, Isaac Deutscher, lifelong Marxist scholar and biographer of Stalin and Lenin, gave a series of lectures in which he summarized the effect of the 1917 Russian Revolution.[13] His lectures are remarkable for their sensitivity to the problem of maintaining freedom of expression in even a humane Marxist society. Yet Deutscher makes it very plain that the openness of the media contributes in part to making a society humane.

(There is a particular poignancy about Deutscher's observations about the need for protection of freedom of expression in socialist societies. A year later, in 1968, an attempt to establish a humane socialist society through freedom of speech and discussion in press and television became a major factor in the Soviet intervention and repression in Czechoslovakia.)

In western democratic societies, the practical possibilities for dealing with what Crossman calls the new Political Revolution, the capacity to control thought, are more immediately hopeful. The need is to bring a greater sector of conduct under constitutional standards. To constitutionalize the media would be in harmony with the American liberal tradition of hostility to censorship and to arbitrary control over opinion.

The need is to approach freedom of the press as something more than negative. This need brings me to a third source in the American Constitution for the statutory recognition of a right of access—the First Amendment itself. The Bill of Rights has not traditionally been considered as a source for legislation but as a safeguard against the state. But the process of constitutional interpretation in our system is a never-ending one. A source of continuing fascination for me is that our much vaunted freedom of the press, at least as far as the states are concerned, is only as old as that 1925 Supreme Court decision. It will certainly take another Supreme Court decision to authorize squarely a right of access statute under the First Amendment. Burying the issue as a matter of interstate commerce will not settle the question of whether the First Amendment has an affirmative dimension. Similarly, proceeding through the Fourteenth Amendment's back door, section five will only lead back to the fundamental question—the constitutional meaning of freedom of the press in our time. Therefore, I would begin where any analysis must ultimately end—in the First Amendment.

The First Amendment should be interpreted as having an affirmative dimension. Legislation pursuant to that affirmative or positive dimension should be deemed authorized by the First Amendment itself. To rely on the Bill of Rights as sources of as well as barriers to legislative power is, admittedly, a revisionist approach to constitutionalism. Since the idea of access is a response to the concern for interchange of ideas and the vitality of the public order upon which the First Amendment is based, I consider it more faithful to the basic constitutional tradition to predicate access on the First Amendment itself.

Expert use of constitutional dialectics utilizing the Fourteenth Amendment or the commerce clause might well be the more constitutionally cautious way to implement freedom of the press. But since the real purpose of access is to implement the First Amendment, I would prefer that legislation so doing would be based upon it and nothing else. Such an approach would establish a new interpretation of freedom of speech and press which would enable groups and individuals to cope best with the new restraints on freedom of expression that have followed the rise of the mass media.

8 /

Marcuse, Mill, and Agnew

Marcuse and Repressive Tolerance

THIS IS AN UGLY TIME FOR REASON. THE LIBERAL EMPHASIS ON process, on dialogue, on juxtaposing attack and counterattack, are all receiving only what Herbert Marcuse has called "repressive tolerance".[1] It is a tolerance given only because no one thinks that the things tolerated can actually result in any change. It might be a different story if dialogue or dissent seemed any real threat to established authority and majoritarian supremacy.

There is a sense in which Herbert Marcuse, the philosopher of the New Left, is unfathomable to the pragmatic, process-oriented American. Marcuse says there is objective truth. Although that may not be an extraordinary thought to someone like Marcuse who came to intellectual maturity in the 1920s in Weimar, Germany, it is an unnerving idea to one reared in the pragmatic liberalism of America—as unnerving as his belief that contemporary tolerance cannot be tolerated.

But, although Marcuse's manner of expression is sometimes unfamiliar, his basic critique accurately illuminates some con-

75

temporary problems in freedom of expression and common reactions to them. Marcuse's extraordinary essay "Repressive Tolerance" indicates that guarantees effective and meaningful are lacking, or worse, even denied. Still, I believe that Marcuse's core idea—that tolerance is repressive—is a false paradox.

Tolerance as an objective is not at fault. The critique should instead look to the reform of existing institutions that use tolerance for self-serving ends. Marcuse understands, apparently as well as Brandeis did, the instrumental role of freedom of expression in democratic society. A democratic society, as defined by Marcuse, is one in which the people participate in the evolution of policy.

Such individual participation is possible through the testing of ideas in the "open marketplace of ideas and goods."

Marcuse is an admirer of free and equal discussion only if it is rational. Rational discussion he describes as "the development of independent thinking, free from indoctrination, manipulation, extraneous theory." In the beginning, American constitutionalism, a child of the enlightenment, assumed as a matter of course that the fruit of freedom would be reason. But in twentieth-century American thought, little consideration is given to the content of discussion. This shift from the continental or eighteenth century emphasis on reason has at least two causes. One is the enormous influence that the nineteenth century liberalism of John Stuart Mill, with its emphasis on relativism, has had on the American constitutional approach to political ideas. The other great influence on free expression theory has been that of American pragmatism which has emphasized process and been relatively disinterested and skeptical about content. It is no accident that Justice Oliver Wendell Holmes, the architect of the marketplace of ideas concept of freedom of expression, grew to intellectual maturity when pragmatists such as Charles Peirce and William James were major figures in American philosophical life.

The new media class has the opportunity to influence and tutor a mass society without any particular rational connection to that society, merely because they control access to the means of expression. They neither possess, nor must they attain, special qualifications for their task. There is almost an element of chance in the present power position of the contemporary owners and controllers of the media. Spiro Agnew has complained that network news people are not elected. It is a radical idea, but an arguable one. There ought to be some rational basis in a democratic order for influence when it is wielded by those who are neither elected nor accountable. The public sense of nonparticipation has bred a crisis of confidence in the media. Increasingly, discussion in America is considered free but unequal.

Marcuse concedes that democratic tolerance, even as presently distorted, is "under all circumstances" more "humane" than an institutionalized intolerance which sacrifices the rights and liberties of the living generations for the sake of future generations.

However, he thinks there is an alternative. He has a fantasy: it is a dream of creating a subversive majority. If the ways to such a development are blocked then new arrangements should be made. What are they?

They would include the withdrawal of toleration of speech and assembly from groups and movements which promote aggressive policies, armament, chauvinism, discrimination on the grounds of race and religion, or which oppose the extension of public services, social security, medical care.

Who is qualified to make such distinctions? Everyone, he says, who has learned to think rationally and autonomously. (Personally, I have never found that to be a numerous class.) Plato spoke of the reign of philosopher-kings. In the writings of John Stuart Mill, Marcuse says, every rational human being participates in the discussion and decision—but only as a rational being. Who are these rational beings? They are few in number and not necessarily the elected representatives of the people. (So much for Agnew.)

In other words, an intellectual elite are the people who can be trusted to war against repressive tolerance or discriminatory tolerance. How will this elite set tolerance aright? Marcuse's recipe is a simple one:

> Liberating tolerance, then, would mean intolerance against movements from the Right, and tolerance of movements from the Left.

Marcuse has little patience with the established formulas of American constitutional interpretation. He thinks that the clear and present danger doctrine is outmoded. Action now follows propaganda so quickly that an approach which requires much time to operate will no longer work. The purpose of the clear and present danger test was to give maximum opportunities for expression, except where expression might lead to such precipitous action that there would be no opportunity for balancing counterdiscussion.

For Marcuse the "whole post-fascist period is one of clear and present danger." Therefore, "true pacification requires the withdrawal of tolerance before the deed, at the stage of communication in word, print, and picture."

Marcuse's hostility to the concept of the marketplace of ideas cannot be underestimated. He writes: "Different opinions and 'philosophies' can no longer compete peacefully for adherence and persuasion on rational grounds." He believes that in present-day competition of ideas, the false is bound to prevail. Small and powerless minorities are bound to fail in such competition even when they are permitted access; and they are more important in his view than the "preservation of abused rights

78

and liberties which grant constitutional powers to those who oppress these minorities."

Marcuse's position certainly fits him as the ideologue of the New Left. He would, I believe, find an access-oriented position to freedom of expression as romantic as I find the now dominant marketplace of ideas theory. He does not wish to repair. He wishes to overturn, to destroy, and to capture existing institutions. What he proposes is intolerance in the name of dissent. That this proposal is made in the name of true tolerance may demonstrate the nervous breakdown now afflicting our traditional attitudes to freedom of speech and press.

Access to the media is important because it gives men a sense of the legitimacy of existing institutions. To implement a right of access is to give an institutional form to tolerance. But institutionalized tolerance is just what Marcuse is bitterly hostile to, because it disarms the dissenters, the militant opposition. It gives them the illusion of having an impact on the social order while in fact having none.

Marcuse wishes to substitute "precensorship" for the "more or less hidden censorship that permeates the free media." He preaches that faith in process should be exchanged for involvement. To the extent that the ideal of free and fair discussion includes no judgment about what is desirable or undesirable, to that extent it is neutral. But he fears its neutrality will fool the people. The public are not told what is the good side. The neutrality of the process will nearly always be allied to that which is regressive, to use Marcuse's word.

Marcuse and the present operators of the media have something in common: a very low estimate of the common intelligence. But democratic processes are based on an optimistic faith in the nature and capacity for development of man.

The central paradox of freedom of expression is that what is permitted in the abstract is not easily realized in practice. Marcuse writes:

> The tolerance which was the great achievement of the liberal era is still professed and (with strong qualifications) practiced, while the economic and political process is subjected to an ubiquitous and effective administration in accordance with predominant interests. The result is an objective contradiction between the economic and political structure on the one side, and the theory and practice of toleration on the other.

The relationship between access to the media and citizen participation in government and society is a key point. It is difficult to bring vital ideas to bear upon "the formation of public opinion"; Marcuse sees this as an indication that an elite presently manipulates and formulates opinion. His solution is to substitute "a dictatorship of an 'elite' over the people." Why? Because the people are no longer free. To the charge that he is suggesting a dictatorship of the intellectuals, Marcuse responds that we now have a dictatorship of nonintellectuals—"politicians, generals, and businessmen."

If under democratic relativism it is assumed that no one possesses the absolute truth, Marcuse argues that such a position is maintainable only if the people are "capable of deliberately choosing." He complains, "Under the rule of monopolistic media—themselves the mere instruments of economic and political power—a mentality is created from which right and wrong, true and false are predefined whenever they affect the vital interests of the society."

The present neutrality is therefore dehumanizing and indoctrinating at the same time. Impartiality reinforces the status quo—and that, to him, is an indictment of tolerance. For people to find out what is really true, to break out of what he calls media predisposition, people would have to be freed from the prevailing indoctrination. How can and should this be accomplished? He answers: ". . . the trend would have to be reversed: they [the people, the audience] would have to get information slanted in the opposite direction."

Equal time or access as a neutral value is not for Marcuse. He does not protest the absence of dissent and controversy. He writes: "All points of view can be heard: the Communist and the Fascist, the Left and the Right, the white and the negro, the crusaders for armament and disarmament." His complaint is that the stupid opinion is given as much time as the intelligent one. In the realm of ideas, he is an aristocrat and a totalitarian.

There is a basic difference between a freedom of the press theory intended to give access to the public and one which complains of lack of access but is really interested in domination and control. Marcuse maintains that existing institutions are incapable of securing the kind of change which he desires. The majority has been too conditioned. Therefore, no matter how greatly access opportunities are expanded for the radical, the militant, and the disaffected, there can be no change. Marcuse does not want the present structure to be made more susceptible to change. He wants to replace the managers of the present apparatus with the ideologues of the New Left. This desire is critical to Marcuse's thought.

John Stuart Mill

What would spew forth from Madison and Jefferson if they knew how Madison Avenue has used the First Amendment as a barrier to the eccentric, the disruptive, and even the upsetting? Similarly, what would John Stuart Mill think of the media managers' use of his libertarian philosophy? Mill is often quoted to provide intellectual armor for the media industry's position that censorship equals freedom, when it is applied by private agencies. In reality, Mill's thought is not so comforting to the media; it has something relevant to say about the rise of private governments like the newspaper chains and the broadcast networks.

To read Mill himself is illuminating. His writing reveals that, although the power he knew was government, it was fear of power more than fear of government which animated his thought. His essay, "Of the Liberty of Thought and Discussion," manifests an enormous concern to maintain the integrity of debate and of ideas. His emphasis is not on private freedom from government censorship, although he undoubtedly considered that important. His concern is to assure debate and the interchange of opinion. His true emphasis is disclosed in the very first sentence, where he says a defense of "liberty of the press" is no longer necessary as a safeguard against corrupt or tyrannical government.

Mill's ideas about political discussion are not less relevant today because so much power over opinion is technically in private hands. He says, "Complete liberty of contradicting and disposing of opinion is the very condition which justifies us in assuming its truth for purposes of action." [2]

Each television network holds licenses in the largest and most lucrative markets in the country. Although governmentally licensed, the networks are technically owned by private stockholders. Yet these private entities can thwart "complete liberty of contradicting and disposing of opinion" as much, if not more, than any governmental unit in America. Mill would have seen through this situation, for his fundamental concern was the threat posed by power of any sort to free discussion.

Diversity of opinion, Mill says, is useful for at least two reasons. One is that the received opinion may be false and some other opinion true. The other is that if the received opinion is true, a conflict with its opposite will give greater clarity to its truth.

Notice that this analysis assumes that there is such a thing as truth. What is it? That's a hard question in our idea-ravaged age, a time of corrosive skepticism and of faltering faith. Any process designed to lead to truth makes us uneasy, since we are doubtful we could recognize what is true. Since we are no longer confident that debate will lead to truth, we tend to be less idealistic about the process of debate. Here indeed is radicalism's quarrel with liberalism. The revolutionary fervor of Herbert Marcuse is not nourished by any optimism about the inherent capacity of the majority of the people to find their way to the humane socialist society. As an Englishman and liberal, Mill of course had a different goal for society, but a similar skepticism. To apportion broadcast time on behalf of an opinion according to estimates of the size of the group that already holds it would have horrified him:

> On any of the two open questions just enumerated, if either of the two opinions has a better claim than the other not merely to be tolerated, but to be encouraged and countenanced, it is the one which happens at a particular time and place to be in a minority.

Reflect on this passage and consider what Mill would have thought of the continuing effort to limit television's equal-time requirement to the candidates of the two major parties. What would Mill think of the law passed in 1960 which in effect permitted television to give time to the presidential candidates for the two major parties and no others? [3]

The startling longevity and adaptability of Mill's thought is evident. The necessity for a mass society to be challenged by genuine debate on basic presuppositions is insisted on. The relationship of free discussion to a tough, stable society is recognized. Exclusion of the fringe opinions, so tempting to insecure societies, is accordingly protested.

Like Herbert Marcuse, Mill upholds the primacy of rationality. Writing in the sunshine of Victorian liberalism and optimism, Mill believed in a "preponderance among mankind of rational opinions and rational conduct." Writing out of the deep pessimism of the radical German intellectual, Marcuse does not believe in the possibility of rational discussion in the modern world: no private voice seems to him able to compete with the media voice.

As a matter of routine, the television networks by which we communicate with one another on the whole shut out the great ideas. Governments or quasi-governments like the American mass media always prefer the bland. The high value placed on blandness in nineteenth century England appalled Mill no less than the acme of the television culture represented by *The Beverly Hillbillies* troubles us. Blandness in Mill's time had its roots in the theological bias of the state, a bias from which nineteenth century England was only slowly turning. Blandness in our time has an overt commercial motivation: the pursuit of the largest audience. But the consequence—that only the trite is safe—was the same; and Mill found it detestable.

To a present-day reader what is contemporary about Mill is his emphasis on openness. Mill wrote in language of great relevance:

> Where there is a tacit convention that principles are not to be disputed; where the discussion of the greatest questions which can occupy humanity is considered to be closed, we cannot find that generally high scale of mental activity which has made some periods of history so remarkable.

Mill would have understood the trend toward participatory democracy, toward representation of a diverse society by the diverse components within it and not by the featureless consensus of politicians and mediating journalists. He believed in opinion in a way that contemporary idea-packaging makes atavistic or anachronistic.

For Mill the structure necessary to resolve conflict of opinion was the presentation of arguments by "persons who actually believe them in earnest, and do their utmost for them." The conviction that the exchange of opinion must not be a stage play is basic to Mill's thought. The Supreme Court in 1969 in *Red Lion v. FCC* therefore caught the essential Mill when they cited exactly this passage in their decision approving a right of reply in broadcasting.[4]

Whether in the modern mass society state it is possible to realize the type of integrity in opinion-making that Mill believed possible and desirable is a matter of both profound doubt and challenge. It may be a serious question whether restlessness in ideas should even be encouraged in a mass society that is dissatisfied, alienated, and frightened. But overemphasis on either of these doubts leads to a nihilistic communications policy that is itself dangerous. To give up hope for a real life of ideas in the media is to leave the media where they are—in the hands of businessmen whose practices are motivated by commercial instincts but are easily taken over by repressive ones. If democratic procedures are not yet entirely window-dressing for repression and control, we must be optimistic in the sense that Mill was. We must believe in the desirability of being thrown "into the mental position of those who think differently. . . ."

The Phenomenon of Agnew

Spiro Agnew is the greatest media critic of our day, if attracting attention is the criterion. The significance of his assault on the media is that it emphasizes by contrast the relative silence of the right in American life. To say this may seem paradoxical, since Agnew is praised or abused as the new—and loud —voice of the right.

When Agnew ran for Governor of Maryland against George Mahoney, liberals campaigned and raised money for him, in reaction to the not so subtle racist implications of Mahoney's campaign slogan, "Your Home is Your Castle." Today for liberals, for radicals, and for the media, Agnew is Antichrist. To juxtapose liberals, radicals, and the media establishment is odd, but it is a necessary juxtaposition if the Agnew phenomenon is to be understood.

Agnew has pointed out that the basic decisions for the network news programs reaching nearly 40,000,000 people are taken by about a dozen people. Even if that dozen were the equivalent in wisdom of Plato's guardians, it does not need a very profound political philosopher to wonder whether so few should have so much power. The underlying motivation for Agnew's criticism of the media is doubtless questionable. We surmise that Agnew is more concerned about an editorial bias which he finds objectionable rather than about the principle of too few men holding such great power.

While concentration of power within the media is criticized by Agnew, the Nixon appointees to the Federal Communications Commission, Wells and Burch, both have supported proposals which will make it easier for present licensees to retain their licenses and harder for new entrants to get into the field. Similarly, although blandness, partisanship, and inadequate national and foreign news coverage are characteristic of many newspapers in one-newspaper towns across the country, Agnew's special targets have been the New York-based television networks, the *New York Times*, and the *Washington Post*.

Agnew believes that there is a liberal establishment which dominates the media.[5] As a practical matter of economics, if one looks at the most influential communications outlets generally and newspapers particularly, the charge is probably not true. If one considers only the opinion-making media—that is, the network news departments and the editorial writers who write for the papers read by the nation's leadership—it has some measure of validity.

The dead center which in the past the media could safely occupy is now a lonely position. The intellectual community and the government in power distrust each other. Many media people are more influenced by the ideas of the intellectual community than by the blandishments of government leaders, particularly when the government leadership lacks the style to which media people are particularly responsive. Recognizing the abyss in the center, and the lapse of consensus, the opinion-making media have fallen back on their own ideas, which largely reflect the liberal and urban biases dominant in the intellectual community. But this community is not the world inhabited by the voters or of the government in power that they elected. What Agnew said was that the opinion-making media are biased. This has been attacked as a crude attempt to bully the media and destroy freedom of the press. It has been countercharged that Agnew is politically biased, which he undoubtedly is. But his point is that elected politicians properly reflect a political bias while journalists should not.

The remedy does not lie in frightening the media. The remedy is simply to demand inclusion where exclusion is practiced. No one believes that government power is preferable to private. What is objectionable is power itself whenever it is held in too few hands and when those hands are basically not accountable to any larger public. Agnew has suggested that the networks indicate on the television screen when they are engaging in straight reporting and when they are indulging in opinion. The separation of news from opinion is not likely to be easily accomplished nor would such an attempt be very satisfactory. Still, Agnew's statement of media power cannot be shrugged off:

> We cannot measure this power and influence by traditional democratic standards for these men can create national issues overnight. They can make or break—by their coverage

8 7

and commentary—a moratorium on the war. . . . For millions of Americans, the network reporter who covers a continuing issue, like ABM or civil rights, becomes in effect, the presiding judge in a national trial by jury.[6]

Later in the same speech Agnew observed,

The American people would not rightly tolerate this kind of concentration of power in government. Is it not fair and relevant to question its concentration in the hands of a tiny and closed fraternity of privileged men, elected by no one, and enjoying a monopoly sanctioned and licensed by government?

When Agnew says that media power exercised by a dozen men in the service of three major corporations, ABC, NBC, and CBS, would not be tolerated if those dozen were government servants, is he not correct?

As Marcuse's writing indicates, the radical left feels as excluded from the media as do the right and the conservative. As Agnew observed in a speech in May 1970:

It does bother me, however, that the press—as a group—regards the First Amendment as its own private preserve. Every time I criticize what I consider to be excesses or faults in the news business, I am accused of repression, and the leaders of the various media professional groups wave the First Amendment as they denounce me. So I hope that will be remembered the next time a muzzle Agnew campaign is launched. There is room for all of us—and for our divergent views—under the First Amendment." [7]

However suspect Agnew's motives for quarreling with the media may be, his basic point deserves a good deal more thoughtful analysis and intelligent response than it has received. What Agnew has said is that the government leadership and the constituency that elected it feels underrepresented in the opinion-making media. That is not a healthy development.

What must be done is to build diversity into both the private and the public sector. The press has long maintained that everyone should be subject to criticism and oversight. At the 1969 national convention of the Radio Television News Directors Association, I suggested that the press also should be subject to oversight. Later the same day, Dr. Frank Stanton, Chairman of the Board of CBS, quoted what I had said and added: "What a chilling thought." [8] But the reality which Agnew describes and the radical reaction to his remarks is also chilling.

The Task of Media Criticism

Mill's ideas on free expression have become so popular with the media establishment that their meaningful survival is imperiled. Mill's neutral libertarianism has become establishment dogma. In their reaction to this development, Marcuse and Agnew are really allies. For their common criticism is that tolerance is establishment dogma but not establishment practice. Their radically different reactions reflect, of course, their own vantage points in society. For Agnew the problem is that a media establishment challenges the political establishment, and that media power is illegitimate because it is nonelected and basically nonaccountable.

Agnew has written that the media should try to report and not to persuade. Marcuse wishes to obtain control of the media just in order to persuade.

To Marcuse, access to the media is desirable but it is only access for the Left that is desired; indeed, ideally, only access for the Left should be tolerated.

Agnew thinks those who are disenchanted with the system should be separated from it. Marcuse thinks that in a repressive society toleration for both sides of a question is *repressive tolerance*.

Marcuse calls for complete control of the media by the Left so that it may persuade and propagandize to create what I call a subversive majority. Marcuse, no less than an advertiser selling a product on television, wishes to manipulate. But he wishes to manipulate not consumer choices but majority political preferences. He would create through the media a majority which will want to subvert the existing order and create a new one. (If there are any ironies in a victim of Hitler's Germany questing for a New Order, nothing in Marcuse's work indicates that he sees them.) The media prevent the new society from emerging. Therefore, the media must be captured in order to make them the instrument rather than the enemy of social revolution.

If one updates Mill, and disavows Agnew and Marcuse essentially while agreeing with them peripherally, what is the implication for the media? To advocate public access to the media is not necessarily to attempt to re-create the vanished world of eighteenth century rationalism with its classic reliance on reasoned discussion, conducted with civility.

Discussion in this ideal sense is a technique used by the members of self-governing society to inform each other of their desires and to persuade each other concerning their separate and differing objectives. To describe discussion in this fashion is almost to confess its hopeless irrelevance to the television culture, where politicians are now packaged like soap. (A *New Yorker* cartoonist pictures a suburban husband saying to his wife that Rockefeller must be spending a lot of money on his campaign because he is beginning to want to vote for him.)

The French political theorist Jacques Ellul is pessimistic about the future of dialogue. The environment is now so permeated with what Ellul calls propaganda that the individual lives in a war zone between conflicting and competing propagandas. Ellul warns that believing individual choice can still endure under such circumstances is childish idealism.[9]

90

Discussion on radio and television, as portrayed by Ellul and others, has not contributed to the exchange of ideas. Opposing propaganda systems do not fight in any direct and open way that Mill would have recognized or approved. Opposing propagandas do not attempt combat at the level of ideas: instead they try to capture the individual. Political debate on television is an attempt to subdue the audience. The members of the audience are intended to choose one propaganda over another (perhaps out of emotional exhaustion) rather than through the exercise of reason.

Pessimism is the fashion in media criticism. Jacques Ellul, for example, comes to conclusions basically compatible with those of the celebrated Marshall McLuhan. McLuhan says that television engenders among its viewers a total involvement and participation that makes points of view obsolete. The public attention span is incredibly short—a consequence, according to McLuhan, of the television conception of time on public opinion. For Ellul the rise of propaganda jeopardizes rational decision-making or choice among ideas by individuals. For McLuhan the medium itself, television, has altered all our print-oriented perceptions and the institutions that reflect them. Indeed, perhaps it has disoriented them.

Obviously there is much insight in what men like Ellul and McLuhan have to say. But the media critics whom I have discussed—Marcuse, Agnew, and Mill—are all in the long run hopeful about the ultimate possibilities of the media. Skepticism about the possibility of a real life for ideas on television is surely short-sighted if the effect is to forestall challenge to those who presently control the media.

What needs to be done in the media? For one thing, let us not replace the hucksters with a dictatorship of intellectuals, as Marcuse asks. It is unlikely that management of the media by a radical elite would take us much farther than we are now. Better to be in the hands of those who only wish to sell soaps and cereals. They are less dangerous than those who wish to sell utopias.

Marcuse is an extreme example of the view that the media should be directed to ideological ends. Among milder exponents of this view are practitioners of the new journalism of involvement, which has stirred younger journalists, particularly in the newspaper press. A mark of their approach is a despair of achieving objectivity in news reporting. They have a point. Complete objectivity is obviously a mirage. Agnew's insistence that journalists stick to reporting and refrain from criticism of political leaders assumes a distinction which in any important sense is doubtful. But even if objectivity in reporting can never ideally be attained, the pursuit of objectivity is less dangerous than the zealous pursuit of commitment. John Hohenberg of the Columbia Journalism School has pleaded for a "greater degree of editorial commitment." [10] But in our angry and divided society, increasing the degree of commitment in the media managers and reporters would only increase the crisis of confidence. There is a new unwillingness to let the lens which looks at American society be directed entirely by CBS or NBC News, even though few would be willing to turn news reporting and the content of television generally over to either Agnew or Marcuse.

In a lecture at the University of Texas Law School, I agreed with Vice-President Agnew that too much media power was in the hands of too few.[11] The law school invited as my antagonist Clifton Daniel of the *New York Times.* We had first met on the *New York Times* program on the National Educational Television Network, News in Perspective, referred to in Chapter 5. Since that time, Spiro Agnew had established himself as a media critic, an event I tried to take note of by observing that some things were true even though vice-presidents said them.

Clifton Daniel saw the humor in the alliance of a conservative vice-president and the liberal professor and observed that since we last met, I had "gained an ally in the person of Vice-President Agnew." Said Daniel: "Mr. Barron has somewhat gingerly embraced this alliance. He is right to be cautious. The Vice-President is not a very good example of a man who has been denied access to the press." [12] Obviously, Agnew and Nixon have instant access. Agnew's real complaint was that the networks had given access to their own newsmen to criticize a President's speech.

Yet the authentic spokesmen for the peace position, the dove Senators, found it impossible at a subsequent time—after the Cambodian intervention—to secure equivalent broadcast time to counterbalance the President. Access only for the government in power and the media in power is not access.

Making the media representative and giving expression to the intensely differing voices among the American public will not be accomplished by substituting government control of the media for private control. The responsibility for providing opportunity for expression belongs to both the governmentally and the privately controlled media.

Operators of the media, whoever they are, must always resist the temptation to capture the media they operate. They can do this by sharing the media with both the disaffected and the complacent and by recognizing that it is beyond their power to always depict American society accurately from their own limited viewpoints. They must be willing to share that portrayal among warring groups and constituencies, who alone can show how things appear to them. The media must play host in a more dramatic and representative way than ever before to the variety and conflict in the nation. Every group must feel that it has an opportunity to plead its own cause in its own way and its own voice. To insist on such participation should be the task of media criticism.

9 /

The Search for an Audience

THERE IS A NEW SEARCH BY DISSIDENT AND PROTEST GROUPS FOR sites where an audience may be found. There is a new awareness that both public and private facilities can play a vital role in stimulating communication of ideas. There is also a new judicial willingness to command access to facilities which previously had not been thought to have possibilities for communication.

These developments reveal the growth of an approach to freedom of expression which affirmatively seeks to develop new opportunities for access. There is a new sensitivity to the positive dimension of freedom of expression. But the willingness of courts to open privately-owned parking lots and sidewalks, and publicly-owned businesses, subways, and bus terminals to the pamphlet distributor and the picketer reveals something else: an awareness of the inability of many in our society to secure access to a public forum.

94

Protest in a Bus Terminal

Over 200,000 people a day use the New York Port Authority Bus Terminal on Eighth Avenue and Fortieth Street in Manhattan. They are passing to and from buses, subways, and streets, and the many shops, waiting rooms, ticket counters, and restaurants in the terminal building. The Fifth Avenue Vietnam Peace Parade Committee and the Veterans and Reservists to End the War in Vietnam did not want to take the bus. They wanted to communicate with the passengers. They assembled outside the entrances and attempted to enter the terminal and distribute leaflets. A policeman told them they were on private property and asked if they were going to buy bus tickets. They replied that they were exercising their constitutional right to free expression. They were turned away.

Ronald Wolin of the Fifth Avenue Vietnam Peace Parade Committee and his associates made other efforts to use the terminal. Wolin sent a letter to the Manager of the terminal requesting permission to distribute handbills and discuss the Vietnam war with passersby. The letter illustrates the new quest for access and the failure of the conventional media:[1]

> The purpose of the activities covered by this request will be to communicate our views concerning the Vietnam war to traveling servicemen and to members of the public within the terminal and to persuade them to join our cause. . . .

> We do not intend to interfere in any significant or substantial way with the operation and use of the terminal for the convenience of bus passengers or other persons who may be passing through or waiting in the building. . . .

> *We intend to conduct our activities inside the terminal because this is the most effective–and perhaps the only effective–way to achieve our purpose.* (emphasis supplied.)

When a policeman told Ronald Wolin that he and his friends were on private property, that policeman was wrong. The protestors were in fact on public property. Further, the bus terminal had permitted the use of its facilities for informational purposes in the past. Auto manufacturers had distributed promotional literature there. But the communication of political views was prohibited on the ground that, unlike the other activities, it was "provocative and controversial."

Wolin went to court and won. The lower federal court concluded that since the bus terminal area was dedicated to a public use it was an appropriate place for the exercise of rights of free expression.[2] A requirement that public property designed for transportation must be permitted to serve as media for political communication is a new and important development. It calls attention to the extent to which property rights are a barrier to maintaining rights of free expression.

To insist on use of the bus terminal as a forum is to ask that facility to share a role long occupied by streets and parks. Acceptance of the streets for non-disruptive political expression required a legal struggle in the United States. Extending the right of political expression to a modern bus terminal is merely extending First Amendment rights into the realities of modern land use.

The Port Authority appealed the decision. Judge Kaufman for the United States Court of Appeals for the Second Circuit agreed with the lower court decision, but took a more broadgauged approach. The fact that a public facility is open or dedicated to public use does not in itself signify a right of access to it. Whether the facility was "clearly available to the general public" was a threshold question, but other questions were also basic. Even if a public facility has made an implied invitation to public use, is it an appropriate place for the communication of political and social ideas? In light of a public facility's primary purpose, is it reasonable to utilize it for the audience it may provide?

In fact the terminal building had been used as a public forum for glee clubs, charitable solicitations, and other nonpolitical forms of communication. Said Judge Kaufman, "To deny access to political communication seems an anomalous inversion of our fundamental values." [3] In constitutional theory it is often said that freedom of speech and press hold a preferred position. They are indispensable to political freedom. For a government facility to admit all expression except political communication is indeed to invert freedom of expression.

But the Bus Terminal case raises hard issues for access. Shouldn't the object of the protest have some relationship to the site of the protest? If an anti-Vietnam war protest is made at a building where the Secretary of Defense is about to speak, the relevance of the site of the protest to the object of the protest is clear. But what does the Port Authority Bus Terminal in New York City have to do with the Vietnam war?

There was a connection. Judge Kaufman said a site might be appropriate either (1) because it is the object of the protest or (2) because it is where the audience may be found. In the Bus Terminal Ronald Wolin had a very special audience in mind— servicemen riding buses to and from Fort Dix, New Jersey. Furthermore, the 200,000 or more persons who daily use the terminal made it an ideal place "to communicate his antiwar protest" to the public in general and servicemen in particular.

Wolin's object was to air his views as effectively as his resources permitted. Judge Kaufman found that his activities were protected by the First Amendment. Kaufman emphasized a cardinal precept of the theory of access: the relationship between the stability and the integrity of the social order and adequate opportunity to participate and communicate within the social order:

97

We should in these times be mindful that to the extent we secure legitimate and orderly access to means of communication for all views, we create conditions in which there is no incentive to resort to more disruptive conduct.

The Bus Terminal case illustrates the paradoxical growth of access *outside* the media, in which public facilities and publicly used facilities are turned into media themselves. But what significance does this have for the mass media? Great significance, for the press and for broadcasting. Title to property does not alone dispose of the public's right to access. Judge Kaufman quoted from a Supreme Court case[4] affording a pamphleteer a right of entry into the streets of a company-owned town in this regard:

Ownership does not always mean absolute dominion. The more an owner, for his advantage, opens up his property for use by the public in general, the more do his rights become circumscribed by the statutory and constitutional rights of those who use it.

If facilities whose main purpose is not communication are required to respond to requests for access, how much greater should the duty be of those facilities—newspapers and broadcast stations—whose entire reason for existence is communication? If the argument of property ownership is insufficient to block a request for access to a shopping center, is the argument not equally hollow when used by privately-owned media whose whole purpose is to serve the community as media of communication?

The Bus Terminal was directed to publish regulations which would provide access for groups like those represented by Wolin and which also insure that the normal operations of the terminal would not be disrupted. Certain basic standards could be established. A limitation, for example, could be placed on the number of persons using the facility for communication purposes at any given time. Clear identification of the places within the facility that could be used for expression was also suggested.

Essentially, the Bus Terminal decision held two things. First, there is a constitutional right to access to a public facility in order to reach a broad audience. Second, such a right must be implemented so that the facility's primary function is not frustrated. The Bus Terminal decision illustrates how practically and easily a right of access to the media could be established.

Rights of entry can be developed which do not disturb either journalistic discretion or hinder the informing or entertaining function of the media. The advent of a right of access to public facilities shows that the courts not only can feasibly handle such a task but that in fact they are already doing it.

The paradox is that a law of access for communication is being developed most successfully in facilities which are not set up to be media of communication. The media have so successfully exploited the hallowed guarantee of freedom of expression to exclude outsiders and underdogs that these groups have been driven to turn nonmedia facilities into forums. The depth of the unsatisfied need for access is revealed by the willingness of the courts to try to meet it.

Ideas in a Railroad Station

The Port Authority case is but one in a rash of efforts throughout the country to use public facilities for purposes of political communication. On September 5, 1966, a group of about fifteen persons entered Union Station in Los Angeles to distribute leaflets protesting the American involvement in Vietnam, primarily to soldiers returning to Camp Pendleton after Labor Day. A police officer asked the group to leave. They refused and he arrested them. The state court found three of the

99

group guilty of loitering under a Los Angeles city ordinance. The small band of protesters appealed. They contended that the ordinance could not be applied to them because they were engaged in protected First Amendment activities. Chief Justice Roger Traynor of the California Supreme Court agreed.

The City of Los Angeles contended that the railroad station was not open to the public for political communication but for only a single purpose—railroad transportation. The protesters argued that places like railroad terminals had succeeded to the role that streets and parks had enjoyed from "time immemorial," i.e. places open to public use for purposes of assembly and discussion of public issues.

In fact, streets and parks have not been open as of right for political dissent from "time immemorial." They have been opened only very recently. Even now, use of the streets and parks for dissent and for communication generally is not unlimited. If the flow of traffic or the public safety is jeopardized, streets and parks may still constitutionally be withheld from those wishing to make use of them for purposes of communication.

Justice Traynor pointed out the newness of the constitutional right to use streets and parks for political and social discussion; but he did so for a reason. To him, the newness of our law of free expression meant that new developments should be expected and new interpretations of First Amendment problems encouraged.

He ruled for the California Supreme Court that the Los Angeles railroad station could not exclude the political protesters. Their right of entry could be terminated only if they interfered with the conduct of the railroads. If they did interfere, "they could legitimately have been asked to leave."

Justice Burke of the California Supreme Court disagreed with extending to mass transportation terminals the First

Amendment law that had developed out of incidents involving streets and parks. In his view, opening terminals to political communication was unworkable because they had difficulty enough serving mass transportation purposes:

> Problems of lost luggage, and lost persons, including the very elderly, the very young, the halt, lame and blind are frequent. The mere presence of Travelers Aid desks in common carrier terminals, to lend assistance to those needing it, is indicative that such stations are places where confusion and distractions abound.[5]

Multiplying the distractions in public places is a necessary but not a welcome development. This new right has been fashioned by the courts at the instance of the alienated and the disaffected to meet a very legitimate need. But the need to make communications media out of noncommunications facilities exists because of the default of the real media.

Opening Up the Shopping Center

Enforcing a right of access within public facilities is, as a matter of constitutional law, much easier than in private facilities. Rights of free expression presently hinge on a rather rigid private–public dichotomy. The artificiality of this distinction is increasingly being recognized, and, again, the first place of development has been within private facilities not usually considered media of communication.

The Logan Valley Mall is a privately-owned shopping center near Altoona, Pennsylvania. Some union members were trying to picket a store there. The owners, Logan Valley Plaza, Inc., insisted, and the state courts agreed, that to go upon private property against the wishes of the owners was trespass which was unlawful. The Supreme Court held in a remarkable opinion that the exercise of First Amendment rights do not end where private property begins.[6]

If the picketers had not been able to enter the shopping center directly, they would have had to picket on paths adjacent to the shopping center. But the picketers wanted to bring to the attention of the customers of the Weis Food Market there that the market's employees were nonunion. The Supreme Court admitted them to the privately-owned shopping center.

What is involved here is the recognition of both a right to an audience and a right of access. Justice Thurgood Marshall, who decided the Logan Valley Plaza case for the Supreme Court, did not go as far as Judge Kaufman did later in the Port Authority Terminal case. Judge Kaufman said that a public facility could be used for communication even when the facility chosen was irrelevant to the purpose of the communication, so long as the relevant audience was there. In Logan Valley, the object of the picketers was to communicate with the customers of a store in the shopping center whose facilities were being used for picketing. The Court took note of the crucial role of the shopping center in modern urban life. In the automobile-centered suburb, the parking lot of a shopping center is the gateway to the amorphous Instant Downtowns which surround our larger cities. A shopping center in a metropolitan district that lacks radio, television, or press facilities *specifically* serving it may be in fact the best and only place to reach the nearby population on a local issue. A revolution in residential patterns requires changes in constitutional patterns as well. That change is occurring.

The Supreme Court refused to permit a private property defense to prohibit the use of shopping centers for purposes of communication. Candidly, the Court pointed out that by 1966, 37 percent of all retail sales in the United States and Canada were being rung up in shopping centers. To say that these shopping centers were offlimits to ideas was unthinkable:

These figures illustrate the substantial consequences for workers seeking to challenge substandard working conditions, consumers protesting shoddy or overpriced merchandise, and minority groups seeking non-discriminatory hiring policies that a contrary decision here would have. Business enterprises located in downtown areas would be subject to on-the-spot public criticism for their practices, but businesses in the suburbs could largely immunize themselves from similar criticism by creating a cordon sanitaire of parking lots around their stores. Neither precedent nor policy compels a result so at variance with the goal of free expression and communication that is the heart of the First Amendment.

The public–private dichotomy was dealt a heavy blow by the Logan Valley case. The shopping center to which the picketers sought admittance was in private hands. Where then was the state action? The Court said the exercise of rights of free expression to "streets, sidewalks, and parks and other public places was long established and that access to such public sites could not be denied across the board."

Then came the clincher. There were some circumstances, according to Justice Marshall, where "property that is privately owned may at least, for First Amendment purposes, be treated as though it were publicly held." Access to property for purposes of communication is therefore not dependent on whether property is private or public but whether "it is ordinarily open to the public." The underlying concept seems to be that when property is open to the public for every purpose except the presentation of views unwelcome to the owners, it should be open to the public for that purpose also. This dedication-to-public-use theory has been applied to public property. The remarkable and pioneering feature of the Logan Valley Plaza decision is that the Supreme Court applied this theory to private property also. In fairness, it should be pointed out that on its facts the Logan Valley Plaza case could have been decided by a conventional state action approach. Since the state court had enjoined the picketing, the state judicial action furnished state action in the orthodox understanding of that doctrine. The Court's reaction, however, seems to be that if its dedication-to-the-public theory strains the traditional conception of state action: so be it.

Superficially, the Logan Valley situation was a humdrum case involving picketing in a suburban shopping center. But the case illuminated the present-day clash of constitutional ideals, the tension between property rights and the rights of free expression. Questions of course remain: Must the protest site and the object of the protest be related? Could an antiwar group use a shopping center? In the Logan Valley Plaza situation, the Court said that since the site of the protest and the object of the protest were related they did not have to decide such a question. But there are hints on how it will ultimately be determined.

The question which the Supreme Court did not wish to face was squarely presented by an issue which arose in Portland, Oregon. Could a privately-owned shopping center be permitted to prohibit protest which did not have a direct relationship to the shopping center?

Lloyd Center in Portland covers fifty acres. The Mall, the principal part of the center, is not crossed by public streets but is open to the general public. The operator, Lloyd Corporation Ltd., prohibits the distribution of handbills within the center.

On November 14, 1968, some persons distributed handbills announcing a meeting of the "Resistance Community" to protest the draft and the Vietnam war. Private security guards told the group they would be arrested unless they stopped.

Public use of Lloyd Center had been uneven. Schools had been invited to hold football rallies. Service organizations, such as the Volunteers of America and the Salvation Army, had been permitted to solicit contributions. Not so the March of Dimes or Hadassah, the Women's Zionist Organization. Presidential candidates have been permitted to make speeches in the mall, but Oregon Governor Tom McCall was denied permission to make a political speech there.

In the court case, the center contended that it was not open to the public but that visitors were invited only for the purpose of shopping. Oregon federal judge Gus Solomon ruled that the center parking facilities and sidewalks served the same purpose as streets and sidewalks in a public business district.

Taking another tack, the center said that the handbills being distributed violated the Selective Service laws. If that was true, responded Judge Solomon, arrest and prosecution is the remedy, not the "prohibition of all speech."

The center contended that the Fifth Amendment guarantee that no person "shall be deprived of . . . property . . . without due process of law" would be violated if groups could use its facilities to disseminate views against the wishers of the owners. Balancing the rights of political communication against property rights, the court decided for the former. In a participatory democracy, said Judge Solomon, information must be uncensored. This last is a vital point. The establishment of access to facilities dedicated to a public use has created an outlet for the uncensored idea. The courts have held that no advertising manager, no editor, and no security guard should be permitted to ban *all* political handbills, or some political handbills but not others. The only requirement insisted on is that the political communication not disrupt a facility's primary activities.

Antiwar protest at a Portland shopping center does not relate directly to any activity of the shopping center. The court ruled that it didn't matter. Emphasizing the community's need for uncensored information, Judge Solomon said whether or not the Logan Valley conception could be stretched to permit protest unrelated to the site, the First Amendment certainly could.

He rendered a judgment that the antiwar group had a right to distribute handbills within the mall and that the Lloyd Corporation was bound not to interfere with that right.[7]

The Federal Court of Appeals affirmed Judge Solomon's decision[8] but in June 1972 the Supreme Court ruled that there must indeed be a relationship between the object of the protest and the site of the protest.[9] It thus took the first backward step in what had been a steady movement toward expanding the right to protest on private property dedicated to public use.

The four new Nixon appointees to the Court—Justices Powell (author of the opinion), Blackmun, and Rehnquist, and Chief Justice Burger—joined with Justice White to rule that distribution of handbills on shopping malls was not protected by the First Amendment if the handbills had nothing to do with any purpose for which the center was designed. The decision marked a new subordination of the values of free expression to those of private property.

The Logan Valley precedent still stands—protest related to the site, even if it is privately owned and operated, is protected by the First Amendment—but there is a new emphasis. The need and right of free expression is now likely to be considered less important than whether the site chosen is private or public property. The majority of the Court denied that the property of a large shopping center is "open to the public" in the same way as is the "business district" of a city, and that a member of the public could exercise the same rights of free expression in a shopping mall that he could in "similar public facilities in the streets of a city or town."

Justice Marshall, joined by Justices Brennan, Douglas, and Stewart, filed an angry dissent. There was no need in the Lloyd Center case, they argued, to decide if there must be a relationship between the object and the site of the protest. The Lloyd Center had already been generally opened to First Amendment activity. They stressed the need for opportunity of expression for those "who do not have easy access to television, radio, the major newspapers" and the usefulness of shopping center protest as an inexpensive substitute for those thus lacking access to the media.

Justice Marshall scorned the majority's concern for the property interests involved: he wrote that "common sense would indicate that speech that is critical of a shopping center or one or more of its stores is more likely to deter consumers from purchasing goods or services than speech on any other subject." The Justice, who wrote the majority opinion in the Logan Valley case, made clear his opposition to requiring a connection between the subject and the site of the exercise of free speech. He concluded, "When there are no effective means of communication, free speech is a mere shibboleth. I believe the First Amendment requires it to be a reality."

Nevertheless, the Lloyd Center case is now an obstacle on the path to the right of access for ideas. The odds are that now the crucial distinction will no longer be whether a facility can provide an audience important to the resolution of a problem but whether the facility in question has a direct relationship to the problem.

A Right to an Audience

When Judge Traynor held that a protest group could use the Los Angeles railroad station so long as the primary purpose of the station is not obstructed, he observed that, after all, the railroad could not complain since the railroad station could hardly make a claim to privacy. But what about the right of privacy of the passengers? The Supreme Court has been forced to grapple with this competing constitutional claim. In 1967 Congress enacted a federal antipandering statute which provided that every private person who receives "pandering advertisements" offering for sale any materials which he "in his sole discretion believes to be erotically arousing or sexually provocative" may request the Postmaster General to prohibit further mailings.

Some mail-order businessmen, book publishers, and mailing list brokers sought to have the statute struck down. The law was enacted to allow householders to shield their mail boxes from pornographers. The publishers and mail-order houses challenging the law contended that they had a right to communicate which the statute abridged. The government defended on the ground that those utilizing the statute had an equally precious right, the right to privacy. The Supreme Court upheld the statute and said essentially: if there is a right to communicate, it does not go so far as to compel entry into a householder's mail box.[10]

In the federal antipandering law case, the Supreme Court struck a blow for autonomy in the area of communications. Autonomy has an intimate relationship to access. The Court confronted the reality of modern mass mailings and said,

> Everyman's mail today is made up overwhelmingly of material he did not seek from persons he does not know. And all too often it is matter he finds offensive.

The mailing case makes the householder "the exclusive and final judge of what will cross his threshold." Such a result, the Court conceded, "undoubtedly has the effect of impeding the flow of ideas, information and arguments which, ideally, he should receive and consider." But to look at the right of the mailer without looking to the right of the recipient is really to protect only the communicator in the communications process. It was this limited approach to the communications process which the Court repudiated when in the great broadcasting case, Red Lion, the Court insisted that the rights of the viewer and the listener were not only protected by the First Amendment but that his interests and not those of the broadcaster were paramount.

A new era has arisen in U.S. communications policy. The laissez-faire approach to freedom of expression has failed because it is too exclusive: it is best equipped to protect the mailer, the broadcaster, and the publisher. But that arrangement made the householder-viewer-listener captive to the common assault of the former. The days of submission of the individual citizen to the barrage of the media lords and mail-order houses in the name of the First Amendment are drawing to a close. The legitimacy of such submission is now very much under constitutional attack.

The whole theory of individual decision-making is based on voluntary individual participation. The Supreme Court concluded in the federal antipandering law case that to hold that an addressee could not constitutionally give notice that he wished no further mailings from a particular mailer would be the equivalent of saying that "a radio or television viewer may not twist the dial to cut off an offensive or boring communication and thus bar its entering his home."

The Court said something else which should give us pause in the light of the railroad station and bus terminal and shopping center cases: "Nothing in the Constitution compels us to listen to or view any unwanted communication, whatever its merit; we see no basis for according the printed word or pictures a different or more preferred status because they are sent by mail." In reconciling the right to privacy and the right to communicate, each right gains strength depending on the locale in which it is to be exercised. The right to communicate in public facilities exercises a stronger claim than an individual's right to be free from exposure to ideas which he finds distasteful. In the home, the individual's right to privacy exercises a stronger claim than the mail-order businessman's right to communicate. As Chief Justice Burger put it: "That we are often 'captives' outside the sanctuary of the home and subject to objectionable sound does not mean that one must be captives everywhere."

The constituent elements of the right of privacy—solitude, the right to be let alone, the right to choose to hear—are challenged by the developments which make media out of nonmedia. Many people in our society simply wish to be let alone. They have a bus or train to catch and they wish to catch it in the easiest, least distressing way possible. They do not wish to participate in the bitter social debate of our time. They simply wish to get home for dinner.

The claim for an audience can be respected only if the audience to be sought is not captive. Yet the throngs who mill through the bus terminal or the railroad station are in a sense captive. They are forced to hear protest about an issue they may or may not be in sympathy with. To turn our public facilities into media by default jeopardizes privacy in a way that establishing a right of entry to the legitimate private media does not. The newspaper reader may refuse to read. The television viewer may refuse to watch. But the homeward-bound traveler accosted by handbills and speeches in public terminals is a participant against his will. Establishing entry into the legitimate media is a healthier and saner course than building substitute communications media out of facilities not designed for such service.

A person is not a sponge who has a duty to absorb as much information and ideas as can be fed, intravenous-like, into him. At least in his home a man can choose to remain free from the sounds of the distracting world—free alike from the propagandizing of commercialism and politics, and free also from the world of ideas. Such a conclusion is not incompatible with an access-oriented approach to the media. Emphasizing the right of participation of the audience makes sense only if the members of the public choose to participate. If they cannot choose to participate, the right to communicate becomes merely the right to propagandize. There is a right to an audience. There also is a right to choose to leave an audience. The right of access is, and must be, an act of choice.

The Court's contrast of the householder helpless to bar mailings of obscene advertisements with the same householder's freedom to turn off the radio or television is only superficially accurate. A mother's dependence on television, the electronic babysitter, may be so great that she has no real power of choice to reject the commercial-packed network cartoons. Only when an alternative is present does a real power of choice emerge. The flight of children to public broadcasting's *Sesame Street* illustrates that where a real alternative exists network television will be forsaken.

As Harry Boyle, Vice-Chairman of the Canadian Radio-Television Commissions, has observed:

. . . modern communication has substituted for the immediate and real environment, present and perceived by the senses, another environment reproduced from reality. This environment is made available simultaneously to greater and greater numbers of individuals over greater and greater areas by fewer and fewer selectors of the programmes shown. For children in particular, but for all people in general, observing this interposed environment is almost their central day-to-day mental experience and one of the most persistent and insistent stimuli to their emotions.

The license to broadcast is then almost the heaviest obligation that society can allow individuals to bear.[11]

A family which watches television may wish they had another kind of television to watch. Marshall McLuhan's thought that the medium is the message is only the beginning of wisdom. People do watch television and they want to watch television.

That people allow themselves to be an audience should not lead to any quick conclusions about either their contentment with the message of the media, or as McLuhan would have it, their indifference to it.

The interdependence of a right of access and the exercise of free choice should be emphasized. The Supreme Court has held people cannot be "communicated with" in their homes against their will. Conversely, in a case involving the right of individuals to keep allegedly obscene materials within their homes, the Supreme Court said that the Constitution protected the right to receive information and ideas. This conclusion is sensible. One must have access to information if he wishes but access must be voluntary. Communication must be by consent. Presently it is not.

Developments which attempt to compensate for advertiser-dominance of mass media by turning public buildings, shopping centers, and railroad and bus terminals into media of protest cannot satisfy, in the long run, the community's need for access to the real communications outlets—the press, radio, and television. Judicial willingness to admit unwelcome political and social ideas to public facilities should be realized for what it is—desperate evidence that the true forums for speech are insufficiently open.

The use of the judiciary to commandeer public or private nonmedia facilities as a viable forum for protest is, I believe, fundamentally just an episode. The important forum for communication in a mass society is the mass media. To place legal obligations on other facilities because of the incapacity or unwillingness of the media to respond to a felt need cannot in the long run be adequate.

The Search for an Audience

Constitutionalizing the Gatekeeper

At the door of the opinion process is the person who may be called the gatekeeper. He is the news editor of a broadcast station, the managing editor of a daily newspaper, the editor of a wire service, or the advertising manager of any communications medium. To reach an audience, an idea must get past him. The power the gatekeeper presently enjoys and the manner in which his power might be constitutionalized are revealed in the developing law of access to public facilities.

An illustration of the behavior of the gatekeeper is found in the experience of the Students for a Democratic Society with the New York City subway system. The S.D.S. sought to buy subway advertising space for posters opposing participation in the Vietnam war. The ad they wanted to run showed a picture of a scarred child. The text was this:

> WHY ARE WE BURNING, TORTURING, KILLING, THE PEOPLE OF
> VIETNAM?—TO PREVENT FREE ELECTION.

> PROTEST this anti-democratic war. WRITE PRESIDENT Lyndon B. Johnson, The White House, Washington, D.C.

> GET THE STRAIGHT FACTS
> WRITE
> Students for a Democratic Society
> 119 Fifth Avenue, New York, New York 10003

> This 10-year-old girl was burned by napalm bombs.

The excuses offered by the advertising department of the New York City Transit Authority to avoid accepting the ad were not very different from those that might be offered by any media advertising department to justify rejecting an ad it finds disturbing. There wasn't enough space. The posters were too controversial. The posters would provoke vandalism. In any event, acceptable advertising was limited to commercial advertising, public service announcements, and political advertising in connection with elections.

But what is a public service announcement and what is a controversial public issue are themselves matters of controversy. The subway authority had accepted posters proclaiming "Radio Free Europe—She Can't Come to You for the Truth" and "Read *Muhammed Speaks* Newspaper."

The students took the New York Transit Authority to court and asked that the subway be required to accept the posters for display. The subway asked the court to dismiss the students' case. The court refused and held that the subway authority's advertising company could not accept some posters and refuse others for reasons that conflicted with the guarantee of freedom of speech.[12]

A new view of the First Amendment, making access for provocative and challenging speech a basic constitutional goal, is found in this case. The court clearly indicated also that merely avoiding all controversial political discussion in advertising would not necessarily be permissible. The court's implication is that if as public a facility as a subway banished all controversial issue advertising, such banishment might be a violation of government's own First Amendment obligations.

Since the subway was governmentally-owned and operated, constitutional duties could be applied. From an access point of view, government was restraining expression. Accordingly, some governmental gatekeepers may now be held accountable to obey their own standards—that is, they are required to accept, within reason, public service advertising on an even-handed basis if they accept any such advertising. But the gatekeeper in the privately-owned media is still essentially accountable to no one.

In 1966, the Supreme Court was confronted with the issue of whether the grounds of a jailhouse could be used to protest the arrest of students for trying to integrate public theatres in Tallahassee, Florida. The sheriff had warned the crowd off the driveway leading to the jail entrance. The student crowd stood its ground and demonstrators were then arrested and convicted for malicious trespass. In a close 5–4 decision, the majority of the Court held that the jails had never been open to the public for protest in the past and that, with regard to such a facility, the state "no less than a private owner of property, has power to preserve the property for the use to which it is lawfully dedicated." [13]

Justice Douglas wrote a dissent in which he bitterly protested the unfettered discretion of the sheriff, the gatekeeper in that situation. He objected to permitting the "custodian" of public property to decide "when public places shall be used for the communication of ideas." Such absolute discretion in the "custodian" of public property places "those who assert their First Amendment rights at his mercy." But the gatekeepers of the private media presently operate under an equally unconfined discretion. In fact, a fundamental reason for the new focus on the role of the custodian of public property concerning the communication of ideas is the practical inaccessibility of the real communications media to protest groups such as those who sought to use the jailhouse driveway in Florida and the subway platform in New York. Justice Douglas recognizes the real origins of the present struggle to turn public buildings and facilities into forums for protest:

> Conventional methods of petitioning may be, and often have been, shut off to large groups of our citizens. Legislators may turn deaf ears; formal complaints may be routed endlessly through a bureaucratic maze; courts may let the wheels of justice grind very slowly. Those who do not control television and radio, those who cannot afford to advertise in newspapers or circulate elaborate pamphlets may have only a more

limited type of access to public officials. Their methods should not be condemned as tactics of obstruction and harassment as long as the assembly and petition are peaceable, as they were.

To constitutionalize the gatekeeper's function does not mean that a right of entry for any idea or any group is or should be guaranteed to any forum. In the subway authority case, the court remarked that reasonable regulations were perfectly in order. Constitutionalizing the function of the gatekeeper demands merely that he articulate the standards for admission to his forum and that he fairly apply them. The irony, as I have noted, is that this development has begun in public facilities which have become the media of desperation. They are now the ultimate forums for those "who do not control radio and television" and for those "who cannot advertise."

10 /

Crime as a Forum

In the winter of 1968 I received a phone call from a New York civil liberties lawyer, Marvin Karpatkin, who had an interesting idea. Could crime make a forum? If crime were resorted to in order to enter forums to express ideas for which access otherwise would be barred, should the crime be excused? Karpatkin had a client who dramatized a new use for the theory of access to the media.

Peter Kiger, a young Quaker, had written a terse note to his draft board in Newcastle, Indiana:

> Please send me a new classification card (1-Y I believe). I do not know the whereabouts of the one which you sent to my home in Dunreith, Indiana, in 1963; and I wish to burn one in sympathy with other people who have done so.

The draft board obliged and sent Kiger a duplicate of his draft card. He was good as his promise. On March 24, 1966, he burned it. Since Kiger and his companions burned their cards at a press conference in New York City, the action was reported in three New York daily newspapers and on major radio and TV stations.

Karpatkin's defense of Kiger was that since the card had been burned in order to reach an audience, the First Amendment should protect him when the law tried to punish him. Karpatkin got his idea from his work as a lawyer in a famous card burning case. On March 31, 1966, David Paul O'Brien and three companions burned their draft cards on the steps of the South Boston Courthouse. O'Brien was indicted, tried, and convicted. The Federal Court of Appeals disagreed and found O'Brien guilty but on a different theory. The United States appealed to the Supreme Court. Representing O'Brien at the Supreme Court, Karpatkin argued that O'Brien's act of draft card burning was protected by the constitutional guarantee of freedom of expression. Draft card burning, contended Karpatkin, was symbolic speech and therefore not punishable.[1] The Supreme Court did not agree and ordered O'Brien's conviction reinstated.

But Justice Harlan wrote a separate opinion which suggested that an access-oriented view of First Amendment rights might sometimes serve as defense to a criminal prosecution. Harlan said that he wished to make it clear that First Amendment claims could be considered when government regulations had the "effect of entirely preventing a 'speaker' from reaching a significant audience with which he could not otherwise lawfully communicate." When Karpatkin was representing Kiger, Harlan's language in O'Brien came back to him. Should crime be forgiven when its purpose was communication otherwise denied?

The extent to which violation of law was symbolic communication oriented to changing public opinion was fully illustrated by Kiger's own situation. Kiger was twenty-six when he burned his draft card. The likelihood at that point that he would have been drafted was virtually nonexistent. Kiger had been in the same draft selection group since August 12, 1964. No person had been ordered for induction or alternative civilian service out of that group during that time. Kiger's contention was that the government's need to protect draft cards was much less in his case than in that of David O'Brien. O'Brien had been twenty-two and classified 1-A, which meant he was available for immediate induction. Kiger was not only practically speaking ineligible for the draft, he was classified 1-O, the conscientious objector classification (his letter was mistaken). Moreover, Kiger's whole effort had been directed to entering the media. He didn't burn his card merely to express his own opposition to the war but as a means to reach an audience. Communication, not arson, was his objective.

The Committee for Non-Violent Action sent a press release to the mass media announcing that Kiger would burn his draft card on March 24, 1966, at the Committee's offices in Beekman Place, New York City. In the middle 1960s draft card burning was still a freak event; the press turned out in full—thirty to thirty-five reporters representing radio, television, and the press. News stories about the incident appeared in the *New York Herald Tribune*, the *New York Post*, and the *New York Times*, which had at that time a combined circulation of 1,450,000.

WCBS–TV and WNBC–TV showed films of the draft card burning on the six o'clock and the eleven o'clock evening news. The earlier news shows reached a minimum audience of 600,000 viewers, the latter about 800,000 viewers. Radio stations WCBS and WMCA, with total listening audiences of about 200,000, also broadcast the event.

The wire services carried the story to newspapers and radio and television stations across the country. Peter Kiger, a young Quaker from Newcastle, Indiana, had discovered the secret of access to the press. Since he made less than $50 a week, he could hardly have bought his way into so much publicity. A full-page advertisement in the *New York Times* alone costs around $7200. A minute of time on a network television news program costs between $1500 and $3000.[2]

Kiger had tried more conventional kinds of protest. He had distributed literature and made speeches against war. He had walked on weekly peace vigils in Times Square. But nothing he had done had won him as large an audience as engaging in a single criminal act.

Kiger's argument presented by his counsel, Karpatkin and Alan H. Levine, was that his guarantee of free speech would not have been really "effective" unless he had done what he did. Therefore, since he was really exercising his free speech rights, he could not be held criminally liable. Federal Judge Frederick Van Pelt Bryan found this ingenious argument simple to dispose of. Kiger had other ways to communicate which were lawful. Judge Bryan denied "that a person is free to violate a criminal statute in order to get his message carried in the press and on the air." As far as he was concerned, the struggle for access to the media was not going to prevail at the expense of the criminal law. The facts were clear: Kiger had burned his draft card in violation of law. Therefore, the judge held, he was "guilty as charged."[3] When Karpatkin and Levine urged their access theory to the Federal Appeals Court, that court also rejected it.[4]

The trouble with access as a defense in criminal prosecution is that it proves too much. When Puerto Rican revolutionaries tried to assassinate President Truman from a congressional gallery, they shot at him not as personal enemies but to dramatize the cause of Puerto Rican independence and to place it in the press. Assassins may do their terrible deeds out of a mad desire to end up on page one. It would be absurd to acquit them on that basis.

Actually it was his inability to get attention in the print media rather than government regulation which created Kiger's access problem. In a sense, the government gave Kiger access to the media. If draft card burning were not illegal, the media would not have been interested in reporting it.

Another difficulty with relying too heavily on Harlan's opinion was that Harlan very clearly indicated that O'Brien's situation was not a case in which government regulation might prevent a speaker from reaching a significant audience with whom he could not otherwise lawfully communicate. Harlan observed that O'Brien could manifestly have conveyed his message "in many ways other than by burning his draft card."

Lack of access can lead to crime but surely a wiser solution to that problem is to make provision for access rather than to use lack of access as a defense. Resort to crime in such cases reveals the need for legitimate and structured access to the media. When crime gains an entry that conventional dissent is not granted, the consequences are disheartening and illuminating. The jaded standards of the media stand revealed.

Kiger argued frankly to the court that his draft card burning was newsworthy only because it was a criminal act. Newsworthiness on TV, argued Kiger, is determined by potential dramatic impact. Ideology may be communicated with the warm approval of the media moguls if it is sufficiently surrounded by entertainment or novelty to guarantee audience attention. Instant access was given Kiger on WCBS–TV for burning his draft card, but if he had had enough money to buy time for a spot announcement expressing opposition to the war, it would not have been granted. CBS had refused to sell spot advertising for social or political opinions.

The fact is that having funds to purchase political advertisements often has little to do with actual access. Even offered money, a newspaper or a TV station may refuse to give space to a point of view. In fact, the easy access Kiger obtained to page five of the *New York Daily News* by burning his draft card in

1966 makes an ironic contrast to the results when less criminal means were tried to express the anti-Vietnam war position in that paper. In May 1970 ninety *Daily News* staffers collected nearly $1,000 and tried to purchase an ad in their paper expressing their opposition to American intervention in the war in Indochina and the *News* refused to publish it. The *New York Daily News* had been a proponent of administration policy in Vietnam and Cambodia. Advertising managers of the *New York Daily News* refused to give a reason for not publishing the ad.[5]

If there is no success in the movement to open up the media, if the present trend toward that goal does not continue, consideration will continue to be given to modes of expression, even if criminal, undertaken to secure an otherwise unobtainable entry into the machinery of public opinion. If the only way to penetrate the media is by exploiting that blend of the hurdy-gurdy and the violent which the media managers find irresistible, perhaps that will have to be considered in deciding whether nominal crimes were really events in the opinion process meriting constitutional protection.

In any event, crime is being used to secure a forum in American society. Peter Kiger is not the only example. Pediatrician Benjamin Spock, Yale Chaplain William Sloan Coffin, Michael Ferber, Marcus Raskin, and Mitchell Goodman were tried in Boston on a charge of conspiracy to counsel, aid, and abet resistance to the draft. But how, the defense lawyers argued, could there be a conspiracy? Justice Harlan had said in a 1957 Supreme Court opinion that "every conspiracy is by its very nature secret." The defendants in the Spock trial had written and spoken their views in *public*. Out of their efforts came a statement, "A Call to Resist Illegitimate Authority." Significantly, the Call was sounded at a press conference in New York City.

When activity such as aiding and abetting draft resistance, deemed criminal by the state, is undertaken in public to influence public opinion, should the openness of the activity affect the issue of its criminality? The trial judge certainly didn't think so.

But in the Federal Court of Appeals, Judge Coffin in a separate opinion allowed that public lawbreaking was a rather special case. He said the Spock group had placed itself "at the mercy of the marketplace of ideas." Possibly, the public would be appalled at the views expressed by the group. But their entry into the marketplace was candidly designed to be a public-opinion event. For Judge Coffin, these circumstances merited some protection for the defendants under the guarantee of freedom of expression.

In fact, the Spock defendants' whole effort was to influence a national debate. Was it unreasonable to ask therefore that such an event should be given First Amendment protection? Speaking for the majority of the Federal Court of Appeals, Judge Bailey Aldrich thought it *was* unreasonable. Unlike Judge Coffin, he refused to find the "present agreement pasteurized because it was exposed to the light"; this, said Aldrich, would "in effect" be "granting a right to public association which is not given to free speech itself." [6]

Furthermore, Aldrich remarked acidly, the defendants, before trial, had "publicly asserted that they were placing their own necks on the block." In his view, "They should not now be heard to say that no axe was involved."

But if we examine what actually happened in the Spock case we see that the case may well illustrate the acceptance in fact of a theory that crime committed in order to secure access to opinion should be excused. Five defendants were indicted in the Spock case. One, Marcus Raskin, was acquitted by the jury. The court of appeals itself held that the evidence as to two of the other defendants, Benjamin Spock and Michael Ferber, was insufficient to prove that they had the requisite intent to engage in conspiracy, and acquitted them. New trials because of error by the trial court were ordered for the defendants Mitchell Goodman and William Sloan Coffin. The government then dropped the prosecutions; so in the end all five men were free.

Crime can indeed not only make a forum but it can lead the forum to a conclusion of no crime. The extent to which the Spock trial was a public-opinion event in which the defendants successfully served as proselytizers of protest in an anti-Vietnam war debate was shown in 1971. At that time Ramsey Clark, who had been U.S. Attorney General when the indictments were drawn up against the Spock defendants, agreed as a lawyer in private practice to serve as defense counsel for the pacifist Berrigan brothers.

The idea that a desperate need to communicate should sometimes halt or mitigate criminal prosecution is a creative one. But it illuminates the problem of access far more than it resolves it. The need for access to the media must be given less negative legal recognition. It is more sensible to make provision for opening up the media on terms less expensive to society. Bus stations, subways, shopping centers, and railroad terminals have all been opened up to dissent by the courts in order to give ventilation to viewpoints which otherwise had found it difficult to secure expression. By so doing, the pressure on the social fabric is relieved. The courts find it more difficult to let a need for access become a defense for crime. Nevertheless, the use of crime to penetrate the media reveals how relentlessly the search for an audience has been pursued in contemporary America. The search has had some practical success even if it has not yet been given theoretical recognition.

For the news value of crime to become an inducement to commit it is a paradox. One of the reasons that freedom of discussion holds a primary place in American society is to make lawbreaking unnecessary. Justice Brandeis stressed the interconnection between a healthy and secure public order and the reality of freedom of expression. He wrote that fear breeds repression; that repression breeds hate; and that hate menaces stable government. Choosing his words carefully, Brandeis continued: "The path of safety lies in the opportunity to discuss freely supposed grievances and proposed remdies. . . ." [7] In our society this discussion is effective only in the mass media. It is the path of peril to allow crime to become the price of entry into the dominant forums of public opinion in this country. If lawbreaking is necessary to secure opportunity for expression, then the case for authorizing public entry to the media is demonstrated.

11 /

Broadcasting—

The Half-Opened Media

THE RISE OF BROADCASTING HAS BEEN A DIRECT CHALLENGE TO the classic noninterventionist approach to the marketplace of ideas. The metaphor, *marketplace of ideas*, is attractive; it has helped to shape our ideas concerning the whole existing American opinion process. The modern realities of press monopoly and concentration of control have not yet penetrated popular understanding. The myth is still current that "the press" and "the marketplace of ideas" are interchangeable entities. But the mythology is increasingly under attack. The very nature of broadcasting was ultimately bound to make apparent the limits of traditional laissez-faire approach to the exchange of ideas. The dozen television channels of the VHF spectrum were and are a limited access medium. As a federal judge said of radio during broadcasting's infancy, "Obviously there is no room in the broadcast band for every business or school of thought." [1]

As a result, in approaching the electronic media, one treads on very different legal terrain than with the press. Unlike newspaper publishers, broadcasters have legal obligations to their viewers and listeners. Three of these obligations demand our attention: the fairness doctrine, the equal time rule, and the personal attack rules. The fairness doctrine requires just that—fairness in presenting controversy on radio and television. It requires broadcasters to provide reasonable opportunity for the presentation of conflicting viewpoints on controversial issues of public importance.

The fairness doctrine does not give any specific group or viewpoint a right to command air time. But it does provide a basis by which groups or individuals representing a viewpoint opposed to one that has been broadcast can sometimes secure rebuttal time. A key point is that the fairness doctrine applies only when the station has started the fray. If the station has ignored an issue, there is nothing to rebut and the fairness principle cannot be invoked.

The fairness doctrine was set forth in a 1959 amendment to section 315 of the Federal Communications Act.[2] That section also states the equal time requirement that has become part of the American language. The equal time rule requires that if a broadcaster permits a legally qualified candidate for a public office to use his station, he must also give equal opportunities to all other candidates for that office. What does "legally qualified candidate" mean? The FCC has interpreted this phrase to mean a person who has publicly announced his candidacy.[3] For example, if X is running as a legally qualified candidate for Congress for the tenth congressional district of Virginia and station WAVA–FM gives him time to broadcast, then that station must afford an equal opportunity to broadcast to all other publicly announced candidates for that office.

Fairness and equal time are the best known and perhaps the most important programming obligations of broadcasters. The fairness doctrine, however, has spun off an additional requirement; the so-called personal attack rules provide a right of reply.

A personal attack is defined as an "attack on the honesty, character, integrity or like personal qualities of an identified person or group."

When a personal attack is made, the broadcaster must notify the person or group attacked of the date, time, and identity of the broadcast within a week. He must deliver a script or tape (or lacking these an accurate summary) of the attack. Finally, he must give the person or group attacked a reasonable opportunity to respond over his station.

Broadcasting is less open to debate than this account of the broadcaster's obligations might suggest. On Tuesday, April 28, 1970, President Nixon gave a nationwide television speech announcing U.S. military intervention in Cambodia. The speech nearly brought the house down and did bring down the campuses—on the heads of the administration.

Peace senators opposed to American involvement in Indochina and Vietnam sought television time to answer the President's speech. Only one network provided time and that network charged for it.

Did the senators and various peace groups opposing the war in Indochina have any legal right to time to reply to the President's speech? The disappointing answer was that there was no such right of reply.

The equal time concept did not apply because President Nixon was not running for office and there was no legally announced candidate opposing him.

The fairness doctrine was no help. The broadcasters must provide reasonable opportunity for the presentation of conflicting viewpoints, but that does not mean that every controversial subject broadcast must be specifically answered. The fairness principle requires only that there be an overall balanced presentation of conflicting viewpoints.[4] If over the three-year license period the broadcaster gives reasonable coverage to both the interventionist and the peace positions, the fairness doctrine is satisfied.

Finally, the personal attack rules did not afford the dissenting Senators or anyone else a right of reply on television since President Nixon had not attacked any person or group in his speech. It would seem that, although better than the case with the press, the legal picture in broadcasting is still inadequate.

Nevertheless, broadcasters envy the lack of obligation of their newspaper brethren. Characteristic is an editorial in *Broadcasting*, the industry house organ, lamenting the existing obligations. "The First Amendment," said *Broadcasting*, "should protect the broadcast media . . ." and called for a nationwide poll "asking the simple question whether radio and television should be accorded the protection of the First Amendment, like newspapers or magazines." [5] *Broadcasting* states the industry ideal and the newspaper reality—no public service obligations whatever. Presently, the First Amendment protects the newspapers, not their readership. In broadcasting, however, the First Amendment has been held to grant some right of participation to the audience as well. A system of broadcast regulation has made possible some entry to broadcasting by the public. These rights are not easily enforced; they are not always taken advantage of; and the agency bound to enforce them, the FCC, has not always been eager to do so.

But a panoply of public rights to broadcasting does exist and can be developed to provide still more access for the audience. Broadcasting is at least a half-opened media.

12 /

Broadcasters and

Controversy

Today editorial commentators on radio or television de-clare somewhat piously after each broadcast editorial that the station invites responsible spokesmen for opposing viewpoints to respond. Do not think that this expression of gracious fairmin-dedness is a welcome illustration of the survival of civility in modern life. The station makes this announcement because it must, to comply with broadcasting's famous "fairness" principle.

The present-day fairness doctrine in broadcasting traces its origins to a controversy about whether broadcast stations should be permitted to editorialize as newspapers do. In 1941, the FCC faced the problem of broadcast editorials when the Yankee Net-work station, WAAB, applied for a license renewal. In the late 1930s the station had broadcast editorials urging the election of various candidates for political office or supporting one or an-other issue in public controversy. The FCC, in its Mayflower doctrine growing out of the case, deplored the practice of radio editorials. The question—Can a broadcaster be an advocate?—was answered with a very loud *no*. Apparently the FCC didn't want broadcasters to editorialize because no one knew quite where the use of radio for partisan purposes would stop. The FCC then felt that the broadcaster's duty to the public was fulfilled by objective and informative reporting:

> Radio can serve as an instrument of democracy only when devoted to the communication of information and the exchange of ideas fairly and objectively presented. A truly free radio cannot be used to advocate the causes of the licensee. It cannot be used to support the candidacies of his friends. It cannot be devoted to the support of principles he happens to regard most favorably.[1]

These remarks might have fallen out of a Spiro Agnew speech. Thirty years later our faith in the possibility of such absolutely objective reporting is much shaken. The Vice-President has raised anew the argument against the broadcaster as an advocate, perhaps for different purposes but certainly for much the same reason. The limited number of broadcast frequencies makes wide public participation in their use impossible and puts enormous power in the hands of those who are selected to control them.

The reluctance shown by the FCC in 1941 to see radio used for partisan ends reflected a feeling which is slowly beginning to revive in the American approach to broadcast policy: aversion to partisan political exploitation of the license to broadcast.

By the end of the 1940s, the Commission had come to a new way to deal with the problem of allowing freedom to the citizens who owned broadcasting stations without denying freedom of expression to the many millions who did not. The FCC decreed in 1949 in its *Report on Editorializing by Broadcast Licensees*[2] that broadcasters should both editorialize and be obliged to represent the various conflicting currents of opinion in their discussion of public issues.

The change came because the rule against editorializing simply wasn't realistic. A broadcaster could easily influence opinion through his programming choices. If spokesmen were granted broadcast time to advocate views which the broadcaster shared but could not himself express, nothing was accomplished except to hide from the public the broadcaster's true preferences and prejudices. Better the overt advocate, said the FCC, than the "covert propagandist." Permitting the broadcaster to editorialize on an issue as long as he also aired contrasting viewpoints was supposed to result in a vital exchange of opinion.

The 1949 *Report on Editorializing* demonstrated a new maturity in American communication policy. The notion that political and social controversy could be objectively presented by a detached electronic journalism was abandoned. The broadcaster could now participate in the conflict of controversial public issues—but he would have to recognize a duty to admit others to participate as well, even though he disagreed with them.

Thus, the broadcaster's right to editorialize gave rise to the public's right to hear a fair presentation of other sides of controversial ideas of public importance. Unfortunately, the fairness doctrine was only a paper victory for the audience.

Broadcasters have not rushed to editorialize in any tough or effective way. Their zeal has been far more energetically spent in attracting new advertisers than in attracting controversy. Perhaps there are signs of change. On January 22, 1969, a newspaper-owned Boston television station, WHDH, lost its license in a rare FCC proceeding.[3] The new applicant for WHDH's frequency contended that since WHDH was owned by the Boston *Herald-Traveler*, the FCC's policy of seeking diversification in the control of the mass media would be better served by an independent voice. WHDH's defense was almost comical, although both the FCC and the Court of Appeals discussed it with straight faces. WHDH said that since it was owned by a newspaper, it had never editorialized since it began operations in 1954. In other words, WHDH had refrained from magnifying its parent paper's influence by taking no stands at all.

The FCC and the Court of Appeals both concluded that this was no defense, since broadcasters were required to give reasonable broadcasting time to controversial issues. But what was significant was that the FCC did not seem to think it strange that a television broadcaster had for sixteen years ignored the FCC's regulations on editorializing. Neither did the Court of Appeals seem particularly shocked by the continuous violation of a regulatory standard. It limited itself to the mild remarks that failure to editorialize showed the problems which arise when a newspaper operates a television station in the same community.[4]

The editorializing situation in broadcasting may therefore be described as follows. Broadcasters may and should editorialize, but it is of no great moment if they do not.

And still a basic feeling exists in the land that broadcasting has a duty both to present events fairly and to inform the public accurately of the controversies of the moment. Americans sense that the issues which absorb and divide us should be rationally and representatively discussed on radio and television. The development of the fairness principle in broadcasting has greatly stimulated these attitudes, as it has given notice that broadcasters have an obligation to the public and that it is one of legal duty and not of grace.

Yet, there have been profound dissatisfactions with the fairness doctrine. Until recently, the fairness doctrine has been more preached by the FCC than enforced. When I first studied the matter nearly a decade ago, I made the following observations:

However, evaluating the fairness doctrine from the point of view of a case-count which inquires only as to whether violations have ever actually been punished, rather than merely rebuked by a Commission letter, does not present a clear picture of the actual effect the doctrine has had on broadcast programming. It has been aptly noted that the persuasive influence of the fairness requirement on network programming may be considerable. Indeed, there appears to be no hostility in the broadcast industry to the principle of the fairness doctrine. Surveys that have been undertaken demonstrate that broadcast licensees prefer a programming standard which states a broad policy, leaving licensees generally free to make determinations as to implementation of the policy. For example, a poll taken of broadcast licensees indicates their preference for a fairness doctrine approach to the problem of broadcast opportunities for rival candidates rather than the present "equal-time" requirement.

Of course, this satisfaction on the part of broadcast licensees with the fairness doctrine's approach to broadcast regulation may be just another indication of its general ineffectiveness.[5]

Yet while the flavor of these conclusions was to urge more strenuous enforcement of the fairness doctrine, some parts of the broadcast industry had a quite different objection. Their unhappiness with the fairness doctrine has nothing to do with how severe FCC enforcement is. The industry cleverly argues that the very existence of the fairness doctrine has a dampening effect on expression and vigorous political discussion. It thus hits the fairness doctrine where presumably it lives, right in its promise to bring diversity of opinion to broadcasting. The contention is that since airing a controversial program or editorial may result in an obligation to offer reply time—and free reply time at that—the broadcaster is not encouraged to make a balanced presentation but rather to steer clear of controversy altogether.

The broadcasting industry seems to feel that it is a rare controversy worth risking a license over. Reuven Frank, when he was executive vice-president of NBC News, said the worst thing that could happen was to have some subject avoided because the broadcast journalist would not think it worth the trouble it would stir up. Rather than risk law suits and angry letters, Frank said broadcasters might resort to such self-censorship as would "restrict broadcast journalism to a mixture of the dull and frivolous." [6]

That threat seems rather empty. If Marshall McLuhan is correct about the intimate involvement and participation fostered by television, television and the real world are inevitably involved in continuous action and reaction. Controversy cannot be banished.

Even if such banishment were possible, it is not to the interest of the broadcasters to bar from the airwaves the unpleasant issues that divide us. Failure to provide balanced presentation of controversial issues can carry a heavy price. In 1969, in the Red Lion case, when the Supreme Court unanimously upheld the constitutionality of the fairness doctrine and the personal attack rules, Justice White gave the industry a short lesson in broadcasting law. Broadcast licenses, he said, conferred no ownership rights on broadcasters. A license gave a broadcaster the privilege of temporary use of a frequency. Unless renewed, he said tersely, a license expires in three years.[7]

What was particularly heartening for those who had despaired of breaking the cynical alliance between corporate interests and First Amendment freedoms was the acuity with which the Supreme Court penetrated the industry's use of freedom of the press to do what they protested was being done to them—censor admission to the airwaves. The First Amendment, said the Supreme Court, gave no rights to broadcasters "to prevent others from broadcasting on their frequencies."

The Court said grant of licenses could be conditioned on a "willingness to present representative community views on controversial public issues." A new era was being announced. Ignoring debate might be a shrewd policy no longer. If a broadcaster responded to public issues onesidedly or blandly, perhaps he would not be renewed when his three-year license period was up.

American broadcasting has travelled a long road from the 1941 Mayflower doctrine which forbade broadcasters to editorialize, to the Supreme Court's 1969 decision that broadcasters had a duty to present controversy and could forfeit licenses if they failed in the performance of that duty.

In 1970, the FCC refused to renew a license because of onesidedness in treating controversial public issues. Fundamentalist preacher Carl McIntire lost his application for license renewal of station WXUR in Media, Pennsylvania, in a groundbreaking decision. Fairness violation had never before resulted in a license loss.

Blandness remains a far more abiding characteristic of American broadcasting than onesidedness, however. In the fall of 1970, Barry Cole of Indiana University reported to the FCC that of 150 network affiliates included in a study, 60 failed to carry any public affairs at all.[8] No station, radio or television, has yet lost its license on renewal for blandness. But laws do exist that would make this possible. The challenge is to use this law— to use it to encourage a change in existing broadcasting or, failing that, to secure a change in existing broadcasters.

13 /

The Roar of Red Lion

The Background

THE GREAT CASE MENTIONED IN THE LAST CHAPTER BEGAN QUIETLY in a small town in Pennsylvania. In the fall of 1964, radio station WGCB–AM–FM, Red Lion, Pennsylvania, carried a program by a right wing clergyman and publicist, the Rev. Billy James Hargis. The fifteen minute program was part of *The Christian Crusade* series. In it, Hargis discussed the 1964 presidential campaign and a book by Fred J. Cook about Republican presidential candidate Barry Goldwater. The book, *Goldwater—Extremist on the Right*, made it clear that its author was not an admirer of Barry Goldwater. Hargis made it equally clear to his listeners that he was not an admirer of Fred Cook. Listen:

Now who is Cook? Cook was fired from the New York *World Telegram* after he made a false charge publicly on television against an unnamed official of the New York City government. New York publishers and *Newsweek* magazine for December 7, 1959, showed that Fred Cook and his pal Eugene Gleason had made up the whole story and this confession was made to the District Attorney, Frank Hogan. After losing his job, Cook went to work for the left-wing publication, *The Nation.* . . . Now among other things Fred Cook wrote for *The Nation* was an article absolving Alger Hiss of any wrong doing . . . there was a 208-page attack on the FBI and J. Edgar Hoover; another attack by Mr. Cook was on the FBI and Central Intelligence Agency . . . now this is the man who wrote the book to smear and destroy Barry Goldwater called *Barry Goldwater—Extremist on the Right.*

Cook asked for time to reply to Hargis' remarks and he asked further that reply time be furnished at the expense of WGCB. The request for free time was a special wrinkle in fairness problems. WGCB's response was to send Cook a card setting forth its rates. Tired of haggling with the station, Cook filed a complaint with the FCC. The FCC informed WGCB of the complaint against it and asked it for a response.

After a further exchange of letters, the FCC arrived at a fairly clear position. The station could ask Cook if he was willing to pay. But once the person attacked says he is not willing to pay, then the station has to put him on. Clearly this position does not encourage people to pay for broadcast time. And if there is anything broadcasters like less than engaging in lengthy correspondence with the FCC about personal attacks, it is having to furnish free time.

The FCC probably was thinking of the high cost of network time when it made reply time mandatory even if the person attacked refuses to pay. If a person attacked on a network had to pay network time rates, few could afford to reply. But networks are far less inclined to indulge in personal attacks than are small stations. Small stations where costs are much lower therefore have an opportunity to bring some heresy into broadcasting by providing outspoken programming. (This situation underlines the problem that ideas are being priced out of the marketplace.

A manufacturer of a mouthwash can reach millions because he has the wherewithal to buy advertising time, but spokesmen for ideas seldom have the resources to reach the media audience.)

In Red Lion, the FCC made up its mind. If the choice was between placing a financial burden on the broadcaster or leaving the public uninformed, then the balance must be tipped in favor of the public. After all, broadcasting is a public service medium owned by the public and only temporarily leased to the broadcasters.

The FCC issued an order formalizing its ruling that Red Lion had an obligation to give Fred Cook free time for reply. Red Lion appealed to the United States Court of Appeals in Washington, D.C. This brought to the test what had been one of the great undecided issues in broadcast regulation: was the fairness doctrine constitutional?

Broadcasting industry folklore had it that the fairness doctrine was unconstitutional. It had never been squarely tested in a federal court. Contending that the fairness doctrine violated the First Amendment, the broadcasters' counsel trotted out all the old constitutional arguments. Fairness was too vague a standard. Broadcasters were supposed to present controversial issues of public importance fairly. But what was a controversial issue? What was an issue of public importance? Who knew?

The judge in the Federal Court of Appeals, Edward Tamm, was not impressed. He did not consider the fairness standard that difficult to understand or observe. The Federal Communications Act required at several places that broadcasters perform in the "public interest." That phrase had never been held invalid because of its generality of expression. Section 315 of the Federal Communications Act, which set forth the fairness standard, required that broadcasters should afford "reasonable opportunity for the discussion of conflicting issues of public importance." That language was much more specific and precise than the public interest standard.[1]

The industry, somewhat shocked, decided to bring suit in another court of appeals, hoping there would be a conflicting opinion and thus to bring the matter before the Supreme Court. The strategy worked. A suit was lodged before the United States Court of Appeals for the Seventh Circuit in Chicago, reputedly a more conservative forum than the U.S. Court of Appeals for the District of Columbia. The Radio Television News Directors Association lodged a petition for review of orders of the FCC concerning reply time for political editorials or personal attacks.

RTNDA strongly urged that the personal attack rules inhibited freedom of the press. The Seventh Circuit agreed.[2] The reasoning was that broadcasters would be unwilling to broadcast freewheeling comment and political editorials if they were required by FCC rules to go to the expense of providing a transcript of possible attacks and to donate time (free time, yet) for a reply. Similarly, a broadcaster would be inhibited from speaking out on controversial issues if he had to provide time to air unorthodox views in response. Finally, it was predicted that the broadcaster would avoid controversial issues of public importance because of the difficulty of determining what FCC rules require in a given situation.

In English common law, the classic understanding of freedom of the press was that it was freedom from prior restraint. Prior restraint is governmental action designed to prevent publication of material. (The principle achieved public attention in our day with the controversy over publication of the Pentagon Papers.) Broadcasters contended that if issues of public importance could not be aired unless they were ready to make equivalent free time available for countering the paid time, discussion and controversy would disappear from broadcasting. The station owners contended that they would have to become first censors of all public interest broadcasts.

But the broadcasters were not in fact required to submit transcripts or tapes of any broadcast to the FCC or to any other government agency. Judge Tamm in the U.S. Court of Appeals in Washington had turned the tables on the industry litigants. Tamm reasoned that if there were no fairness doctrine, the rights of those in Cook's situation would be the ones curtailed: rather than creating censorship, the fairness doctrine alleviates it.

To counter Judge Tamm's ruling, the RTNDA suit challenged the validity of the personal attack rules. The Federal Court of Appeals in Chicago approved the industry argument that those rules were inherently vague, and that they encouraged broadcasters to act as private censors, and held the rules unconstitutional.

In the Supreme Court the score was 1–1 and the stage was set for a tie-breaking decision. In a case that made broadcasting history the Supreme Court joined the two cases and came down squarely in favor of broadcast regulation, affirmative duties to the public on the part of broadcasters, and a broad right of reply in broadcasting.[3] The decision said the fairness doctrine and the personal attack rules were not only consistent with the First Amendment but that they implemented it. The Supreme Court's decision in Red Lion was a body blow to the laissez-faire approach to freedom of the press in the United States. The simplistic concept of liberty of the press as the absence of any legal obligation by the broadcaster to the public was struck down.

The industry money and energy expended in these cases before the Supreme Court was great. Distinguished counsel, some of them academics with impressive civil liberties credentials, filed briefs as friends of the court in support of the major networks and against the "fairness doctrine." Former Solicitor General of the United States and Harvard Law School Professor Archibald Cox was retained by the Radio Television News Directors Association to aid in getting the favorable decision of the Chicago Federal Court of Appeals affirmed by the Supreme Court.

I doubt that many of those who had, on the industry side,

long preached the unconstitutionality of the fairness doctrine had actually expected the fairness doctrine or the personal attack rules to be held unconstitutional.[4] Both decency and fair play obligated broadcasters to present opposing viewpoints on controversial issues and to permit response to personal attacks. Nevertheless, the actual decision of the Supreme Court was very disappointing to the industry and the scope of the opinion was a surprise. The decision's radical thrust rocked broadcasting. It was studded with indications that the Court was disenchanted with the existing structure of broadcasting and that, as far as the Court was concerned, there was nothing sacred about that structure. The airwaves were operated by private broadcasters and networks, but the Court thought this was due more to a lack of realistic alternatives than to any property rights of the broadcasters. The Court emphasized that Congress had great latitude and power to improvise with regard to broadcast regulation.

Rather than parcel out licenses to a small number of broadcasters in a nation of 200,000,000 people, the government could as well require that every frequency should be shared by "all or some of those who wish to use it." Conceivably each person in the country could be assigned a "portion of the broadcast day or the broadcast week." The suggestion that there could easily be an alternative to the system of private broadcasting was heresy and, considering the source, important heresy at that.

The Supreme Court has thus brought the curtain down on broadcasting's greatest act: the fantasy that the program decisions made by the executive hierarchies of ABC, NBC, and CBS represented the inexorable and historic unfolding of the constitutional guarantee of freedom of the press. In the decision justifying the personal attack rules and the fairness doctrine, a conservative former Attorney General, Justice White, used language which broadcasters were more accustomed to hearing from their radical critics than from the Supreme Court. He said in effect that the FCC's mechanisms for reply, personal attack, fairness, and equal time were not only consistent with the First Amendment, they were required by it. Otherwise station owners and "a few networks" would be able to "make time available only to the highest bidders." Rebuttal time, and free rebuttal time at that, was essential. Without it broadcasters would be able to "communicate only their own views on public issues, people, and candidates."

Private Censorship

The Court thus plainly repudiated one of the dogmas that the broadcasters hoped would be reaffirmed. The dogma was that censorship could be called freedom of the press if it was done by private hands and not by government. The fact that the power to decide what would be heard was gathered in remarkably few hands was little remarked as industry counsel and publicists had long succeeded in keeping attention on the genuine evils of government censorship. Private censorship was mentioned only as the lesser of two evils in an either/or proposition. The Supreme Court has at last refused to let broadcasters use the First Amendment as a cover for their single-minded hucksterism. The First Amendment, the Court said, does not provide a sanctuary for "private censorship in a medium not open to all."

Liberty of discussion has classically been secured by protecting the property rights of the communicator. The older emphasis on property is now being replaced by attention to the rights of the public to information and participation in open discussion. An entirely new climate is evident in the Court's remark that, in regard to the First Amendment, "those who are licensed stand no better than those to whom licenses are refused."

But even beyond that, the Court stressed that the purpose of broadcasting is to benefit the public, an idea which is rapidly taking root in the other media as well. Broadcasters are licensed not in order to vent their own ideas but to serve as fiduciaries of the channels for representative community views and voices which would otherwise not have access to the air. In stern language, the Supreme Court warned that a broadcaster has no constitutional right "to monopolize a radio frequency to the exclusion of his fellow citizens."

When it is understood that the broadcast license is not private property, it seems obvious why broadcasters must serve as hosts to public dialogue and debate even though they would rather show cartoons. If the license is not property, if its purpose is not primarily to enrich the licensee but to benefit the community, then it becomes easier to understand why a broadcast outlet has to provide for response when controversial issues, political campaigning, and personal attacks are broadcast by a station. In such circumstances, according to the Court, the public has "collective rights" to have the media function consistently with the First Amendment. It can no longer be claimed that freedom of the press is served by protecting the absolute discretion of the individual broadcaster.

The Rights of the Viewer and the Listener

Paradoxically, the concentration of ownership in the news media has at last served to identify the real purposes of the guarantee of freedom of expression. In the eighteenth century, publishers were protected in expectation that they were sufficiently numerous and contentious that protecting their property would result in vigorous and robust debate. Today, protecting the property of the new electronic press has not led to diversity. Therefore, a new understanding of "freedom of the press" has become necessary. In Red Lion, the Court revolutionized First Amendment thinking when it said: "It is the right of the viewers and the listeners, not the right of the broadcaster, which is paramount."

The primacy of the audience, the rights of listeners, is a pioneering concept which is not yet fully developed or understood. In the past, admittance to public debate has been essentially at the disposal of the media gatekeepers. Broadcasting spokesmen have hoped that their private status would divert attention from the enormous potential for social harm inherent in their monopoly situation. But the diversion tactic is failing. The Supreme Court particularly noted the advantage that the prestige media have in shaping and commanding mass opinion.

Perhaps the long term answer to the need for dialogue and diversity in the media lies in the rise of community antenna television and in better utilization of UHF television outlets, as yet unused or poorly used. But for now, it is network dominance of the programming of the commercial VHF television stations which is the great contemporary reality in forming American public opinion. The sheer fact of network success demands legal obligation.

The existence of competing media could not be treated, in the Court's opinion, as a complete solution to the need for diversity and dialogue. Existing broadcasters have secured an immense government-conferred benefit. As the Court saw it, "Long experience in broadcasting, confirmed habits of listeners and viewers, network affiliation, and other advantages in program procurement give existing broadcasters a substantial advantage over new entrants, even where new entry is technologically possible."

The Coming of Age of Access

The Red Lion decision can be explained by conventional theory. Legal responsibilities may be imposed on broadcasters which may not be imposed on newspapers because of the inherent limitations in the spectrum. But although the Court gave lip service to the conventional doctrine, it was obviously intrigued with the idea of a right of access to the media as a basis for evaluating media policy and analyzing First Amendment problems.

The Court in Red Lion gave three reasons for finding the fairness rule and the personal attack rules constitutional:

(1) the scarcity of frequencies,

(2) public ownership of broadcast frequencies, and

(3) "the legitimate claims of those unable to gain access to those frequencies for expression of their views."

This last reason is certainly the most fascinating, the most radical, and the most fertile idea for the future. It may open the way for freedom of expression in broadcasting to reach a far larger congeries of rights.

Perhaps the most challenging sentence in Red Lion is the following: "It is the right of the public to receive suitable access to social, political, esthetic, moral and other ideas and experiences which is crucial here." Red Lion has displaced a previous authoritative statement on broadcast regulation, *National Broadcasting Co. v. U.S.*, a 1943 Supreme Court decision.[5] That decision involved an attempt by the FCC to regulate network contracts, by which local stations were being denied their initiative and independence. The networks contended that the FCC had only the power to regulate technical and engineering aspects of broadcasting. The Supreme Court then rejected the network argument that the FCC had no power to impose modest substantive responsibilities on the industry as it rejected the network argument in 1969 that the FCC had no power to provide a legal requirement for dialogue.

Why could conditions and responsibilities be imposed on broadcasters and not publishers? Justice Felix Frankfurter gave a short answer for the 1943 Supreme Court: "The radio spectrum simply is not large enough to accommodate everybody." Broadcast regulation was possible, constitutionally speaking, because the number of applicants for broadcast licenses exceeds the number of broadcast frequencies. Some standards therefore had to be developed to keep stations from interfering with each other. The task of selecting applicants was entrusted by Congress to the FCC, which was to choose for each available frequency the applicant most likely to operate in the public interest. It was also the task of the FCC to give content to the statutory phrase, "public interest."

Twenty-six years later the Supreme Court again cited the limitations of the spectrum to justify broadcast regulation. But the Court was obviously troubled by a sense that the problems of liberty of expression in broadcasting are not caused just by the limited available number of frequencies. Economic factors are as much a limitation in securing access to broadcasting as technological ones. At stake in the Supreme Court decision concerning a small radio station in Red Lion, Pennsylvania, was not only whether providing reply time was constitutionally required but also whether the reply time could be obtained free. It was on the latter issue that WGCB had appealed and it was on that issue that it was defeated.

Concepts like fairness, equal time, and opportunity to reply to personal attacks would be needed even if broadcasting were not a technologically limited medium. In fact, TV broadcasting could be less of a limited access medium than is the daily newspaper industry. Many American cities have not utilized, or have underutilized, UHF frequencies. Facilities to use these frequencies can be built at competitively minimal cost, compared with the financial resources needed by a new entrant into the daily newspaper market in any large (or even medium-sized) American city.

The Meaning of Red Lion

The first and most immediate significance of the Red Lion decision is that it held the fairness and personal attack rules to be entirely consistent with the First Amendment. This means that public rights in broadcasting have now been given a security never before enjoyed in the entire history of broadcast regulation under the Federal Communications Act of 1934. A licensee can no longer plug into a network, take his rake-off from the advertisers, and call his performance the exercise of First Amendment rights.

Secondly, the validation of the fairness and personal attack rules ought to give new strength and heart to those entrusted with the regulation of broadcasting. Over the years, the FCC has blown alternately hot and cold over the issue of enforcing the fairness doctrine. One of the reasons for its vacillation has been a concern that requiring broadcasters to be fair somehow might violate freedom of speech and press.

Thirdly, the relationship of the broadcaster to his license has now been clarified in plain words. The broadcaster has no property rights in the frequency he is temporarily licensed to operate. His personal financial investment is not as important as the nation's dependence on the quality and character of broadcasting.

Fourthly, Red Lion marks the beginning of a new chapter in the understanding of problems of freedom of expression in the United States. The owners and operators of the communications media owe positive obligations to their viewers, listeners, and readers. Freedom to petition and freedom of speech can be as easily suppressed by the new media class as by government. The Supreme Court has recognized this reality and made it clear that private censorship is no less antithetical to First Amendment values than government censorship. The work of the Su-

148

preme Court in the Red Lion decision demonstrates that the First Amendment still has enough resiliency to be the instrument of its own protection. Freedom of the press, print and electronic, can be required—even from the press itself.

14 /

The Unfairness of Fairness

THE FAIRNESS DOCTRINE HAS LONG SERVED AS A LEGAL HANDLE TO insure that ideas have an entry to broadcasting. But it is a slippery handle. When a specific right of reply to a specific program or spokesman is wanted, the fairness principle is particularly defective. The decision as to which group or spokesmen should represent a particular viewpoint is entirely the broadcasters'. For example, Senator McGovern of South Dakota, an announced candidate for President and a long-time critic of the war, had no right under the fairness doctrine to answer President Nixon's Cambodia speech.

The basic defect of the fairness doctrine is the primitive level on which it functions. Only if someone says X may someone else say anti-X. This hardly leaves room for the spontaneity that gives excitement to the clash of ideas. There should be some less ponderous way to stimulate discussion of fundamental social issues and problems.

The fairness principle imposes some obligation on broadcasters to allow fair debate. But some issues simply do not get debated. It is here that the fairness idea needs to be enriched by the concept of access. The performance of broadcasters should not be judged just on how meticulously or generously they apportion reply time. They should also be judged on how well they meet an affirmative obligation to give access to controversial issues of public importance in the first place.

The bare language of Section 315 of the Federal Communications Act of 1934 can be interpreted as imposing much weightier obligation on broadcasters than compliance with the fairness doctrine. The law obliges broadcasters "to operate in the public interest and to afford reasonable opportunity for the discussion of conflicting views on issues of public importance." Surely this language is compatible with requiring broadcasters to originate debate and seek out controversial issues for presentation on radio and television. Presently, Section 315 is interpreted as merely recording Congressional recognition of the fairness idea. Of course, at renewal time a broadcaster who has evaded controversy may be attacked for carrying insufficient public issue programming. The risk such a broadcaster takes is nonrenewal of his license. But few broadcasters in nearly forty years of regulation under the present law have ever been forced to pay that penalty. Only recently has the pattern changed.

But since the fairness rule has been the only avenue for entry as of right to television, a new effort in the 1960s has been developed to expand its scope. In December 1966, a young Manhattan lawyer, John W. Banzhaf III, asked WCBS–TV in New York City to provide time for antismokers to reply to the pro-smoking views of the cigarette commercials.

Banzhaf pointed out in his letter that the cigarette advertisements, with handsome and beautiful protagonists involved in attractive situations, implied that "smoking is socially acceptable and desirable, manly and a necessary part of a rich full life." This was a point of view and a controversial one. The question was whether CBS was therefore obligated to make its facilities available "for the expression of contrary viewpoints."

Banzhaf's request illuminated the whole regulatory approach to ideas in broadcasting. Ideas that influence, that mold society and opinion, do not exist solely or even very significantly in the world of Sunday afternoon panel shows. The form of the spot commercial is ideally suited to the art of persuasion, as was proved when *Sesame Street* adopted it with immense success to sell the alphabet rather than commodities to children.

The question of whether advertisements were subject to the fairness doctrine was not a new question, but it had always been a difficult one. In 1946, a broadcaster's license renewal had been challenged on the basis that he had sold time for liquor commercials but had refused to sell time for broadcasts promoting abstinence. The FCC gave notice that broadcasters were not relieved of the duty to be fair just because a controversy concerned advertising. After delivering this sermon, the FCC then dutifully renewed the license.[1]

The idea that cigarette advertising, and advertising generally, can be treated as a controversial idea strikes at the breadbasket of modern American mass media. But for a Hutterite or an Amishman, all advertising may be a controversial idea. Television's idealization of "getting and spending" may very well suggest a lifeview that they disagree with in the most fundamental sense. If, as is sometimes said, the media really exist to facilitate the movement of commodities, the possibility that Ralph Nader would have a right to ask for reply time to point out the safety faults of some new automobile is something that should, and perhaps yet will, send shivers up Detroit spines.

WCBS–TV rejected Banzhaf's request for time. The station said the fairness doctrine did not apply to advertisements and, anyway, they had given time to the antismoking position. Had they not in recent months carried (free!) five announcements against cigarettes by the American Cancer Society?

Banzhaf then complained to the FCC. To the horror of two industries—tobacco and broadcasting—the FCC agreed with him. The FCC held that advertisements which promote the use of a particular cigarette as enjoyable are controversial.[2] Why? Apparently because both government and private sources have asserted that use of cigarettes is a threat to health. The FCC insisted that its decision was good for one trip only: reply time was "limited to one product—cigarettes." But surely the door had been opened. The FCC had conceded the impact of television on social behavior.

But the social damage that can result from presentations like the cigarette commercials cannot necessarily be ameliorated by a rebuttal. There are not two sides to cancer. Some things are objectively undesirable, as the FCC itself seemed to recognize when it first proposed to prohibit cigarette advertising on television altogether. Congress underscored this view by enacting a law to prohibit all cigarette advertising on television after January 1, 1971.[3]

When Banzhaf's request for television time to counteract cigarette advertising reached the United States Court of Appeals in Washington, the judge, David Bazelon, wrote an opinion sustaining the application of the fairness doctrine to cigarette advertising. Bazelon stressed in his decision that, although the FCC was justified in applying the fairness doctrine to cigarette advertising, the FCC also had authority to order rebuttal time for antismoking groups on the basis of its duty to enforce the public interest.

That is, hazards to health threatened by public acceptance of smoking placed a duty on broadcasters to provide free time for reply to cigarette commercials. It is an arresting idea. Can all advertising be tracked? Is not all communication a hazard to something or someone? Both the FCC and the U.S. Court of Appeals apparently feared the dilemmas raised by such questions. Both struggled therefore to confine their ruling to cigarette advertising.

But it is hard to put shackles on a stimulating idea. The anti-smoking decision does take a social responsibility approach to freedom of expression and so moves beyond the traditional laissez-faire idea that the broadcaster or the publisher should be the sole arbiter of content in his medium.

In the Banzhaf case Judge Bazelon pointed out that free debate was not assured when "only one party has the financial resources and interest to purchase sustained access to the media." Such a contest was "not a fair test of either an argument's truth or its innate popular appeal." Debate is not self-executing. One side frequently has financial resources and a compelling economic interest that its opponents cannot equal. By requiring substantial time for antismoking information to counteract cigarette advertising, Judge Bazelon thought that the "purposes of rugged debate" would be "served not hindered by an attempt to redress the balance." [4]

It is significant in the Banzhaf case that both the FCC and the U.S. Court of Appeals recognized that some issues need airing even though exposition might not be demanded by formal operation of the fairness rule. Until this case, the fairness doctrine had not been applied to television commercials. The seriousness of the smoking issue obviously influenced the decisions. Indeed, on appeal, Judge Bazelon mentioned that the First Amendment interest in debate would be served by some mechanism to provide expression in an area "where the public stake in the argument is no less than life itself."

The first tentative step was to provide time for free commercials against smoking. The technical basis for the rule was ostensibly the fairness doctrine. More critically, the reason was the recognition that the antismoking position simply needed access.

Need for access to television can sometimes create a right to it. In establishing this, the Banzhaf case represents a major victory. It is always hard to open a door just a little bit. In August

1970 a group called Friends of the Earth contended to the FCC that WNBC–TV in New York City was obligated to make free time available for antipollution groups to reply to automobile advertisements. Obviously cigarette smoking is not the only issue in our society that merits access to the media. Many do. The FCC is reluctant to set out criteria to indicate which issues merit access. But that task must be undertaken.

If the FCC is considered too inept, too political, or too unwilling to do the job, a right of access to broadcasting enforceable in the federal courts should be provided by statute. Alternatively, a right of public access to the broadcast media can be enforced by the courts on the basis of an access-oriented reading of the First Amendment.

Keeping the cigarette advertising reply time decision from spreading to other fields is proving difficult. The result is that broadcast regulatory policy is slowly whittling down the traditional limitations on the scope of the fairness doctrine. The effort to make fairness do the work of access is illustrated by a recent example.

Hill's department store was an advertiser on WREO in Ashtabula, Ohio. Its ads promoted the usual service, selection, and bargains. What was unusual was that Retail Store Employees Local Union 880 was on strike against the store. The union undertook to support its campaign with one-minute spot announcements publicizing the strike.

At first the union had no difficulty in buying time, but as time went on the station seemed less willing to sell. On the other hand, the store had no problem in buying its radio ads; 322 advertisements were carried by WREO between February and April 1966.

Finally WREO refused to sell the union any more time. The union filed a complaint with the FCC. The station then offered free time to both parties for a roundtable discussion of the issues involved in the strike. The union rejected this offer and asked the Commission to order the station to sell it advertising time to state its cause.

The big question was why did WREO stop selling ads to the union. On appeal, Judge Bazelon, for the U.S. Court of Appeals, speculated on the possibility that economic pressures by the department store were responsible. Under the circumstances, Judge Bazelon said, the record did not support renewal of WREO's license.[5]

Judge Bazelon said it was a breach of public interest to carry the ads of one side to a labor dispute while freezing out the other side. The key term here is *public interest*. If that concept can be used to build rights of access and reply, we can put aside the largely disappointing effort to make the fairness doctrine do work for which it was never designed. In Bazelon's view, the public interest may be violated when a radio station allows a store to buy ads urging the public to patronize it yet refuses the store's striking employees "any remotely comparable opportunity to urge the public to join their side of the strife and boycott the employer."

Bazelon's use of the cigarette advertising ruling in the WREO case is hopeful for the future of access to broadcasting. It illustrates that the FCC's effort to keep fairness out of advertising questions is beginning to fall apart. In analyzing his own decision on the cigarette advertising case, Bazelon indicated that the crucial factor was whether advertisements carried "implicit" messages. Is there a right of specific response to "implicit" messages in advertising? Bazelon has opened the way to such a conclusion.

One of the ironies of the recent impetus toward access is that the same broadcasters who once sought to invalidate the fairness doctrine now praise it. In comparison with the personal attack rules and with the movement for access, fairness looks good. In a speech at the American Bar Association's 1969 convention in Dallas, Richard Jencks of CBS praised the fairness doctrine for emphasizing that "the choice of viewpoints to be presented, and of spokesmen to present the viewpoints" is within the broadcaster's discretion.[6] (Such industry affection for the fairness doctrine had not stopped CBS from filing an *amicus curiae* brief with the Supreme Court in the Red Lion case, asking for a declaration that the fairness doctrine violated the First Amendment.)

In Dallas, Jencks extolled the fairness doctrine over the personal attack rules. Under the personal attack rules, if the injured person wishes to reply, he must be given a right to reply in his own words. This upsets Jencks. He praises the gatekeeper who in the newspapers and in broadcasting makes the "final decision as to the selection, order, priority, and emphasis of the day's views." [7]

But journalistic discretion, the journalist's expert sense of "newsworthiness," is not being cast aside by access as Jencks fears. The choice is not either to carry anything anyone submits or to give broadcasters absolute domination of the air waves. The movement for access is designed only to achieve greater media responsiveness to community desires for direct participation. That is what the personal attack rules permit.

In a panel discussion on the right of access and reply to the media at that 1969 ABA Convention, Commissioner Kenneth Cox of the FCC defended the idea that radio and television might serve more usefully and creatively as forums for public discussion and information than they presently do.[8] Cox pointed out that the FCC's seminal paper, the 1949 *Report on Editorializing by Broadcast Licensees*, made clear that fairness involved something more than mechanical provision of reply time when requested. The licensee, the Report said, has an affirmative duty to encourage the broadcast of controversial issues.[9]

If vital issues are not broadcast or given attention as a consistent policy, it doesn't matter whether the reason is commercial avarice or ideological prejudice. Consistent denial of access for such views should be as much a factor in consideration of the license renewal application as the fairness doctrine now is.

Former Commissioner Cox reads Red Lion as providing a public right "to employ privately owned media for the expression of the significant views of the community." Cox likes the idea of letting licensees make the initial selection of issues and spokesmen for different points of view. The FCC can review this determination. But he urges broadcasters themselves to seek out the critical issues and the groups and individuals appropriate to discuss them.

Cox feels the Federal Communications Act provides a right of access and that the Red Lion case indicates that the Supreme Court reads the law that way too. Certainly Section 315 can be read as providing access more clearly than as requiring fairness. The initial decision maker should be the licensee. The FCC role as evaluator and reviewer comes later. But if program content analysis shows a station devoting less than one percent of its time to public affairs, its performance should be seriously re-examined at renewal time.

Some precise FCC rules requiring access for issues of public importance which have been underrepresented in the licensee's programming would help to minimize broadcaster evasion of the fairness rule. Access will block the escape hatch in the present operation of the fairness rule. Avoidance of controversial matters altogether to evade the fairness doctrine would no longer be worth the risk if a station had clearly defined access responsibilities.

Access is more important than fairness, but a right of access harmonizes with enforcement of the fairness principle. First there must be an obligation to present the "problems which beset the people." Then there must be a duty to present them fairly.

15 /

The Movement for

Access to Television

HE SUMMER OF 1970 SAW INAUGURATED AN INTENSE CAMPAIGN for access to television. The President of the United States' easy access to television to urge support for an unpopular war in Indochina dramatized the lack of access of the rest of the country. Even the highly placed were prevented from responding to him on that issue on television. Fourteen senators—led by George McGovern of South Dakota and Mark Hatfield of Oregon, and including eleven other Democrats and one other Republican, Charles Goodell of New York—filed a complaint with the FCC in July 1970. Technically relying on the fairness doctrine, the senators argued that the First Amendment gave them a right of access to respond to Nixon's pro-war telecasts. They demanded that the networks provide time to any substantial group of senators opposing the President "whenever the issue is one in which the Senate has a role to perform in seeking resolution of the issue."

McGovern and other sponsors of the Hatfield "end-the-war" amendment had asked the networks to sell them time to present their views. NBC sold them a half-hour which was used to solicit funds. But NBC as well as ABC and CBS turned down requests for more paid time. The network position was that they had satisfied the fairness requirement in covering the peace issue in other time allocations. The networks contended that the position of the "peace" senators had been made clear in interviews and regular news broadcasts.

Two other organizations, the Committee for Fair Broadcasting of Controversial Issues and the Business Executives' Move for Vietnam Peace, urged that broadcast of five TV addresses by the President in seven months brought the fairness doctrine into play. The FCC took these and other pleas for access up together on August 14, 1970. It rejected the request of the senators for mandatory television time for rebuttal, saying it was unable to find any basis for "singling out any 'substantial group' of Senators as being entitled to respond." [1]

The FCC also rejected the requests of the Business Executives Move for Vietnam Peace for a substantial block of uninterrupted time controlled by BEM to answer the President's viewpoint. They and other complainants were told that the broadcasters, and only the broadcasters, had the responsibility to determine the appropriate spokesman to represent a point of view on television.

But the determination to keep matters of television reply and rebuttal firmly in broadcaster hands was soon thwarted by the broadcasters' own comically unsuccessful attempts to resolve problems of entry to television for protest. At the same time the FCC rejected the request of fourteen United States Senators and others for television time, it also dealt with a complaint against network behavior which grew out of a CBS decision voluntarily to give twenty-five minutes on July 7, 1970, to Democratic National Committee Chairman Lawrence O'Brien to answer President Nixon.

CBS pleased no one. O'Brien and the Democratic National Committee immediately demanded free network time for every Presidential press conference and public statement. The Republican National Committee, furious about O'Brien's use of the reply time, then asked CBS for free time to answer him. Republican Congressman Broyhill of North Carolina objected to O'Brien's partisan appeal for funds on the program. Republican Senator Gurney of Florida said CBS and the Democratic Party were in an "unprecedented" and "illegal direct collaboration." Reflecting on virtue's rewards, CBS President Frank Stanton reminded everyone that all CBS had wished to do by putting on O'Brien was to minimize the "risk of imbalance" and to treat "public issues fairly."

The Republican National Committee next complained to the FCC that the Democratic broadcast was partisan and dealt with "which party should be in power" rather than the issues upon which the President had expressed himself. The FCC agreed and ordered CBS to make available "a reasonable period of time to the Republican National Committee or some other appropriate Republican party spokesman selected by CBS."

Sources as disparate as the conservative and hawkish newspaper columnist William S. White and liberal dovish Senator Mike Mansfield protested CBS' decision to offer the reply time to Chairman O'Brien. White said O'Brien, a nonelected party functionary, was simply not a suitable choice to reply to the President of the United States. Senator Mansfield said that the claims for a right of reply on television to the President were being overdone. After all, Mansfield observed, the President had a duty "to go on television and make statements from time to time."

The CBS decision to put up Larry O'Brien to answer Nixon is a good demonstration of the need for more clarity, precision, and authority in dealing with the problems of access for the political opposition when the President uses television to defend administration policy.

How to grant access without actually granting access was the FCC's dilemma. How to provide the antiwar sentiment in the country some outlet on television without appearing to grant access to *any* particular issue or group as of right? The FCC tried to obscure the fact that the necessary remedy lay in a shift from fairness to access theory. The FCC posed the problem in what presumably was hoped would be inscrutable bureaucratese: "Are reasonable opportunities afforded when there has been an extensive but roughly balanced presentation on each side and five opportunities in prime time for the leading spokesmen of one side to address the nation on this issue?" Despite the camouflage of jaw-breaking prose, the FCC had moved in a new direction. In view of the overexposure of President Nixon's pro-war views on television, the FCC ordered that some sort of specific access was required: "We believe in such circumstances there must also be a reasonable opportunity for the other side geared specifically to the five addresses (i.e., the selection of some suitable spokesman or spokesmen by the networks to broadcast an address giving the contrasting viewpoint.)"

The FCC said that "in light of the fact of five Presidential speeches on this issue, we believe that more is required of each of the networks in this respect (i.e., affording prime time for a speech by an appropriate spokesman for the contrasting viewpoint to that of the Administration of the Indochina war issue.)" The FCC therefore ordered that, "at the least, time be afforded for one more uninterrupted opportunity by an appropriate spokesman to discuss this issue with the length of the prior efforts in this area of uninterrupted presentations." Once again, the FCC left the networks the choice of the appropriate spokesmen for one more uninterrupted opportunity to answer the President.

The Access Hit Parade

The FCC thus admitted the Indochina war issue to what Nicholas Johnson has sardonically called the Access Hit Parade. Johnson was referring to the fact that, although the FCC professes not to recognize a right of access to television, some issues have managed to secure access as of right. Anticigarette announcements had been the first entrants to the Access Hit Parade. The position of the Indochina war issue was shaky, but it was definitely in the parade.

The amount of broadcast time afforded to the pro- and anti-Vietnam war positions had perhaps been roughly equivalent. But was that sufficient when the President had had five opportunities to take his views to the nation on prime time television from November 1969 to August 1970? In answering this question, the FCC moved farther than it ever had in the past in the direction of requiring access for political and social commentary. The FCC violated its own rule that what was crucial was reasonable opportunity for the overall presentation of contrasting views, rather than equality of presentation for specific issues. The FCC ruled in this case that some suitable spokesman should be given television time to present the position against the war in Indochina. In other words, for the first time the FCC ordered a specific right of reply for a specific issue. Realizing that it was opening the door to a general right of access for controversial issues, the FCC insisted that all it was doing was providing a "reasonable opportunity for the other side." In its efforts to make the Indochina war issue unique, the FCC anxiously insisted that "our holding here is based upon the unusual facts of this case—five addresses by the outstanding spokesman of one side of an issue." [2]

Nicholas Johnson in a separate opinion agreed with the FCC decision to order one specific reply to the President but disagreed on the supposed "uniqueness" of the situation. Johnson believed that "every broadcast of an uninterrupted Presidential address gives rise to an obligation to present contrasting viewpoints."

Dean Burch tried to sum up what the FCC had done in disposing of the access complaints against the three major networks by insisting that traditional approach to the fairness doctrine had in no way been altered: "It still relates to issues, not to people, and requires a licensee to make reasonable judgments in good faith as to the presentation of viewpoints on controversial issues of public importance."

An amusing aspect of the ruling was that the press reported what the FCC had actually done rather than, as Chairman Burch would have liked, the FCC's explanation. The AP's story stated: "The FCC has ruled broadcasting networks must give opponents of President Nixon's Indochina War policy equal, prime-time rebuttal." Said Chairman Burch, this "simply wasn't the case": all the FCC had asked for was "reasonable opportunity." Among the papers whose interpretation of the ruling was criticized by Burch were the *Christian Science Monitor*, the *Chicago Sun-Times*, the *Boston Globe*, the *St. Paul Pioneer Press*, and the *National Observer*. Burch challenged the *New York Times* story of August 15, 1970, that broadcasters were required to give "uninterrupted premium exposure" to the opponents of the President. The *Times* said this decision "was the first of its kind and appeared likely to alter Mr. Nixon's use of the medium." Burch claimed that the FCC had not said "what the *Times* said it said."

Newsweek was chastised for saying—accurately, in my opinion—that a "new fairness doctrine" was being created. The new doctrine was really a modified right of access for certain selected issues. The disquiet of the FCC over the press's recognition of a new access development is of course readily understandable. It realized that it would soon be besieged by groups claiming a right of reply on other issues. The FCC does not want to have to face up to the selective character of its Access Hit Parade. Meanwhile, the pressures for direct entry to television continue.

The Fulbright Proposal

In August 1970, Senator Fulbright introduced a proposal to provide some media access for congressional opposition to the President. Fulbright proposed that a "reasonable amount of public time" be made available to "authorized" House or Senate representatives "to present the views of the Senate and House on issues of public importance." This proposal was inspired by the inability of congressional opponents of the Cambodian intervention to secure television time from the networks to rebut the President.

Fulbright believes that the network practice of extending free television time to the President whenever he requests it has dramatically and negatively altered the constitutional balance of power between the Congress and the Executive.

Senator Fulbright's proposal would amend section 315 of the Federal Communications Act of 1934 by inserting a new subsection at the end which would read as follows:

(d) Licensees shall provide a reasonable amount of public service time to authorized representatives of the Senate of the United States and the House of Representatives of the U.S., to present the views of the Senate and the House of Representatives on issues of public importance. The public service time required to be provided under this subsection shall be made available to each such authorized representative at least, but not limited to, four times during each calendar year.[3]

Fulbright's bill is an access bill. Senators and Congressmen are to be given time to present the views of the Senate and

House regardless of whether the broadcaster has provided occasion for any right of reply under the fairness doctrine. Like all solutions, the proposal raises its own problems. The bill says broadcasters shall provide "public service time." Is that paid time? Who is to say who are the "authorized representatives"— a representative group authorized by vote of the Senate or the House? If that is the case, won't the majority position in each house merely be reinforced?

Another difficulty with Senator Fulbright's proposal is that it tends to give an overriding advantage to incumbent politicians. The constant public exposures which mandatory television appearances would give to congressmen presently in office would greatly disadvantage their opponents in subsequent elections.

Despite the new problems raised by his proposal, what Senator Fulbright wants is clear. He wants to break the President's "near monopoly on effective access to the public attention." Fulbright has given a precise summary of the immediate access to television enjoyed by the President:

> The President can command a national television audience to hear his views on controversial matters at prime time, on short notice, and at no expense to the Federal Government or to his party.[4]

Senator Fulbright realizes the problem of access to television is greater than just securing a right to be heard. Prediction or accusation, scandal or sensation, he says, make the media immediately available to a politician: "What you cannot easily interest them in is an idea, or a carefully exposited point of view, or an unfamiliar perspective or a reasoned rebuttal to a highly controversial presidential statement."

The Fulbright proposal exemplifies still another approach to access. Nicholas Johnson of the FCC would like access to television to be secured as an individual right. FCC Chairman Burch takes a far more limited view of the broadcaster's duty to provide access: Access for a few very important issues is apparently all that he would require. Still, it is remarkable that the FCC chairman now thinks there is a duty to provide some access.

Access for institutions, specifically congressional ones, is Fulbright's approach. But can there be an institutional position on Vietnam in the Senate or the House? Realizing the lack of an institutional position on some matters, Fulbright has suggested that the Senate should first vote on whether to use television time for a particular issue.[5] If it is obvious that the Senate is divided, then Senators representative of each position should speak. Unfortunately, the actual language of the bill says nothing about providing access for such diverse senatorial or congressional views on issues.

A more fundamental problem is whether televising a debate can fulfill Fulbright's fundamental purpose to allow Congress to match the communicating power of the Presidency. Can a debate between two senators equal the singleness of view or purpose which the Presidential appearance can convey? The President is one and the Congress are many.

Television news commentators have attempted to provide a kind of rejoinder to the President by subjecting Presidential television speeches to detailed and sometimes harsh criticism. The howls of Spiro Agnew have put that practice in decline. CBS's solution of picking another political person to respond to the President is a good example of the inadequacy of relying on journalistic judgment, expertise, and discretion to deal with access. Surely the selection of O'Brien was, as William S. White said, absurd. The networks are too vulnerable, having shown too little courage and too poor judgment in the past, to be entrusted with such decisions as a matter of grace.

In protesting a rising "juvenile egalitarianism" in the demands for television time to reply to the President, William S.

White has asked menacingly, What will television do when the millions who voted for George Wallace demand time to "answer" the President? That is a good question. The way it should be answered is to give those millions a television voice. The access problems of the nonelected and the nonincumbent are much more serious and much more critical than the access problems of Senators. The fact that United States Senators have attracted much media attention in their pursuit of access illustrates that theirs is a comparatively minor problem.

Nevertheless, access for the political opposition to the administration in power is a special access problem. It must be resolved by precise congressional or agency standards. One alternative would be a rule that the nominee of the party having secured the next highest number of votes in the national election should have a right to answer the President's political appearances on television. Such a rule would forestall charges of media bias—for example, if Humphrey had been given time to answer Nixon on Cambodia as against some more outspoken antiwar critic. Oppositionist sentiment not represented by the views of the nominee of the other political party would, of course, still have a right to access to television under general fairness or access standards.

If such an approach seems unconstitutionally to freeze out the nominees of all but the two major parties, perhaps access for time to answer the President could be worked out on a formula which relates votes obtained in the last national election to the amount of broadcast time a presidential nominee would be entitled to. Such an approach would provide a clear right of specific reply on television for all the opposition. At the least, the Fulbright proposal has focused attention on the need to grant a right of rebuttal in the media for the elected political opposition to the President.

Time for Ideas?

One formidable group finally became bored with entreating the broadcast moguls for broadcast time—the Democratic National Committee. Instead of asking, as it had earlier, for a right to reply to the President, on May 19, 1970, it asked the FCC to create a general right of access to television time for the presentation of political and social commentary.

The Democrats had wanted to buy segments of a half-hour or more of television time to solicit funds and to comment on contemporary controversial issues. They met a wall of resistance from individual stations and from the networks. CBS took the position that it would sell time for political purposes only during political campaigns. ABC said it had a policy against solicitation of funds except for charity.

And so the Democratic National Committee filed with the FCC its request that the Commission prohibit broadcasters from refusing to sell time to "responsible entities" such as the Democratic National Committee "for the solicitation of funds and for comment on public issues."

The right to purchase time for comment on public issues, the FCC said, was a fundamental question but it was not an open one. The law has long denied such a right. The request was regarded by the FCC as a challenge to licensee control of programming. In its view, balanced presentation of controversial public issues was a matter of broadcaster judgment.

The FCC ruled that broadcasters were not legally obliged to sell anyone time segments of a half-hour or more for political and social comment.[6] However, in somewhat indecisive language, the FCC did agree with the Democratic National Committee that it should have a right to buy political spot announcements to solicit funds.

The Democratic National Committee had wanted recognition of a much broader right of access. The Supreme Court in Red Lion had just given the members of the public a new right —the right of access to broadcast facilities. Therefore, the Democrats argued, a right to purchase segments of broadcast time for discussion of political and social issues now existed.

The FCC would say only that it would regard a network refusal to sell spot announcements for political parties, even though unrelated to an election campaign, as arbitrary. If unable to appeal to the media public for political contributions, the political parties would necessarily become even more dependent on wealthy contributors. Commissioner Nicholas Johnson said cuttingly that the reason the Commission was willing to recognize political commercials for funds was that commercials and commercialism was something the Commission could understand.

Why did the FCC refuse to recognize the right of a public group to buy its own time and put on its own show? As we have seen, making blocks of time available as of right for purchase by groups or individuals would be an opening wedge for a common carrier concept of television. A common carrier concept—the idea that at least some broadcast time could be purchased as of right with the network or the broadcaster having no more right of oversight than the phone company does over a phone conversation—was anathema both to the broadcasters and the FCC. But the FCC took care not to seem to base its stand on mere industry protectionism. The trouble with the common carrier concept, it said, was that there was no obligation to present the other side. If the parties seeking to buy time all share the same view, the common carrier concept becomes a vehicle for one-sidedness. That would be a particularly severe problem if broadcast time was completely at the command of the highest bidder.

Nicholas Johnson observed in response that the opinion process belongs to the high bidders now. Putting a part of the broadcast day up for sale, he thought, might at least equalize things. In a dissenting opinion, Johnson said he would require broadcasters "to accept programming of a political nature, if offered, in an amount up to 5 percent of their prime time evening schedule on a first-come, first-served basis." On the basis of "four hours of prime time every evening (from 7:00 p.m. to 11:00 p.m.)," Johnson reasoned that "calculating 30 days per month" such a requirement would provide "six hours per month to 'pure access'" to politicians and citizen groups.[7] Johnson's thinking appears to be that if there is no right to free grants of time to public groups, at least there should be a right to purchase some time.

The broadcast day is finite and a 5 percent limitation on access is reasonable. However, network time rates are extremely high, higher than the rates for advertising in a small town newspaper. The high rates of the broadcast networks and the time limitation do tend to screen out ideas in favor of propaganda.

Present television commercials are nearly all propaganda about commodities. But the way to minimize this phenomenon is not to prohibit alleged propaganda about ideas. This would hardly lead to the suitable access for ideas of which the Supreme Court spoke in Red Lion.

But access to broadcast time need not be granted on the basis only of an applicant's capacity to purchase it. Otherwise the scope for censorship will have been only narrowed and not removed. For an issue to secure entry to television now it usually must have some money in back of it. To remove broadcaster approval and make money the only arbiter of entry might be improvement in limiting broadcaster power, but it would hardly be a complete or satisfactory solution. If some broadcast time is to be assigned to the public, a certain portion of it should be assigned without a price tag.

Here, of course, is a rub. Which issues should have free access? If television should go off the money standard, what should be the guide?

Folksinger Pete Seeger has tried to answer the question. Reserve 20 percent of television time for the public sector, he recommends. Divide the country into TV regions and let the people in each region vote for delegates to a national annual Public Sector Television Conference. Through rights to television time and trade-offs between delegates, programming for the public sector would emerge. Seeger's proposal recognizes the deep-rooted national hunger for greater direct public participation in the media. Says Seeger: ". . . the air belongs to everyone. To sell it to the highest bidder makes as much sense as selling Grand Canyon to the highest bidder." [8]

Utopian as Seeger's proposal may sound, it reflects a vital instinct that direct public participation in television is a social necessity whose urgency is at last being understood. Exclusion of the public from direct participation in television stimulates the prepackaging of opinion. The rough and tumble of real conflict need not always be filtered through handsome network news commentators or distorted by the bizarre and therefore televisable antics of the most extreme sectors of public opinion.

In the Democratic National Committee case the FCC said that dispensing information was the ultimate goal of broadcasting. The FCC believed the Supreme Court in the Red Lion case had asked broadcasters to do two things: (1) to devote a reasonable amount of time to political and social issues; and (2) to make that presentation fair. Few will quarrel with that. But a basic issue remains unclear. Does devoting a reasonable amount of time to political and social issues assume that spokesmen for such views have a right to present them on television in their own words and in their own way? Justice White had upheld the constitutionality of the fairness and personal attack rules in part because of the "legitimate claims of those unable without government assistance to gain access to those frequences for expression of their views. . . ."

There was much controversy concerning the impact of Red Lion on the FCC when it decided that the broadcaster had no obligation to sell time for political and social comments to anyone who wished to purchase it. Red Lion did not require unlimited access. But I believe a dispassionate reading of Red Lion offers more support for the access or common carrier concept than the trusteeship concept. Broadcaster trusteeship is a euphemism for complete broadcaster control.

The Court's position in Red Lion was that it is within the power of the FCC to impose either a common carrier concept or a trusteeship concept of regulation on broadcasters. But the receptivity of the Court to "time-sharing" in broadcasting is made very clear. The point was emphasized that the creative possibilities for increasing public participation in broadcasting through regulation were unlimited.

The issue is whether partisanship has rights of entry to broadcasting apart from broadcaster willingness to welcome it.

For the present, the FCC concedes that ideas have a place on television, but it agrees with the broadcasters that the scope of the ideas, and even their entry to television, is a broadcaster decision. In the Democratic National Committee case, the FCC gave a conservative and limited reading to the Supreme Court's great broadcasting decision.[9] The broadcaster is not a common carrier duty-bound "to sell time to all comers on public issues." The broadcaster is instead a public trustee who must choose "representative community views and voices on controversial issues." In the FCC's view, the Supreme Court chose "the right of the public to be informed" over the "right of any individual or group to speak."

Access is ordered, under this view, not for the public but for disembodied ideas. There is to be access on television for ideas, but not for those identified with the ideas. The gatekeepers are to be the same broadcast industry personnel who have always insisted that they had no obligations whatever to provide access. Choosing its example carefully to discomfit the largely liberal attackers, the FCC asked rhetorically in its Democratic National Committee opinion: Suppose the oil industry wanted to buy time to discuss oil depletion? The FCC insisted that decisions about who could purchase time should be made in the public interest and not be controlled by the power or the affluence of the group seeking access to television. This is an argument the networks had particularly urged. Their intense objection to a right to purchase broadcast time brings us to the economics of the matter. If a broadcaster has to sell time to whoever wants it for the espousal of a particular viewpoint, the broadcaster may yet, under the fairness doctrine, have to give free time to the antagonists of the purchaser.

The gist of the objection to the establishment of a right of access, to a right to buy time for political and social comment, is clear: Access and fairness together place too heavy a burden on the broadcaster. In its response to the Democratic National Committee, the FCC indicated that diversity of opinion on the air was being achieved by alternatives more satisfactory than compulsory access to television time. Cable particularly, the new promised land of television, received warm words from the Commission: "Because of the potentially great number of channels, cable opens up the possibilities of common carrier channels, public access channels." The FCC insisted that, although indirectly these new developments might lead to greater access for issues, neither issues nor broadcasters have a right of access. Rather, said the FCC, it is the public which has a right to be informed.

Nicholas Johnson struggled to apply to broadcasting the new court decision admitting dissent to public parks or transit systems. The difficulty is that the broadcast media exist under certain public service obligations regarding the content of their programming; no such complications arise in recognizing a right of access to a bus terminal or a railroad station.

In perspective, the Democratic National Committee's access request appears very modest. Only groups which were "representative" would have a claim to television time. Entry would still be on the basis of meeting station and network rate charges for time. Nevertheless, the request was considered unthinkable, suggesting as it did that there was an obligation on the part of the broadcaster to sell time for political and social issues to some who wished to purchase it. CBS had a specially pious reason for opposing such an obligation: Sale of time for programs on controversial issues would reduce the time available for news, sports, and entertainment programs!

A phrase that has bounced around descriptions of broadcast programming for many years is lowest-common-denominator. The folk terms for television—the idiot box or the boob tube—revealed the low popular estimate of the art.

Must the broadcaster, or more accurately the network executive, fulfill for eternity his present role in the system of deciding what denominator is in fact the lowest; what programming is least offensive and perhaps most appealing to the greatest number of people? In the past, public issue programming has rarely been considered to be in this category. Public issue programming has been reserved for Sunday afternoon or early morning or late at night. NBC's *First Tuesday of the Month* or CBS's *Sixty Minutes*, like Edward R. Murrow's famous *Person-to-Person*, were welcome cases of information and excitement providing a bitter contrast with the usual broadcast fare.

Yet, when it was proposed that ideas be sold as freely as soap and have as ready access to broadcasting, the industry struggled to "save" public issue programming (or at least to save broadcaster control over programming). If programs could be bought without restriction, how, the opponents of access asked, would we be sure of having enough public issue programming? But the public has certainly not been surfeited with such programming in the past.

Access to ideas cannot be realized without some respect for the importance of their authenticity of expression. Recall how in his Red Lion decision Justice Byron White quoted John Stuart Mill's observation that justice is done to issues when they are delivered by persons "who actually believe them; who defend them in earnest, and do their very utmost for them." Relating this thought to the broadcast media, Justice White observed: "The expression of views opposing those which broadcasters permit to be aired in the first place need not be confided solely to the broadcasters themselves as proxies." Surely those remarks have to be interpreted as supporting freedom for the television controversialist from the waffling hand of the broadcaster. The Jesuit scholar, Walter Ong, has emphasized the benefit of actual confrontation between controversialists: "The word moves toward peace because the word mediates between person and person. . . . So long as two persons keep talking, despite themselves they are not totally hostile." [10]

The choice for television is not either for every channel to operate as a common carrier or for it to be a law unto itself. In the contemporary American system neither choice is acceptable or desirable. The challenge is to broaden public participation in television without destroying the valuable counterpoise to government power provided by private operation. The need is to give ideas a right to television time.

A Beachhead for Access

The Democratic National Committee appealed the FCC refusal to require broadcasters to sell advertising time to groups or individuals wishing to speak out on controversial public issues.

The U.S. Court of Appeals in the District of Columbia reversed the Commission.[11] The court ruled that a "flat ban on paid public issue announcements was in violation of the First Amendment at least when other sorts of paid announcements are accepted." The broadcaster still had the right to exercise judgment and control in public issue programming and the sale of advertising time. No specific right of access to any group or individual was authorized by the court. The crux of the decision was that the ban on the sale of advertising time for public issue announcements was invalidated, and therefore a *general* right of access to advertising time on broadcast time was recognized. The task for the FCC would be to develop the procedures and regulations which would determine "how many 'editorial advertisements' will be put on the air."

The Democrats were joined in the appeal by Business Executives' Move for Vietnam Peace, 2,700 business owners and executives opposed to the Vietnam war. BEM wanted to initiate a blitz advertising campaign urging immediate American withdrawal from Vietnam and from overseas military installations. They wanted to buy time for spots on the all-news Washington radio station, WTOP. Although WTOP sells a great number of short advertisements, the station refused to take the BEM ads. Why? As a policy matter, WTOP refuses to accept advertising espousing views on controversial public issues. BEM complained about this policy to the FCC. The FCC rejected BEM's contention that WTOP should be ordered to sell it time.

The Business Executives' Movement for Vietnam Peace group then joined the Democratic National Committee to challenge FCC refusal to alter broadcasting policy prohibiting the sale of time for the dissemination of controversial issues. BEM's position differed somewhat from that of the Democratic National Committee. The Democrats had asked the FCC to give a declaratory ruling that a "broadcaster may not, as a general policy, refuse to sell time to responsible entities, such as DNC, for the solicitation of funds and for comment on public issues." BEM had a specific right of access complaint. They contended that WTOP had failed to cover anti-war views fully and fairly.

The battle lines were sharply drawn. The Commission maintained that the fairness doctrine was adequate to satisfy First Amendment demands. Significantly, the fairness doctrine would not give either the Democrats or BEM a right to buy broadcast time. The Democrats and BEM said that fairness was not enough, that access had to be provided as well.

A pioneering decision written by Judge Skelly Wright shows how creative decision-making can make free expression rights in the media effective. There is no reason that what Judge Wright has done for access in the electronic media cannot be accomplished by the courts for the print media as well.

The Democrats and BEM sought a "limited right of access to radio and television for paid public issue announcements." The court agreed there was such a right of access although it was limited. Where was the locus of the right? Judge Wright candidly confessed that it would have been possible to locate it in the Federal Communications Commission's public interest standard or the statutory-regulatory fairness standard. But Judge Wright preferred to identify a limited right of access to broadcasting in the First Amendment.

The decision was not a complete breakthrough. "Normal programming time" was not at stake. If broadcaster-controlled time were at stake, the court reasoned, the constitutional position of broadcasters would have been stronger. But the "open section" of broadcasting was what was at issue. Advertising *belonged* to advertisers rather than broadcasters. In this view, limiting broadcaster discretion over advertising time really does not infringe the free speech rights of broadcasters.

A common argument from an odd pair of allies, the networks

and "the defender of the public interest," the FCC, emerged in the Democratic National Committee case: the public have a right to be confronted with the spectrum of ideas but the public have no right of direct participation in the life of ideas in broadcasting. The court rejected this argument because it discounted the most important First Amendment right of all, "the interest of individuals and groups in effective self-expression."

Editorial advertising is a most appropriate standard bearer for access to broadcasting. Advertising, by definition, depends on the initiative of the would-be advertiser. Recognition of the public issue advertiser-applicant's right to control the content of the time he purchases has established an important beachhead for direct public entry into broadcasting. Yet, the new beachhead does not directly challenge or disturb the editorial discretion of broadcast journalism. The advantage of introducing access to broadcasting by means of a right to purchase editorial advertising has the additional virtue of permitting the fairness doctrine and the access principle to co-exist. Fairness will still be the rule for normal broadcaster-controlled programming. But access as a general right is established for editorial advertising.

On the other hand, broadcasters are still not to be considered common carriers. The new decision does not oblige broadcasters to "accept any advertising message that is submitted." Broadcasters may place an outside limit on the total amount of editorial advertising they will sell. Further, broadcasters are given discretion as to when they will broadcast the editorials submitted, although they are warned not to exclude them from prime time.

Suppose that one group tries to monopolize editorial advertising time. Outside limits, Judge Wright suggests, might then be placed on the amount of advertising time that would be sold to one group or to representatives of a "minor viewpoint." This last comment highlights the fundamental distinction between the access concept and the common carrier concept. The access concept involves some editorial judgment.

A major issue to be resolved concerning access to television is how can the access principle be honored without being destroyed by obligations imposed by the fairness doctrine. For example, if assuring access for an editorial advertisement generates requests for advertising time from its antagonist, wouldn't broadcasters be threatened with financial ruin? Could an anti-pollution society advertisement be met with an oil company apologia? Judge Wright answered this question by assuming that the FCC would not interpret the fairness doctrine so rigidly as "to throw licensees out of business."

Wright believed that by issuing guidelines the FCC could make the necessary judgments to balance the access demands with the even-handed presentation of controversial issues required by the fairness doctrine.

A final question must be asked: Did BEM or the Democratic National Committee actually win anything from the court decision? The U.S. Court of Appeals ordered that the two groups should be permitted to reapply for advertising time. Their applications should be accepted said the court "unless their presentations are found to be excludable under the FCC guidelines."

Access to advertising time for groups like BEM and the Democratic National Committee is by no means now assured but surely it is now much more likely. The burden is placed on the broadcaster. He must show that very substantial harm would flow from acceptance of editorial advertising in order to justify rejecting it. Although the broadcasters are still not under a common carrier concept of broadcasting, the decision does deal a heavy blow to the idea that the broadcaster is the trustee for the community and that, therefore, he is the sole determiner of who shall have access to the air.

In these respects, the Democratic National Committee decision is a victory for a modified right of access. Although Judge Wright properly tried hard to confine his ruling to the facts, it is clear that the decision could be a beachhead for the implementation of public access to broadcasting.

A broad proposition is now established. Commercialism cannot be preferred over ideas. A preference for commercialism is now recognized as rank discrimination. But the decision avoids difficult questions: Does the First Amendment radiate a preference for ideology? Further, why should the right to petition for entry into broadcasting be restricted just to that segment of broadcast time which broadcasters choose to allocate for advertising?

The fact that no specific right of access has as yet been won was vividly pointed out by the fact that a different panel of judges in the United States Court of Appeals for the District of Columbia had earlier in the Green decision rejected the specific claims of access of two peace groups.[12] A Quaker group and a serviceman's group asked stations in Washington and San Francisco to give them some free time so that they might inform the public of available alternatives to military service. The cases differ from the requests to buy advertising because of the different questions raised. What do you do when a group seeks broadcast time for the presentation of an idea and the group has no money? Since both the Washington and the San Francisco stations had carried recruiting advertisements for the armed forces, these groups contended that the fairness doctrine demanded equal opportunities for discussion of the alternatives to military service.

The FCC declined to order the stations to donate time to the two groups. The Court of Appeals agreed with the FCC. The fairness doctrine was concerned with keeping the public informed. It was not concerned with giving any particular advocate or group time to present its view as of right. The Court of

Appeals said that the issues of the Vietnam war, the draft, and the military service have been ventilated for years on every television and radio station in the land.

The Green decision was an effort to make the fairness principle do the work of access to the media. The court agreed with the FCC that no "individual member of the public has the right of access to the media."

The Quakers and the GI peaceniks were denied free time for antimilitary announcements, because broadcasting had reached the saturation point on the Indochina war issue.

The Quaker antimilitary recruitment case and the Democratic National Committee case are a strange pair of cases to be decided by judges on the same federal court of appeals in a single summer. The Green case, decided June 18, 1971, says the broadcasters have no duty to provide free time to the Quakers who sought to counter military recruitment ads. On August 7, 1971, the court said a right of access to advertising time existed and guidelines should be set forth to implement the right. The Green case itself posed a question: by what calculus did the court of appeals conclude that the antiwar issue had been sufficiently ventilated and that, therefore, access was not necessary for antimilitary announcements? It was a question the FCC would have to consider if it was to fulfill the mandate of the Democratic National Committee case.

On July 1, 1971, the FCC responded to an environmentalist complaint about some Esso institutional ads on television. These ads insisted that an Alaskan pipeline could be built without ecological damage. Esso's advertising, the FCC ruled, involved a controversial public issue which environmentalists had a right to answer.[13] In a similar development, on August 17, 1971, the Friends of the Earth won an access victory before a federal court of appeals panel consisting of Judges Roger Robb, and Carl McGowan. Judge Wilbur Miller dissented.[14] Relying on the Banzhaf case, the court of appeals told the FCC to reconsider the request of the Friends of the Earth for counter-commercials to serve as antidotes to Ford's Mustang and General Motors' Impala ads. These cars were what made air pollution a problem. The FCC had tried to confine the rule allowing reply time to cigarette advertising by saying that situation was unique. The court of appeals had taken the same tack. Judge McGowan was now asking, Why unique? Pollution is for the asthmatic what cigarette smoking is for the lung cancer sufferer —a peril to life. From the Quaker point of view, war, no less than the Impala or the Mustang, is a peril to life. The developments in the environmentalist cases contrast sharply with the result in the Green case. Judge Wright in Democratic National Committee said that the broadcaster has the burden of showing why acceptance of the proferred ad would be hurtful. It is hard to see why giving the Quakers time for their point of view would have been hurtful.

A Crossroads for Access

On June 9, 1971, the FCC announced that it would undertake a review of the fairness doctrine. The progression in broadcast regulation from fairness to access occasioned the new review.

In announcing the new inquiry, the FCC declared its devotion to two principles, the fairness doctrine itself and the principle that broadcasters "were *not* common carriers who must accept all materials offered by any and all comers." Furthermore, the FCC pledged to take into consideration the decisions in the pending court cases on matters involved in the fairness proceeding.[15]

In one respect, the Democratic National Committee case has already affected the pending FCC review of fairness. The FCC, in its notice of inquiry in the fairness doctrine review, announced its continuing devotion to the trusteeship concept of broadcasting. The National Association of Broadcasters could not have stated the broadcaster position better: "The individual licensee has the discretion, and indeed the responsibility, to determine what issues should be covered, how much time should be allocated, which spokesman should appear, and in which format."

This concept of broadcasting has been properly scored as a recipe for paternalism in the Democratic National Committee decision. No longer are broadcasters alone the masters of every minute of broadcast time. The opening up of advertising time for access is bound to affect the rest of broadcast time.

In its announcement of the fairness doctrine review proceeding, the FCC cataloged the range of access and fairness problems. For example, the problem of counter-commercials was included for re-examination. The FCC called attention to its record of disapproval of the view that the licensee must make free time available "in a set ratio in part or during prime time evening hours" for countercommercials. Nevertheless, with manful openmindedness the FCC asked: Should there be a duty on the part of broadcasters to carry material opposing or arguing the merits of product commercials? Another matter agonized over in the announcement of the fairness review was that "spot announcements may not add substantially to public knowledge." The hilarious (or bitter) rejoinder, of course, is: do commercials, which are also spot announcements, contribute to public knowledge? The Commission agreed that from the larger perspective of the fairness doctrine, consumer and public health groups might be entitled to "equal opportunities" to discuss the merits of products and services hawked on broadcasting.

The FCC said the heart of the issue was whether there was a right of paid access for informing the public why "a product or service advertised over the station's facilities should not be purchased." The FCC's reason for concern in this area is obvious. It fears that the commercial structure of broadcasing could not survive exposing commercials to scrutiny and counterattack.

A major thrust of the fairness review proceeding, the Commission said, was to obtain information on whether it would be appropriate to issue guidelines on questions of access, either on a paid or a sustaining basis, for discussion of controversial issues and for political party fund solicitation. Further, the FCC would like to be informed on what the criteria or guidelines should be. The Commission's heart is on its sleeve in this area as well. It struggled to at least voice the rising public demands that it articulate access criteria, then said, hopefully, that comments in the fairness review proceedings should reflect on whether "the problems in this area" are so varied "that decisions should be left to the judgment of thousands of licensees and, in cases of complaint, to the abjudicatory process." For the FCC, the main question about the access to controversial issues part of the inquiry was a simple question: "Should we re-affirm present Commission policy and practice?"

The reversal by the U.S. Court of Appeals of the FCC ruling that broadcaster dominance over advertising time was absolute has since answered the question. A re-affirmation of the Commission's expressed preference for fairness and distaste for access is now impossible.

It is clear therefore that the new proceeding must address the need for criteria to implement access. The FCC pointed out that Judge Bazelon in his landmark decision in the Banzhaf case, requiring free time to be made available to counter cigarette commercials, had warned that the rationale of the case should not be used to command free rebuttal time for product commercials generally. What would be the yardstick for such a task? It would have to be, to use Bazelon's telling phrase, "a more discriminating lens than the public interest or the public health."

Commissioner Johnson wrote a concurrence in the fairness doctrine review proceeding which displayed severe disenchantment with the fairness doctrine. For him the fairness doctrine serves to "legitimize broadcaster frustration of access demands." The fairness doctrine leaves the decision to initiate discussion of controversial issues with the broadcaster, not the public. Johnson charged that the fairness doctrine review proceeding was really a way of putting the brakes on the momentum for access.

However accurate is Commissioner Johnson's appraisal of the intent of the majority of FCC Commissioners, it is now clear that the airwaves are going to be opened up to the public. Citizen groups around the country are insisting on it, and the federal courts are reading that insistence into broadcast regulation.

We now seem about to begin an elaborate search for a methodology to give an immediate reading on the public importance quotient or the controversiality component of a particular issue, so that its case for access to television may be established. Similarly, it is likely that new efforts will be made to determine the particular suitability of a particular group or individual to advocate a point of view. But, in a phrase Justice Felix Frankfurter was fond of using to describe complicated social problems of law and policy, these are non-Euclidean problems. No list of criteria is likely to provide a calculus to identify the deserving groups and issues which merit access to broadcasting.

The pattern for the future is already evident. The FCC is being instructed by the courts that certain segments of the broadcast day are open to public access as a matter of First Amendment compulsion. The licensee has the task of responding to the request for access. The lesson of the Democratic National Committee case is that the Commission should try to draft guidelines to aid the broadcaster in making his response. The case itself indicates the major themes for the guidelines. First, advertising time should be sold nondiscriminatorily. Second, the traditional broadcaster policy of prohibiting the advertising of ideas is illegal. Third, the burden of proof is on the broadcaster to show that he will be hurt if the spot announcement for an antiwar message or an antipollution ad is accepted.

The new challenge to both the FCC and the broadcasters is to discover a sensitivity to access problems that they have not displayed in the past. It is the federal courts that have been unusually sensitive to these problems. Indeed, the law of access to broadcasting has been forged in the federal courts and not in the federal agency established by Congress to seek the public interest in broadcasting. The federal courts of appeal, particularly the U.S. Court of Appeals of the District of Columbia, may be expected to continue to serve as sources of creative policy-making in the access field. If the FCC wishes to regain a lost initiative in this area, it will have to use the fairness doctrine review proceeding, not to hold back a new era of public access to broadcasting, but to usher it in.

Access to Prime Time

The FCC has met the demands for access to broadcasting obliquely rather than directly. The FCC steadfastly has refused to open up the media to the public or to representative public groups as of right. But it has decided to de-emphasize network dominance over the mass audience. Traditional network control over prime time, 7 to 11 p.m., has been dealt a heavy and unexpected blow.

To everyone's surprise, in May 1970 the FCC adopted a "prime time access" rule designed to limit network control over prime-time programming. After September 1, 1971, television stations in the top fifty markets where there are three or more commercial television stations were not permitted to broadcast more than three hours of network programming during the prime time hours.[16] The rule is designed to release some prime television time from network control time so that other sources of creative programming can develop. Unfortunately, the network affiliates have not used the hour to sell or furnish free time for programs developed by political and social groups within the community. There was little reason for the industry to help justify the FCC's belief "that much greater diversity of programs and program sources than presently contained in network schedules is potentially available." The prime-time access rule gives a wide-open choice to the local broadcaster. Although the Democratic National Committee sought to enter television through the networks, the prime time rule could give such groups entry through the stations.

A difficulty is that each network chooses to program a different three hours in the 7 to 11 time period. The local broadcaster sees his problem as keeping his audience during the mandatory nonnetwork hour when faced with competing network programming on the other networks. The pressure therefore is very great to select programming which will be treadmill lowest-common-denominator crowd-pleasers.

This defect could presumably be cured if all the network affiliates in a community were required to program nonnetwork material during the same time period. But, even then, there are other avenues of escape from the FCC's effort to provide for access for creative programming during prime time. What is creative programming? Is it aged videotapes of "I Love Lucy"? It is clear that the struggle has just begun to achieve diversity of programming in prime time television.

The broadcasting industry did not take the prime time access development meekly. Stations in Burlington, Vermont, Louisville, Kentucky, and Albany, New York, as well as the mighty CBS have filed appeals in the courts.[17] CBS argued that the smaller stations will be hurt, although the rule only applies to the top fifty markets, because the networks are cutting back their prime time programming to three hours and the smaller stations simply don't have the cash to develop or to purchase the kind of programming necessary to fill the nonnetwork hour.

CBS tried to draw an analogy between the prime time rule and a hypothetical regulation preventing newspapers from devoting more than a specified percentage of their space to material furnished by wire services like the Associated Press or the United Press International. CBS argued that just as that would be unconstitutional so the prime time access rule in broadcasting is unconstitutional. Ironically, such a limitation would probably be both constitutional and desirable. In fact, few things would contribute more to varying the uniform canned flavor of newspaper copy in one-newspaper towns across the country. The cause of local investigative journalism would be another likely beneficiary.

It is doubtful that limitation on network prime time will in itself immediately succeed in infusing variety, diversity, or, in the FCC's phrase, "creative programming," into commercial television. The important point is that something new has dawned in American broadcast regulation. The movement for access to television has spun off a move to alter the control a few networks have over almost all prime time television. The FCC's effort is to chip away at network dominance and to restore some independence to the local broadcaster. If the prime-time access experiment has failed, the networks should not rejoice. For waiting in the wings is not a pristine restoration of network dominance but rather renewed demands by citizen groups throughout the country for direct entry to broadcasting.

There is a difference between access to a local audience and to a national one. For this reason, a requirement that one hour of prime time be locally originated is of great potential significance. Access problems are likely to be most intense at the local level. The local community usually is served by just one newspaper. Networks which generate the most widely watched shows on local television network affiliates are not likely to focus on local issues at any time when anybody is watching. Reserving one hour of prime time for creative programming specifically directed to the local community is designed to counter network neglect.

The myopic and self-serving view which the broadcast networks take of the whole concept of freedom of expression in broadcasting was revealed in the concerted network attack on the prime-time access rule. CBS, ABC, and NBC all joined in a court test of the rule. The networks argued that a limit on the amount of time a network affiliate could use abridged the network right of free speech. After the Red Lion case, this position had a certain Rip Van Winkle quality. It was the Red Lion case and its emphasis on access that prompted the FCC to try to free some evening prime time for something besides the standard network fare. The United States Court of Appeals for the Second Circuit manifested amazement at the network lawyers' primitive understanding of what the First Amendment should mean for television.

As the court saw it, there was a clash between the access rights of the public and the free speech rights of the networks. The clash was not difficult to resolve. Declaring that the prime-time access rule was valid, that far from prohibiting such a rule, freedom of expression on television demanded it, the United States Court of Appeals rejected the network attack.[18] The whole legal assault of the broadcast networks was easily routed. The public's right to access, said the court, had priority "over all other claims."

Patiently, the court tried to explain to the broadcasters that freedom of expression in the electronic media and freedom of broadcasters to do as they please were not the same thing. Conceding that the prime-time access rule inhibits broadcast licensees from being "able to choose, for the specified time period, the programs which they might use," Judge Hays emphasized for the court that the rule had a broader concern; it "is designed to open up the media to whom the First Amendment primarily protects—the general public." The role beloved by network lawyers, of virtue at bay and defenders of civil liberties in peril, was scoffed at by the court. The networks—purveyors of *Bonanza, Adam-12, I Love Lucy, Green Acres,* and *Bewitched*—argued darkly that the prime-time access rule would limit the capacity of broadcasters to carry programming on controversial issues. This debater's parry brought a stinging judicial thrust: If such a result were in the offing, then it must be based on a "cynical assumption" that the networks were going to cut back on their controversial issue programming.

There was an enlightening by-product of the bitter controversy about the prime-time access rule in the FCC and the courts—a chronicle was provided of the dramatic decline of nonnetwork sources for television programming in a little more than a single decade, from 1957 to 1968. An Arthur D. Little Report showed that programs produced or controlled by networks in evening hours rose during that time period from 67.2 to 96.7 percent. The consequence was that access to network-affiliated stations for independent producers of syndicated programming was virtually closed.

Before 1959 almost half of network programming had been supplied by independent producers who dealt directly with network advertisers. The FCC has pointed out that the decline of independent producers on television and their replacement by network productions is by no means qualitatively irrelevant. The programs independently produced for television—such as the *Telephone Hour,* the *Hallmark Hall of Fame, Robert Montgomery Presents,* and the *National Geographic* documentaries —all secured critical acclaim.

The networks made the argument that the small broadcasters will be hurt by the prime-time access rule because the smaller stations are so dependent on the national networks that the loss of revenue from a half-hour of network programming will put them in economic jeopardy. The FCC responded to this complaint by saying this merely illustrated the pitiful plight of the smaller broadcasters. Unable to exercise the freedom of choice and the responsible trusteeship which are foundation stones of broadcast regulatory policy, the smaller stations were revealed to be mere conduits for programming and programming decisions made in network offices in New York City. Small station dependence on every possible moment of network programming showed how thoroughly network dominance had suffocated local station initiative for developing independent creative programming.

The court victory for the prime-time access rule does not mean that new and inspired programming will now abound on television screens across the nation. Neither will the rise of CATV and its multiple channels necessarily mean a quantum jump in the diversity and quality of television programming. Yet the prime-time access rule, like the development of cable, is a step in the struggle to open up the media, to free it from the tyranny of lowest common denominator programming, and to make a start toward the decentralization of television.

16 /

The Rise of Citizen Groups

BROADCAST MEDIA ARE BEING OPENED TO A MUCH GREATER EXTENT than in the past through the efforts of citizen groups. In 1967, a landmark federal court decision gave new rights to broadcast listeners and viewers throughout the country. Organizations representing the black community of Jackson, Mississippi asked the FCC to grant a hearing permitting a challenge to the application for renewal of television station WLBT–TV in Jackson. The citizen groups argued that the station had continuously taken a segregationist viewpoint and essentially excluded expression of the integration viewpoint. Furthermore, the citizen groups said, the station's programming ignored the interests and tastes of the black population of Jackson except for a token amount of time assigned to Negro churches for religious programming.

The FCC responded that the petitioners were merely members of the public: since citizen groups were not themselves applying for the license of WLBT-TV, they lacked the necessary economic interest in the proceeding. Their rights as listeners, as viewers, as members of the public, were simply not sufficient to furnish the standing necessary to get a hearing.

The United States Court of Appeals of the District of Columbia disagreed; it held that the interest of listeners and viewers was sufficiently great to entitle them to challenge license renewals.[1] The decision gave the public an opening wedge to challenge the stake both bureaucrats and broadcasters had in the status quo. The decision at last armed the viewing and listening public with a tool potent enough to make both the FCC and the broadcast industry take notice of them.

The history of this pioneering decision illustrates FCC solicitude for the industry it is supposed to regulate. WLBT–TV of Jackson had a record of complaints about its programming in racial matters. Back in 1955, it had been carrying an NBC network program on which Thurgood Marshall, then general counsel of the NAACP and now a Supreme Court justice, was being interviewed. The general manager cut off the program and substituted a "Sorry, Cable Trouble" sign. In 1957, the station carried a program on the Little Rock crisis. The participants included white Mississippi politicians who favored the segregationist cause, such as Senator Eastland, Congressman John Bell Williams, Governor Coleman, and others. There were no Negro participants, although all of the white politicians gave their views on what the Negro wants and doesn't want. In 1962 complaints were made to the FCC about the coverage by WLBT and other Mississippi broadcasters of the effort of James Meredith and other black students to gain entry to the previously all white University of Mississippi.

When WLBT's license expired in 1964, the United Church of Christ, representing the black population (nearly half) of Jackson, asked the FCC to order a hearing to allow it to challenge the license renewal application.

Since the church group challenger was not a competitor, existing or potential, of WLBT, the FCC insisted that it did not have the standing necessary to warrant a hearing. However, the FCC did try to mollify the citizen group by granting a short-term one year "probationary" renewal rather than the usual three-year renewal. The reason for even this mild sanction was probably less to punish unfairness than to avoid being compelled to hold a hearing on the complaint. The FCC argued that since it accepted the United Church of Christ's contentions with regard to misconduct on the part of WLBT, no hearing was necessary. But of course an obvious question then arose: If the contentions concerning WLBT's poor performance were accepted, why renew WLBT at all, even for a year?

The reason given was that the public interest demanded the continuation of the television station in Jackson. The real reason might have been that the thought of having license renewal proceedings opened up on the petition of a group of dissident viewers to a hearing and to public and press scrutiny shocked the FCC to the core. The passive living rooms were going active. The prospect that the closed world of government and industry lawyers would be penetrated by public interest groups representing all the preferences of the community was terrifying. Better to agree with the church group that WLBT was a bad apple and apply a mild sanction. Perhaps citizen groups with their bizarre idea that they had the same right as a businessman applicant to fight a license renewal would somehow go away.

But the viewers of Jackson were not bought off. The United Church of Christ took the FCC to the U.S. Court of Appeals and was granted a right to participate in a public hearing. As a result, an important new idea was at large in broadcast regulation. Public interest groups should be accorded the same rights to challenge a broadcaster's performance that competing applicants within the industry had long possessed.

But winning a court decision and winning the day-to-day battle before the government agency charged with regulating an industry are very different things. The United Church of Christ went back to fight on FCC terrain. It proved pretty unfriendly soil. The church group discovered it had won a rather hollow right. They were treated as interlopers rather than as representatives of the public interest. And after the hearing the FCC granted a full term three-year renewal to WLBT.

Once again the United Church of Christ went to the United States Court of Appeals for the District of Columbia, and once again, Judge Warren Burger (now Chief Justice of the United States Supreme Court) read a stern lecture to the FCC. By the time the case had returned to his court a second time, Judge Burger had wearied of reading sermons to the FCC. Burger took the unprecedented step of revoking the license renewal award to WLBT without remand to the FCC. Enough was enough. Speaking of the FCC Hearing Examiner's treatment of the United Church of Christ, he said, "His response manifests a 'glaring weakness' in his grasp of the function and purpose of the hearing and the public duties of the Commission." He added that the public intervenors were performing a public service and "were entitled to a more hospitable reception in the performance of that function."

Harsh language followed from the Commission's persistent attempts to renew the license of WLBT. Said Burger:

> The record before us leaves us with a profound concern over the entire handling of this case following the remand to the Commission. The impatience with the Public Intervenors, the hostility toward their efforts to justify a satisfyingly strict standard of proof, . . . leads us, albeit reluctantly, to the conclusion that it will serve no useful purpose to ask the Commission to reconsider. . . . The administrative conduct reflected in this record is beyond repair." [2]

In this passage is reflected distilled disenchantment with over thirty years of federal regulation of broadcasting. Supervision of broadcasting by a federal agency has largely been the history of the capture of the agency by the industry. By 1969, two years after his first decision in the case, Judge Warren Burger had become wearied beyond endurance with this familiar pattern. His court ordered the FCC to invite applicants to file for the revoked license.

17 /

Media, Pa.: A Success for

the Citizen Group?

THE CITIZEN GROUP HAS MADE A FORMIDABLE START AT OPENING up broadcasting. The public now has a right to question the performance of radio and television licensees every three years at renewal time before the decision-maker, the Federal Communications Commission. As a result of the efforts of the United Church of Christ, a right of access to the broadcasting bureaucracy has been established for citizen groups. The Red Lion case, for its part, assures the public a right of access to radio and television directly.

A battle which occurred in Media, Pennsylvania, shows what an alliance of citizen groups can do to affect the identity and character of broadcasting. On July 1, 1970, the unthinkable finally happened. Because of the concerted efforts of citizen groups, a radio station, WXUR–AM and WXUR–FM, lost its license at renewal time because of failure to comply with the fairness doctrine.[1]

WXUR was a small radio station in Media, a suburban Pennsylvania town of 5,800 people. The operator, Brandywine-

Main Radio, Inc. was wholly owned by the Faith Theological Seminary of Elkins Park, Pennsylvania, presided over by right wing radio preacher Carl McIntire.

McIntire's association with the Media radio station had been stormy from the beginning. When in 1965, McIntire's group first applied for voluntary transfer of control of WXUR to them from its previous owners, bitter protests were raised by community groups who were both hostile to McIntire's right-wing views and suspicious of his professed willingness to give balanced treatment to controversial issues. As a result, the FCC first approved the McIntire group's taking over WXUR only after receiving a pledge that they would provide an equal opportunity for the expression of opposing viewpoints on controversial public issues.

The FCC was by no means unanimous in approving the acquisition. Commissioner Kenneth Cox dissented, noting that the depth of community protests against operation by McIntire was "virtually unprecedented." Commissioner Lee Loevinger agreed with the decision to let the McIntire group operate WXUR but dissociated himself from the pledge required of WXUR by the other commissioners.

Loevinger said the fairness doctrine didn't require fair presentation of issues but only fair opportunity for reply. The question of whether WXUR, which turned out to be a politically right-wing, religiously fundamentalist radio station, had merely to provide reply time or actual and meaningful access for its critics became a major question in the renewal proceeding.

When renewal time came for WXUR, citizen's groups in the local community contended that McIntire's staff had not stood by their pledge. The sheer variety of the groups which participated in the WXUR proceeding demonstrates the pioneer work which had been done by groups like the Reverend Everett Parker's United Church of Christ in stimulating community interest in broadcasting and encouraging community participation in broadcast renewal proceedings. Eighteen civil and religious groups as well as one individual intervened in the license renewal proceeding:

AFL–CIO of Pennsylvania
The American Baptist Convention Division of Evangelism
The Delaware Valley Council of the American Jewish Congress
The Anti-Defamation League of B'nai B'rith
The Board of Social Ministry of the Lutheran Synod of Eastern Pennsylvania
B'rith Sholom
Catholic Community Relations School
Catholic Star Herald
Fellowship Commission
Greater Philadelphia Council of Churches
Jewish Community Relations Council of Greater Philadelphia
Jewish Labor Committee
Media Fellowship House
Media Chapter of the NAACP
New Jersey Council of Churches
Philadelphia Urban League
U. S. Section of the Women's International League for Peace and Freedom
American Jewish Committee
Rev. Donald G. Huston, Pastor, First Presbyterian Church of Lower Merion

The long hearing on whether WXUR should be renewed revealed how WXUR had generated such intense hostility in some sections of the greater Philadelphia community. Thomas Livezy, the moderator of a WXUR call-in program, *Freedom of Speech*, was finally removed by the station management because of his encouragement and apparent approval of the remarks of some of the program's anti-Semitic callers. FCC hearing examiner Godfrey Irion thought that the hearing testimony indicated that liberal viewpoints were expressed fairly frequently by other callers. Some citizen groups thought, on the other hand, that these remarks still failed to provide a truly balanced treatment.

WXUR's targets were many. Eugene Genovese and Staughton Lynd, celebrated figures of the New Left, were among the individuals attacked. Another target of the station was Harvard law professor and former Defense Department official Adam Yarmolinsky, who was called disloyal. Among groups attacked were the black Deacons for Defense and the Flushing Branch of the Women's International League for Peace and Freedom, which was labeled "a Commie group." Under the personal attack rules, WXUR was required to furnish the attack victims notice of the attacks, copies of the transcript, or failing that, tapes and summaries and offer of an opportunity to reply. But WXUR had established no procedures for providing notice and response.

A House Resolution of the Pennsylvania legislature was directed against the programming practices of Dr. McIntire. The resolution contended that until 1960 when he began his broadcast, the *20th Century Reformation Hour,* McIntire had enjoyed little success. McIntire's response shed considerable light on the small nonnetwork affiliated radio station:

> Well, I think maybe that it is true . . . we could not get our story before the public through the networks . . . We found that the press was generally blocked against us and we discovered that by the private radio stations spread across the country, the little stations, that we could get on and talk about those matters in the *free exercise of religion,* and was in that area that we are able to spread across the country, and, as the report goes on to say, broadcasts over 600 stations reach millions of people."

Media, Pa.: A Success for the Citizen Group?

There is much to be said about McIntire's candor here. Network practices certainly do appear to shut out the far-right point of view. McIntire had a real problem of access. He solved it by utilizing the small radio stations. There is another insight in his remarks about communication policy: the name of religion may be exploited to shield the broadcasters from legal responsibilities that may apply when politics are the avowed subject of discussion.

WXUR was not a fairness case where someone had asked for reply time, was denied it, and was now suing for it. The criticism of the station was that it had not striven sufficiently to provide truly credible and convincing opposing positions as a counterpoise to its own generally conservative and rightist line. WXUR shows the new importance of an access-oriented approach to communications policy. The FCC made it clear that a station had an obligation to institute affirmative procedures to make debate and opportunity for reply possible even when no reply had been sought.

The force of the new right of citizen groups to demand a hearing before the FCC where they could bring out the actual performance of a broadcaster is fully illustrated by what happened to WXUR. No competitor had applied for the license. If citizen groups had not been able to ask for a hearing, there simply would have been no reason to deny the renewal. Indeed, there would have been no formal record to justify denial of a renewal application.

So, for citizen groups, there is much reason to take heart from the result in WXUR. In the twenty-one year history of the fairness doctrine no broadcaster had ever got the regulatory axe for noncompliance. It was citizen groups that precipitated the first denial of a broadcaster's application for license renewal in the history of broadcast regulation.

But as with all revolutions, victory was not completely unalloyed. The Philadelphia Chapter of the American Civil Liberties Union was troubled by what amounted essentially to a suppression of opinion—the silencing of McIntire's station and the nonconformist right-wing political/religious opinions advocated on it.

Also, the WXUR case could easily have been handled as a group defamation case. Although it is now known as the first case where a licensee had lost its license for violation of the fairness doctrine, it could just as easily have been the first case in broadcasting to consider the suitability of a broadcaster which attacked racial and religious minority groups. The FCC preferred to treat the racial slurs as a fairness issue rather than as a separate and basic problem of communications policy. But the problem of group defamation in broadcasting was suppressed rather than clarified by the FCC's decision in WXUR.

The objective of the fairness doctrine is ostensibly to encourage "robust, wide-open debate." But, just as some debate objectively informs, some debate can be socially corrosive and inflame a community. How should such speech be dealt with? FCC reaction to this hot potato is instructive. The FCC hearing examiner decided to renew the license of WXUR. He opined that excessive tenderness for individual and group sensitivities was incompatible with the encouragement and continuation of free expression. The FCC reversed the hearing examiner and ordered the WXUR license denied, but not on any ground that dealt with group defamation.

The same classical liberal position which abhors any government intervention in the press, whether to restrain or stimulate freedom of expression, is also opposed to restricting expression even in the area of racial defamation. However, it was the racial slurs against Jews and Negroes and on some WXUR programs occasionally Catholics which evoked the extraordinary community outpouring of hostility. In the summer of 1965, a citizen of

204

Media, Pa.: A Success for the Citizen Group?

Media complained to the Borough Council about WXUR's *Freedom of Speech* program on the ground that it promoted "hate and dissension by attacking minority groups." Moreover, an advertising boycott against merchants who advertised on WXUR was undertaken. After Livezy left the *Freedom of Speech* program, the Media Borough Council decided not to drop plans to seek an FCC investigation into bias on WXUR. The 7800 pages of the record of the agency hearing disclose that the racial slurs occasioned much of the public hostility. The FCC Commissioners did not deal with this problem at all, the fundamental dilemma that some kinds of expression, particularly in the area of racial tensions, are not neutralized but aggravated by reply. Recognition that equal time is not an adequate remedy for racial defamation would have been helpful. A frank awareness that the lack of access to establishment broadcasting, particularly, has necessitated a flight of nonestablishment viewpoints to the small town nonnetwork-affiliated radio stations would also have been welcome. As Hearing Examiner Godfrey Irion remarked of the WXUR proceeding: All favor motherhood and fairness depending upon the circumstances.

For the present, minority group organizations are dubious of the merits of legal prohibition of group defamation. Both the American Jewish Congress and the American Jewish Committee oppose legislation prohibiting group defamation. Of Jewish organizations only the Jewish War Veterans favors group libel legislation. For the present, private censorship takes care of problems of group defamation on broadcasting. The media can be relied on to deny the merchants of hate access to radio, television, and the press. But how reliable or enduring is such a state of affairs?

Superficially, the WXUR situation raises a single issue: Dr. McIntire had not complied with the fairness doctrine. But the decision skirted many of the tough questions. How can a small, poorly financed station specializing in public issues, manage to audit all its programs to conform with the requirement that the subjects of personal attacks be given notice of those attacks and an opportunity for reply? Abstractly, the rule that victims of personal attacks be notified is sound. Large communications entities such as radio and television networks have the personnel and the financial resources to comply. Independent small town radio stations with no network affiliation do not. Should all broadcasters be under the same duty to comply with the personal attack rules with no reference to their financial resources? The Commission didn't say. The FCC decision denying license renewal to WXUR was reaffirmed by the Commission once again on a petition for reconsideration. Whether the Commission will yet illuminate these issues remains to be seen. Meanwhile, McIntire has taken the matter to court.

Most American communities have more radio than any other kind of media outlet (certainly more than VHF television outlets or daily newspapers of general circulation). One solution to problems of access and diversity of opinion would be a frequency allocations policy which would strive to license a Black Panther radio station, a John Birch radio station, or an SDS radio station. An ironic observation by FCC Examiner Godfrey Irion is worth reflecting on—that WXUR offered controversial public issue programming in about the same degree that most stations offer entertainment.

WXUR was acquired by Carl McIntire's Faith Theological Seminary to propagandize, and it did. But it did not take a position by means of designated editorials on public issues. Instead, WXUR's whole program structure reflected a conservative and right-wing approach in politics and a fundamentalist approach in religion. Was it possible for WXUR with its thorough-going ideological approach to broadcasting to meet the requirements of the fairness doctrine? Optimal use of the fairness doctrine really occurs when a station is basically neutral on public and social issues. Where the management and the individual programs carried do have a very special point of view, the offer of reply time in such a context is resisted by the groups and individuals attacked. Individuals attacked or groups attacked, for example, hesitated to appear on WXUR for fear their appearance would (1) legitimize the fringe-type opinion; (2) result in being subjected to further group or personal abuse; or (3) make it possible for the station to continue to be licensed. The last ground presents a paradox. The appearance of the targets of the station's programs makes it possible for the station to renew its license because then it is thereby enabled to assert that it has complied with the fairness doctrine.

Was the WXUR case a triumph for free speech? Probably not. The case illustrates but does not resolve some basic problems in communications policy. For example, it shows how difficult it is to achieve balanced presentation. As citizen groups battle for wider access to broadcasting, the complexities of the meaning of access bear in upon us. The strident voice, unattractive and shrill, is not found in the smooth homogeneity offered by the prestige media, the network-affiliated radio and television station. The voice of real nonconformity on radio is increasingly found in the small nonnetwork affiliated radio station, be it operated by the left-leaning Pacifica Foundation or the rightward McIntire group. In either case, a real and distinct voice with a cutting edge is offered. To apply to these small stations mechanisms for dialogue which are better suited to counter the issue-shy blandness of the prestige media may not be productive.

It is entirely possible that as a general proposition, fairness and access concepts may not make too much sense in the context of the local radio station, even though they make excellent sense with regard to the network-affiliated VHF television station. It is these distinctions which must be reflected on as citizen groups increasingly demonstrate that the kind of broadcasting a community gets is more within the control of the community than ever before.

18 /

Three That Almost Made a

Revolution—Access and

Concentration of

Ownership in the Media

THE CLASSIC LIBERTARIAN IDEA OF FREE EXPRESSION AND TRA-
ditional antitrust policy share the assumption of Judge Learned
Hand that "right conclusions are more likely to be gathered out
of a multitude of tongues." [1] Justice Hugo Black wrote in the
same antitrust context, that the First Amendment "rests on the
assumption that the widest possible dissemination of information from diverse and antagonistic sources is essential to the wel-
fare of the public, that a free press is a condition of a free society." [2]

There are many roads to public access to television. Direct

obligation on the part of a broadcaster to provide access is one route. A policy of inhibiting concentration of control in the media is still another. Both routes have a common destination— freshness and diversity of viewpoint and expression.

Of all the significant broadcast cases of the decade, perhaps the most significant from the point of view of diversification of media control was the case in which the FCC declared that the channel run by Boston television station WHDH, licensed to the daily Boston *Herald-Traveler*, should be awarded to a new applicant.[3]

The United Church of Christ case launched the citizen group as the real foot soldier in the battle for fairness and access. The Red Lion case, by its declaration that access for ideas on television was a public right, legitimized the attack on the broadcast establishment. The WHDH case questioned the idea that once-a-broadcast-licensee, always-a-broadcast-licensee. The triad of cases were three that—almost—made a revolution.

The WHDH Case

Broadcasters had always known that technically all they had was a three-year license to a frequency. But in practice the FCC had given them a quasi-property right in their licenses. In the whole history of broadcast regulation, one could count on the fingers of one hand the licensees that had failed to win renewal.

Then in 1969, the FCC ruled that it would not renew the license to channel 5 of the Boston *Herald-Traveler* television station, WHDH. The channel was awarded to a new applicant, Boston Broadcasting Inc.[4] The action largely turned on the question: should a newspaper own a television station? The legal answer to that was of abiding interest to the owners of the mass media. Many of the most lucrative television properties are owned by cross-media interests. WHDH, an ABC affiliate, was a prime example.

Three That Almost Made a Revolution

In a separate concurring statement in the WHDH case, Nicholas Johnson pointed out that in America's eleven largest cities not a single network affiliated VHF television station is independently and locally owned. All such stations, said Johnson, are owned by networks, multiple-station owners, or a major local newspaper.

The FCC answer about whether a newspaper should own a television station had been characteristically bureaucratic: alternately yes, no, and maybe. Indeed Commissioner Roselle Hyde's comment on his voting in WHDH's previous bouts with the agency illustrated the situation: "On the first round I voted against WHDH. On the second round, I cast my vote for WHDH, Inc." This time, he said because "it is no less difficult for me to choose among these competing applicants—I have simply abstained." But whatever general stands the FCC had taken in the past, the hard fact was that no incumbent television station operated by a newspaper had ever been denied a license on renewal.

Renewal of the existing license was the pattern even in the face of a challenge at renewal time by a competing applicant. Comparative hearings, weighing the merits of the incumbent against those of the new applicant, were sometimes held; the result was invariably to license the incumbent once again. Therefore when the FCC actually refused to renew the license of an incumbent licensee, the broadcasting industry was shaken. Suddenly, the power seemed to have gone out of the industry litany that the broadcaster's investment in a transmitter, good-will, and staff should not be liable to destruction every three years.

The industry considered that, at its broadest reading, the WHDH case jeopardized the life of every existing broadcaster in America. Furthermore, the decision raised another issue: was concentration of ownership of different media in the same hands in the same community now to be a mortal sin? Although there had in the past been FCC musings on the point, the unchallenged existence of media concentration indicated that apparently the FCC had not thought it too undesirable. In this respect, the WHDH decision was a breakthrough.

Oddly enough, when WHDH appealed the decision, Red Lion's emphasis on access and fairness was turned on its head and used as an argument against applying the FCC's policy of requiring diversification of media ownership in the same city. WHDH argued that since all licensees had an obligation to provide balanced presentation of ideas, it didn't matter if the licensee had other media properties. Judge Leventhal in the court of appeals denied that Red Lion had pulled the rug from under the FCC's diversification of ownership policy. Both policies, the policy of requiring balanced presentation and diversification of ownership, worked toward the same end.[5]

Legal recognition of a right of access in no way lessens the need for diversity of ownership. Just because there is now a direct obligation on broadcasters to provide access to the public, the Commission need not be "confined to the technique of exercising regulatory surveillance" to insure that broadcasters would fulfill their responsibilities. The FCC was entirely justified, in Judge Leventhal's view, to choose as broadcasters "those who would speak out with fresh voice," and who would "most naturally initiate, encourage and expand diversity of approach and viewpoint." That a fresh voice is one unconnected with other media in the same community was implicit in Judge Leventhal's opinion.

But some communities have only one newspaper and have better general and balanced presentation than cities that have several newspapers. What is the real consequence when the same ownership operates both a television station and a newspaper in the same community? Does it lead to slanted news? To blocks in the opinion process?

One of the grounds on which the FCC defended its WHDH decision was the fact that the Boston *Herald-Traveler*, owner of

WHDH, had obtained a scoop on a report of the Massachusetts Crime Commission without also publicizing the report over its broadcast stations. Although the newspaper received the draft report four or five days before publishing it, the paper's broadcast station did not learn of it until midnight of the day before.

In the FCC's view, the fact that the newspaper put its own journalistic interests ahead of its television station was a debit. But was it really? The newspaper's attempt to scoop its own TV station may only prove that investigative journalism by the press is far superior to that of electronic media. It may prove that the television station and the newspaper were truly run on an independent basis and the fact of common ownership is irrelevant. I do not mean to minimize the dangers of concentration of ownership in the media. I suggest instead that both diversification of control of the media and a right of access are necessary. Deconcentration of ownership alone is insufficient.

Further, when the Boston *Herald-Traveler* was shorn of its television license, the paper folded and sold its assets to the Boston *Record-American*. Was the WHDH decision, then, a victory or defeat for diversity of ideas in Boston?

The Counter-Revolution: The Pastore Bill and the Policy Statement

The WHDH case gave citizen groups around the country some formidable weaponry. United Church of Christ had allowed the citizen groups to enter FCC proceedings, but WHDH gave these groups an incentive to do battle: renewal of the existing broadcast licenses was no longer a sure thing. When these two developments were added to the Red Lion emphasis on diversity of opinion and access for the public, it appeared for a brief interlude that a new day had begun for American broadcasting.

But a counter-revolution soon appeared. Doing battle for the broadcasting industry was scrappy little Senator John O. Pastore, Democrat of Rhode Island, Chairman of the Senate Subcommittee on Communications. To the applause of the broadcast industry, who feared that millions of dollars in capital investment might go down with unrenewed licenses, Senator Pastore introduced a bill to prevent the FCC from considering "the application of any other person" for a license at renewal time if the FCC first found that the existing licensee had served the public interest. Only if the FCC determined after a hearing that renewal would not be in the public interest could there be consideration of the application of other parties for the license in question.[6]

What was amazing about the proposal was the obvious cynicism about the regulatory process revealed in the language of the bill.

Pastore would have charged the FCC to defend the broadcasters from the very public whose interest the FCC was established to represent.

The Pastore proposal was not enacted, but the counter-revolution continued. The FCC, reflecting for one thing the wishes of its new Nixon appointees, decided to take some of the bite out of WHDH on its own.

Pastore was glad to let the thing die. To Pastore's surprise, his proposal had drawn heavy fire from blacks. A black citizen group, BEST (Black Efforts for Soul in Television), contended that the Pastore proposal would close the field to newcomers; they objected because, at the present time, there is virtually no black ownership of radio and television in the United States.

BEST was not the only citizen group to attack the Pastore Bill. Nicholas Johnson reported that the National Citizens' Committee for Better Broadcasting had said the Pastore Bill would perpetuate excessive concentrations of control. The American Civil Liberties Union said the Bill would "freeze out every under-represented class in American society."[7]

On January 15, 1970, a full year after the announcement of the WHDH decision, the FCC issued a new Policy Statement on broadcast renewals undercutting its implicit challenge to the status quo. The broadcaster's investment, which had provoked shrill defensive cries from the executives of the National Association of Broadcasters and from the editorial pages of *Broadcasting* magazine, was again given the deference to which the broadcasters had long been accustomed. Piously, the FCC observed that the "broadcast field must have stability, not only for those who engage in broadcasting but from the standpoint of service to the public."

In the Policy Statement the FCC said that "if the applicant for renewal shows in a hearing with a competing applicant that its program service during the preceding license term has been substantially attuned to meeting the needs and interests in its area, and that operation of the station has not otherwise been characterized by serious deficiencies, he will be preferred over the newcomer and his application for renewal will be granted." [8]

WHDH was actually capable of several interpretations. In order to arouse its sympathizers in Congress, the industry had contended that WHDH threw every licensee in America up for grabs by any new applicant. Dissenting from the FCC's decision in WHDH, Commissioner Robert E. Lee argued that a renewal applicant should be in a different position from an applicant seeking a broadcast outlet for the first time. He pointed out the great sums expended for facilities and good will which would be forfeited if, as the WHDH decision implied, a new applicant could obtain the license on the basis of making promises that were superior to the performance of the incumbent.

Of course the WHDH case need not necessarily have been given a radical interpretation. It could simply have been held to say that where an incumbent has cross-media affiliations in the same community and the new applicant does not, the new applicant should be preferred.

On all these points the FCC tried to offer sedatives to a nervous industry. The Policy Statement warned darkly that if the substantial investment of the existing broadcaster were not given a preference, there would "be an inducement to the opportunist who might seek a license and then provide the barest minimum of service which would permit short run maximization of profit, on the theory that the license might be terminated whether he rendered a good service or not."

Actually the 1970 Policy Statement showed the bureaucratic genius at work. The FCC had managed to deflect attacks on the status quo in broadcasting from both the left and the right. The Congressional attack from the right, the Pastore Bill, was coopted since the Policy Statement gave preference to the existing licensee. The attack from the left from the citizen groups was outflanked because, if the existing licenses were to be automatically renewed at renewal time, the new right of the citizen groups to participate in renewal proceedings would have little practical effect. There would be no incentive for mounting a long and costly attack on the renewal applicant.

The citizen groups, BEST, and Al Kramer of the Citizens Communication Center (CCC), immediately fought the Policy Statement by petitioning the FCC to adopt a rule proposed by them to clarify the standards in comparative broadcast hearings. The FCC dismissed that petition, but on July 21, 1970, it issued a further explanation of the Policy Statement in response to a subsequent petition by BEST, CCC, Hampton Roads Television Corporation and Community Broadcasting of Boston.[9]

The FCC stuck to its guns and contended that the Policy Statement actually encouraged competing applicants to challenge renewal applicants who have only "minimally served the public interest." The Commission boasted that it was prohibiting upgrading. (After the competing application is filed, a station will sometimes upgrade its programming, i.e., more public affairs, news, religious broadcasts.)

Actually, the 1970 Policy Statement was a far more cleverly drafted document than the Pastore Bill had been. Bureaucrats are apparently better at quiet assassinations than are legislators. The Policy Statement offered the promise of change at renewal time while managing to tinker with the renewal procedure in such a way that a successful renewal challenge would be nearly impossible. The FCC contemplated a two-stage renewal proceeding: if there were a competing applicant for a license at renewal time, there would be a hearing to ascertain whether the incumbent had been "substantially attuned to meeting the needs and interests of its area" and had "not otherwise been characterized by serious deficiencies." In such circumstances, the incumbent would be preferred over the newcomer. Only if a finding of "substantial service" was not made by the FCC trial examiner would the hearing proceed to the next phase, in which the new applicant could actually triumph if he established that he would substantially serve the public interest.

Former FCC staff member Hyman Goldin, now on the faculty of the Boston University School of Public Communication, has said that the failure of the FCC to give any content to the "substantial service" requirement was the abiding defect of the Policy Statement.[10] He believed that a definition should have been attempted by the FCC which would have included specific allocations of time for public affairs programming, "community-involvement," and "quality programming for children." Broadcasters would then know what was expected of them. Better still, broadcasters would be held to a common standard. Hopefully, a common duty to comply with a common standard would raise the overall quality of programming.

The FCC retained Dr. Barry Cole of the Indiana University faculty as a consultant to review the license renewal process. One of his proposals was a suggestion that the FCC undertake an inquiry to establish a definition of "substantial service" as that term is used in the 1970 Policy Statement.[11] The FCC is presently engaged in establishing such a definition.

My difficulty with the Policy Statement cannot be cured in any fundamental sense by giving content to the term "substantial service," although such an effort might be helpful. Long experience with a similar term, broadcasting in the "public interest," has failed to yield a satisfactory definition although it has been in the Federal Communications Act since 1934.

The flaw in the Policy Statement is in the regulatory policy which animates it. It betrays on every page a preference for the present holders of radio and television licenses. This preference is justified on the basis of protecting the investment of the existing businesses. Until regulatory philosophy is more concerned with the programming service of the licensee to the community and less about the future of the licensee's investment, change in American television will be frustrated.

The Renewal Process–Open At Last?

Two citizen groups, the Citizen Communications Center under the direction of Albert Kramer, and BEST (Black Efforts for Soul in Television), led by William D. Wright, took the 1970 Policy Statement to court. The court agreed that the Policy Statement was unlawful, and ordered the FCC to abandon it.[12]

The citizen groups won their case by convincing the court that the Policy Statement was a violation of a 1946 Supreme Court decision, the Ashbacker case,[13] which required that the FCC provide a comparative hearing to determine the merits of mutually exclusive broadcast license applications. Indeed, the Federal Communications Act itself specifically grants a competing applicant a hearing.[14]

The Citizens Communications Center case sent new shock waves throughout the American broadcasting world. Broadcast regulation has been dominated for nearly forty years by an un-written law of renewal. The Citizens Communications Center case rivals the FCC's WHDH decision in striking down the un-written law and restoring broadcasting to the written law: the clear requirement in the Federal Communications Act which prohibits the FCC from giving a broadcaster a license for more than three years.[15]

The 1970 Policy Statement made it very difficult to subject a broadcast renewal applicant to a hearing even in contested cases: If there was no hearing, then, for all their newly won rights of standing, the citizen groups were neatly robbed of a forum where they could show the imperfections of the renewal appli-cant.

The Citizens Communications Center decision did give some small encouragement to the industry. The court said that licensees who had rendered "superior service" ought to be re-newed. This was a concession, of course, to the continual battle over the nature of the broadcaster's license. Broadcasters pointed to the vast sums for which broadcast licenses were traded. Built into the price, they argued, was the expectation of an indefinite license renewal. The court emphasized that broad-casters do not have a proprietary right in their licenses, but did suggest that renewal might be depended upon as a reward for ex-cellence.

Although the court talked about superior service it did not intend to make that issue determinative in renewal proceedings. This view is supported by veteran industry lawyer Marcus Cohn who concluded that even a showing of superior programming by the licensee was not intended by the court to "resolve the issue between the existing licensee and the newcomer." The determi-native factors in making the renewal judgment, Cohn points out, include local residence, integration of ownership and man-agement, diversification of ownership of the media, and superior service. Another factor mentioned by Judge Wright for the court was whether the incumbent broadcaster reinvests his profits "to the service of the listening and viewing public."

The fact that the Citizens Communications Center decision did not make superior service a crucial factor in renewals prompted Cohn to suggest that Congress should amend the Communications Act to permit the FCC to renew some licenses for periods of more than three years. Cohn argues the excellent station gets no reward for excellence. Since broadcast licenses are almost always renewed, the best and the worst broadcasters get the benefit of the same passing grade from the FCC—renewal. Cohn argues that the possibility of being able to secure a license for more than three years might stimulate a desirable competition for excellence.[16]

The suggestion that "superior service" be a factor considered for renewal was a concession to the right, the industry, and the old habits of broadcast regulation. But the Citizens Communications Center decision has sufficient catholicity and counterpoint to offer a promise to the left, the citizen group, and the access approach to broadcast regulation. The court made clear that any approach to renewals which did not offer new interests and racial minorities a chance of entry to broadcasting would be invalid.

But are not the odds heavily in favor of the incumbent even on a superior service standard? The financial means, the broadcast know-how, the ability to meet even an exacting standard of programming excellence are all with the existing broadcast licensee. These formidable advantages make it difficult, if not impossible, for the new applicant, minority or otherwise, to persuade the FCC that his promises should be believed over the incumbent's performance.

Is there a tension, if not an open conflict, between a superior service standard and a public interest conception which insists on a renewal and licensing procedure that will not by definition exclude representation from minority groups such as the black community and the Mexican-American community? Since few would call the present level of broadcast programming performance in this country superior, it can be argued that a superior service standard should call for loss of license on renewal and new certification of new groups and interests with new ideas. If, on the other hand, the superior service standard, as implemented by the FCC, is not to be taken seriously, if it is simply the "substantial service" standard under another name, then once again a court victory has been won for the public interest in broadcasting only to be lost on the level of FCC interpretation and implementation.

The court asked the FCC to clarify the meaning of superior service. On August 20, 1971, the FCC issued a statement on the impact that the Citizens Communications Center case would have in its proceeding on FCC policy in broadcast renewals.[17]

The statement explains the Citizens Communications Center case in an apparent effort to overrule it and ignore it. The rejection of the substantial service standard is minimized. In an appalling exercise of sophistry, the FCC professed to believe that the court may have read " 'substantial' service as meaning minimal service meeting the public interest standard." Therefore, reasoned the FCC, the court's superior service reference was really meant "to convey a contrast with mediocre service." The FCC went out of its way to demolish the plain meaning of superior service as developed by the court. Superior service or substantial service, the FCC seems to be saying, are just labels for the same thing.

Thus, the FCC reads the Citizens Communications Center decision to be a judicial way of saying that the past service of the incumbent licensee is the crucial factor in renewals. The essential fact, in this view, in a renewal proceeding is the incumbent licensee's expectancy that his license will be renewed. The trouble with this rationale is that it is false. The court decision was a sustained attack on the property approach to the broadcast license and the broadcast renewal proceeding.

The question arises: why the commission's hostility, its obduracy, to change in broadcasting? Commissioner Nicholas Johnson suggests that the FCC's protectionist tendencies toward the broadcast industry rise from a misplaced sympathy for the investment of the broadcast licensee. It is an affection that is misplaced because the greatest asset of the broadcaster is something he never earned, and something that, beyond the three-year license he has no rights to—the opportunity to broadcast. Nicholas Johnson describes the "property" of broadcasters with the stinging candor that has won him the badge of honor for federal regulators, a demand that he be impeached by at least two state associations of broadcasters:

> The "forfeiture" that occurs when an incumbent loses to a new competitor is precisely that property value that the Act says shall not be created. The 1952 amendments to the Act simply accentuated this dilemma by insuring a free market in the buying and selling of licenses, subject only to Commission regulation. 47 U.S.C. 310 (b) (1964). An oligopolistic industry (especially in television), profit maximizing behavior, virtually automatic renewal, and a Commission permissive to the buying and selling of licenses have combined to make an industry with very large profits which were then translated into capital gains as licenses were sold.[18]

Of course, a broadcaster is entitled to reimbursement for his capital investment. But once having been granted a license, has he a claim to the real value of the license forever? The FCC prefers not to give too final an answer to this question.

The FCC apparently decided not to seek a rehearing or Supreme Court review of the Citizens Communications Center case. The sympathy for new approaches to broadcast regulation demonstrated in Red Lion has shown that the agency cannot rely on the Supreme Court to chase the citizen groups out of the renewal process.

In the area of broadcast renewals, the court instructions are clear: the renewal proceedings must be opened up, the license is not property, and the license expectancy interest of the broadcaster, although a factor to be considered, should not be the dominant consideration in renewals. The dominant factors should be those specified in the Citizens Communications Center decision: minimalizing advertising, excellent programming, the diversification of ownership of mass media, the integration of ownership and management, local roots in the community, and freedom from dependence on the FCC to implement First Amendment rights.

Yet the FCC in its statement "interpreting" the court decision either played down or ignored these factors. Instead, the FCC indicated that it might measure "superior service" by a mechanical yardstick. The strategy is to set categories for programming—for example, public issue programming, entertainment programming, religious programming—and require that a licensee broadcast a fixed percentage of each programming category. Compliance would be "superior service" programming.

A former broadcasting executive, FCC Commissioner Wells, has taken exception to this approach: "We are naive if we think that the licensee of a television station that is worth millions of dollars will take any chances on falling below a numerical floor. If by meeting or exceeding these numbers he is practically assured of license renewal, there can be no doubt as to the course he will follow."

What Wells is dissenting from is an attempt to quantify the unquantifiable. If 3–5 percent of total programming must be public affairs programming, broadcasters will provide it. But what kind of public affairs programming will it be? Nothing is likely to be improved except the marketability of broadcast common stocks, since undoubtedly such a procedure will produce stability of ownership in the broadcast industry.

Chairman Burch has expressed a willingness "to await the judgment of the case" if general guidelines fail. But what is not appreciated—or at least the FCC has not mentioned it—is the consequence of quantifying programming requirements. This approach does not define the programming categories. The result can easily lead to automatic license renewal and to depriving citizen groups of any influence altogether.[19]

Any mechanical approach to programming which does not precisely define program categories, and which sacrifices a difficult qualitative analysis for an easy but meaningless quantitative analysis will only serve to perpetuate the existing broadcast programming and existing broadcast ownership. This result should be reflected on in light of the many clear statements in Judge Wright's Citizens Communications Center decision that the present holders of broadcast licenses have no proprietary rights in their broadcast licenses.

New entrants will still have difficulty in entering broadcasting if the FCC continues to invalidate court efforts to frustrate an automatic renewal policy. It is a tiresome game. The citizen group loses at the FCC level, wins in court, and is frustrated once again back at the FCC.

But as the Citizens Communications Center case shows, the day of the citizen group in broadcasting is here. People like Albert Kramer of the Citizens Communications Center and Tracy Westen of the Stern Community Law Firm[20] are not going to go away. They will keep appealing and winning in the courts and in the long run the FCC, kicking and grumbling, will have to produce a communications policy that will meet a far wider variety of interests than the typical ones represented by government officials, broadcasters, and broadcast lawyers. Eventually the broadcast renewal proceeding will be an opportunity for renewal of the search for excellence in programming and fair opportunity for all sections of the community to provide it.

19 /

The Petition to Deny—

A Weapon for the

Citizen Group?

WHAT IS THE ROLE OF THE CITIZEN GROUP IN ALL THE FERMENT over broadcast renewals? The truth is that really no one knows. The 1970 Policy Statement dampened the rush to file petitions to deny and competing applications on renewals. After WHDH, no less than eight challenges were presented to television licensees up for renewal. Most of these stations were owned by newspapers, and WHDH was the welcome precedent which offered hope for successful challenge. But the WHDH decision's preference for the new applicant with no other media affiliations over the old incumbent licensee owned by a newspaper was expressly disavowed in the Policy Statement. Perhaps more importantly, the FCC backtracked from its own position in WHDH that the incumbent's investment would not operate as an automatic guarantor of renewal.

The whole area was again thrown into turmoil by the Citizens Communications Center case. Presumably, citizen groups can still intervene in both phases of the renewal hearing under the new decision. But intervention in the renewal proceeding is not, practically speaking, always very useful. Sometimes, there is no competing applicant and therefore no hearing.

If a citizen group is dissatisfied with a licensee's performance and there is no new applicant for the license, it can file a petition to deny the license renewal application. But filing a petition to deny does not grant the citizen group a right to an evidentiary hearing, where witnesses may be called and cross-examined and where the past performance of the licensee can be demonstrated. Without an evidentiary hearing, it is very difficult for a citizen group to show that past programming has not been substantially attuned to the needs and interests of the community.

Wresting an evidentiary hearing from the FCC through a petition to deny is not easy. The struggle of some individual citizens of Salt Lake City to secure a hearing illustrates how unequal such a struggle is. A taxi driver and another person took on the Mormon Church. They challenged the license renewal application of KSL–AM, a radio station broadcasting in Salt Lake City.

KSL, Inc., operator of a TV station, an AM radio station, and an FM radio station in Salt Lake City, is a subsidiary of Bonneville International Corporation, which is wholly owned by the Mormon Church. The Mormon Church also owns one of the two metropolitan dailies in Salt Lake City, the *Deseret News*. KSL–AM is one of the few clear channel stations in the country. It blankets eleven western states.

The Salt Lakers filed letters with the FCC protesting renewal and asked that the matter be set for hearing. The FCC refused, declaring that there was no substantial question of fact requiring resolution. The FCC said it could decide whether renewal would be in the public interest without scheduling a hearing.

Getting a hearing from the FCC is difficult enough for an experienced and sophisticated communications attorney representing a license applicant. It is harder for an underfinanced citizen group or, as in Salt Lake City, an aroused taxicab driver.

The dissident Salt Lakers said two issues warranted a hearing: (1) whether the licensee's programming complied with the fairness doctrine, and (2) whether it would be in the public interest to renew KSL–AM given the concentration of communication ownership of KSL, Inc.

After the FCC denied their request for a hearing, the citizens appealed and lost again.[1] The U.S. Court of Appeals in the District of Columbia emphasized the showing required to make out a fairness doctrine violation:

> Where complaint is made to the Commission, the Commission expects complainant to submit specific information indicating (1) the particular station involved;
> (2) the particular issue of a controversial nature discussed over the air;
> (3) the date and time when the program was carried;
> (4) the basis for the claim that the station has presented only one side of the question; and
> (5) whether the station has afforded, or has plans to afford, an opportunity for the presentation of contrasting viewpoints.[2]

Approached from this standard, the Court of Appeals said, the petition to deny had simply failed to show any fairness doctrine violations and so had failed to justify a hearing.

Such decisions frustrate any real control of or participation in local broadcasting. By withholding a hearing on the merits of the citizen's petition to deny, the citizen is effectively prevented from proving the wrong he complains of. It is as if a litigant in court were denied a trial because his complaint failed to show in advance the merit of his cause. It ought to be the very purpose of the FCC hearing to give the petitioner the opportunity to show the merit of his cause.

For the citizen group attacking a license renewal application, the dilemma is that it is often impossible to tell whether opportunity for presentation of contrasting viewpoints has been afforded by the radio or television station. If the citizen group were able to document its case sufficiently against the renewal applicant in the petition to deny, it wouldn't need a hearing. Yet under the present law, without such documentation, no hearing is required. In Salt Lake City, for example, KSL–AM did not publish a daily program log in any newspaper. As a result, the citizens said, it was impossible to survey the station's general programming, much less be in a position to document in the petition to deny whether KSL–AM had provided balanced treatment of controversial topics.

The situation in Salt Lake was worse compounded because the station took the position that the citizens lacked standing to complain before either the FCC or the courts. KSL's position was that individual citizens had no standing to file a petition to deny a license application renewal. That point was an open question: Judge Burger in the United Church of Christ decision had said that representative citizen groups within the community did have standing to enter FCC proceedings. Whether Burger intended to include individual representative citizens was a good question. The FCC decided not to quarrel about standing. It was easier merely to deny the citizens a remedy, that is, no hearing. The station raised the standing point on appeal, but the Court of Appeals did not pick it up. Instead, it agreed with the FCC that the petition to deny should not warrant the holding of a hearing.

In such a situation one of the purposes of a hearing would have been to conduct a searching inquiry of the station staff, station records, and community experience with the station. All these inquiries would be directed to the basic question of whether the station had satisfied the requirements of the fairness doctrine. It makes no sense to say to inexpert laymen who have no entry to the files of a station that unless they can document in advance a licensee's imperfections no hearing will be allowed. Citizens with a grievance are being denied both the means of showing the grievance and of correcting it.

Shifting the Battleground: Pressuring the Stations at Home

Although the FCC maintains, and so far the courts agree, that citizen groups must make a fairly persuasive showing in their petitions to deny to persuade the FCC to order a hearing to inquire whether there has been substantial service by the incumbent licensee, such groups in the meantime are using the petition to deny as a bargaining weapon to pressure stations across the country into changing programming and personnel practices. If the pressure doesn't work, the petition to deny is still relatively inexpensive. Industry lawyers estimate that it costs somewhere around $5,000 to prepare a petition to deny, with lawyers' fees the heaviest expense. If a citizen group were actually going to file a competing application for a license (something most citizen groups have nothing like the financial resources to do), the cost could reach around $250,000. Even to participate in a comparative hearing to show the defects of the incumbent in an effort to aid a new applicant would cost a citizen group around the same amount. So the petition to deny at $5,000 is really a best buy for the victory often won.

Strangely enough, if the radio or television station licensees simply were to ignore the bargaining attempts of the citizen group, the likelihood of emerging unscathed would be pretty good. The probabilities of a citizen group in most cases winning a hearing through a petition to deny, much less actually securing a license denial—is, as we have seen, very remote. But, like Spiro Agnew, aroused citizen groups have learned a lesson: no one ever lost anything by underestimating the cowardice of the broadcasting industry.

The pioneer among citizen groups in using negotiation to bring diversity and change to television has been the victor in the Jackson, Mississippi, case, Everett Parker's Office of Communications of the United Church of Christ. In groups like his, says Dr. Parker, "Television and radio audiences—the most silent of silent majorities—have found their voices." His group has been continuously active in working to provide access to broadcasting for the black community. Recently it has turned its attention to problems of news avoidance. Although black ownership of television stations is nonexistent, and black radio ownership is rare, black-oriented programs are common, particularly in radio. But that hardly means the existence of a black perspective in broadcasting. Dr. Parker believes broadcasters with black-oriented programs "regard blacks as consumers who are fair game for exploitation by unscrupulous advertisers." [3]

The Office of Communications of the United Church of Christ has been influential in shaping the activities of other citizen's groups in relation to the local broadcasters. With its help, some members of the black community in Texarkana, Arkansas, filed a petition to deny the application for license renewal of KTAL–TV in that city for failing to serve the needs of the community, particularly its black component. KTAL agreed to sign a legal contract with twelve local organizations pledging improved television service to the entire viewing area. Parker, speaking of the protests against KTAL and other stations that his office has aided, said the United Church of Christ does not file a formal petition except as a last resort. Parker said the United Church of Christ seeks friendly relationships with stations. [4]

Sparring with the stations in this fashion has at least for the moment proven more productive than attempting to initiate formal proceedings before the FCC—and it is certainly a lot less expensive. The threat of a petition to deny is giving listening groups leverage to change station employment and programming practices. But the bluff of a petition to deny can in fact be called by the issuance of a piece of paper from the FCC denying the order. Unlike the situation with a competing applicant, the petition to deny does not get the petitioning citizen's group an evidentiary hearing. Yet this last is really what the existing licensee wants to ward off if he can.

As a result of the issuance of the 1970 Policy Statement, the citizen groups in broadcasting are increasingly operating on the basis of informal bargaining and negotiating with the station.

20 /

The Citizen Group

at Work

The Industry Response

THE STRATEGY WORKED OUT IN TEXARKANA, ARKANSAS, HAS BECOME famous—or to the industry, infamous. A citizen group tells a station coming up for a renewal to make certain changes in its programming or hiring practice. If the station does not cooperate, the group will file a petition to deny. An alternative approach is first to file a petition with the Commission and then negotiate with the station.

This technique has drawn angry criticism from broadcasters although it has also brought instant success in many communities. Richard Jencks, president of the CBS broadcast group, criticizing the spate of informal negotiating agreements with stations by citizen's groups, has called the development "broadcast regulation by private contract." [1] This characterization was not meant as a compliment. It seems an odd criticism coming from someone who has long argued that the FCC is a threat to broadcasters' rights to freedom of expression.

There are situations in which Jencks clearly prefers the

FCC's frying pan to an angry citizen group's fire. In fact, Jencks' criticism of citizen groups was provoked by an agreement between Capital Cities Broadcasting Corporation and a well-known citizen group, the Citizens Communications Center of Washington, D.C. Capital Cities Broadcasting sought to acquire WFIL–TV in Philadelphia, WNHC in New Haven, Connecticut and KFRE–TV, in Fresno, California. The Citizens Communications Center filed a petition to deny the attempt to acquire the stations. Capital Cities then filed a pleading before the FCC in which it promised to set aside $1 million over the following three years for programming reflecting minority groups and interests. Moreover, advisory groups in the minority communities in these cities are to have a large role in determining how the money is to be spent.[2]

In the light of the success wrought by direct negotiating by citizen groups with stations, the irony in a network executive urging a citizen group to take its complaints to the FCC is almost too strong. The bureaucratic wall that the Salt Lake citizens ran into at the FCC has a message for the members of the broadcasting public, and the public seems to have received it. The FCC appears to provide an apparatus for accomplishing change without actually doing so.

The Citizens Communications Center in its 1970 Progress Report comments on the rise in face-to-face negotiations by citizen groups to obtain pledges from broadcasters in areas such as minority employment and public affairs programming. Reports the Center, "Often, however, a legal license challenge filed with the FCC has been necessary to encourage broadcasters even to enter such negotiations."[3] The Center is presently working on a handbook discussing the role that negotiations by citizen's groups with local broadcasters can play in influencing changes in television programming. In Atlanta, Georgia, for example, all the stations were challenged at renewal time, and all capitulated. In 1970, the Citizens Communications Center filed a petition to deny the renewal of the license of a southern broadcaster who refused to give news coverage to a local civil rights movement.

In another action, when two former employees of the San Francisco Chronicle Publishing Company took on that media giant and sought to obtain denial of its application to renew its licenses to KRON–TV and KRON–FM in San Francisco, the Citizens Communications Center provided the necessary legal help.[4]

The Chronicle publishes the newspaper with the largest circulation in the San Francisco Bay area. The two employees argued that renewal would not be in the public interest because it would perpetrate the concentration of control of mass media. Before the entry of lawyer Al Kramer's Citizens Communications Center into the KRON case, one San Francisco lawyer donating his time had to battle the legal army employed by the Chronicle—one San Francisco law firm and two Washington, D.C., law firms, a total of seventy lawyers. Since Kramer has been the only lawyer at the Citizens Communications Center for most of its existence, the battle has not suddenly become fair, but at least it has become possible.

Sometimes a station on renewal will receive opposing blasts from more citizen groups than one. Black groups protested the renewal of WHC–TV in Memphis; but so did the Memphis Citizens Council, who protested that WHC–TV was biased in favor of blacks.[5]

For Jencks, such inconsistent protests are the proof of the unwisdom of having citizen groups make demands on broadcasters.

This conflict in the community only reveals the unreal quality of the homogenized blandness in programming dear to the industry. Inconsistent community protests about a local broadcaster's programming testifies to the need for more direct programming by community groups without censorship by the broadcaster. What the industry is really seeing is an attack on the trusteeship theory of broadcasting, the idea that a broadcaster can himself represent the disparate voices of the community.

Authentic debate is the crucial problem. Citizen groups are increasingly financing access to television. Unfortunately, it is sometimes an ersatz kind of access. Recently, Robert A. Maslow of the Businessmen's Educational Fund has offered free to radio broadcasters a daily four-minute program, *In the Public Interest*, taking the liberal-left viewpoint. Designed to balance the effective use of radio by conservative right-wingers, exemplified by H. L. Hunt's *Life-Line* and Carl McIntire's *20th Century Reformation Hour*, the program has been carried by five hundred and ten radio stations since February 15, 1971.[6] Funding for the show comes from the Businessmen's Educational Fund and the World Federalist Fund. Broadcaster enthusiasm for this program is partially attributable to an honest desire for balance in programming. In part, it is also due to a desire to get instant compliance with the fairness doctrine—free!

Paradoxically, broadcasting's credibility problem is in some respect due to such endeavors. For both *In the Public Interest* and *Life-Line* are essentially in the business of funding propaganda. It is doubtful that either effort makes much more of a contribution to the authentic flow on broadcasting of ideas concerning either the nation's or the community's anxieties, aspirations, and divisions.

Jencks' attack on the extra-legal work of the citizen group is two-pronged. First, he questions its long-term implications. He argues that a citizen group by definition represents no constituency but itself. In a political sense, this is true; typically, the citizen group wishes to obtain a slice of programming which will mirror its view of the universe. In our heterogeneous society the number of potential citizen groups is infinite. Jencks believes that television should appeal to a mass audience, to what unites us. If programming must shift from a mass perspective to a representational one, the basic theory of commercial television is undermined.

But for what purpose is this appeal to unity? Surely, there is some movement of ideas on television but it is peripheral compared with the dominant commercial concern for the sale of goods.

There is an earned unity, a just consensus, that comes from the interplay among diverse and authentically expressed views. There is also the specious unity of the Nielsen rating, a unity which is directed neither to what we like, nor what we might aspire to, but only to the lowest point of toleration. The unity which commercial television seeks is a false and delusive unity—a unity that exploits that which is least offensive and therefore what is least relevant.

The crimes committed in appealing to a common denominator in a broadcast audience are continuous. In Atlanta, the owners of classical music radio station WGKA received a purchase offer from some Texas broadcasters who planned to shift its format to popular and light classical music. The FCC approved the transfer and the change of format. After all, more people in Atlanta preferred popular than classical music. A poll conducted by those who wanted to take over WGKA revealed that only 16 percent of the radio audience in Atlanta was attracted to classical music. The poll showed that 74 percent liked "Mace" and "Moonglow" but only 16 percent preferred "The Emperor Concert" and "Petrouchka." [7]

A citizen group in Atlanta was formed to fight the format change: the Citizens Committee to preserve the present programming of the "Voice of the Arts" in Atlanta on WGKA–AM and FM. The broadcasters seeking the transfer of the WGKA license argued essentially that broadcasting in the public interest was basically a question of numbers. The ludicrous results of such an approach were revealed by a community survey on which the Texas broadcasters relied. The survey disclosed, for example, that the sheriff of Fulton County had never heard of the station.[8]

The U.S. Court of Appeals in Washington reversed the FCC order approving the transfer and the program format change. Somewhat stingingly, Judge McGowan said the FCC position might make sense if there was only one radio frequency in Atlanta. In point of fact, there were twenty such frequencies. "Surely," observed McGowan, "it is in the public interest" to accommodate "all major aspects of contemporary culture" so long as "that is technically and economically feasible."

For McGowan and his fellow judges, it was incredible that being a member of a minority in taste should forfeit all one's claims to consideration in the character and quality of broadcasting. McGowan declared that a "minority position" does not exclude classical music lovers from the allocation of radio channels and that the FCC's "judgmental function does not end simply upon a showing that a numerical majority prefer the Beatles to Beethoven, impressive as that fact may be in the eyes of the advertisers.[9]

Judge McGowan suggested that sensitivity to advertising needs rather than any excess zeal for majoritarianism is what has prompted the least common denominator approach in commercial broadcasting. This suggestion very shrewdly hits at the motivation of much of contemporary commercial broadcasting's quest for "unity."

Denying that the creation of unity is the function of the press (both the electronic and the print media), Katherine Graham, publisher of the *Washington Post*, contends that "the purpose of a newspaper" is "not to pull people together but to report all sides of every argument 'as comprehensively and comprehensibly as possible.' " [10]

Implicit in Katherine Graham's observation is the assumption that the balanced reporting will be done by an objective reporter. The cry of the citizen group is that balance does an injustice to their perspective. Their partisanship must be allowed expression in its original zeal and in its native tongue, however disturbing it may be. To leave journalism to an all-purpose, presumably disinterested reporter invites suspicion. Katherine Graham says the critical problem for the press is that it is not believed. True. But part of the public refusal to suspend disbelief is a reaction to the fact that the person reporting all sides of every argument is usually a TV commentator reading the AP news. Whether he's black or white, middle-American or militant, it's still the AP news.

Hollie West, a black reporter writing in Mrs. Graham's own newspaper, describes the problem. A small television chain, Metromedia Television, started a special program called *Black News* in its New York City station, WNEW–TV, and its Washington station, WTTG–TV. Miss West reviewed the Washington debut of the program. She found the black anchormen "no 'blacker' " than "black anchormen on regular news shows." But, complained Miss West, there was no interpretive reporting, just the same "quasi-objective, bland copy", the same reliance on the wire services. The program was scheduled for 3:30 p.m. to compete with (or surrender to) NBC's *Baseball Game of the Week*.

Miss West was suspicious: "Is the station serious or is it trying to dodge the possibility of the Federal Communications Commission accusing it of being irrelevant to the black community?" The Metromedia venture gives the impression that "blacks are in ultimate command of the program," but, Miss West concluded, "the truth is that white executives are in charge, and the show is a token offering to a populace whose majority is black." She concludes that "the network would do better to integrate the 'Black News' program staff and make an honest effort to report news from the entire community." [11]

Diversity in broadcasting can be successfully achieved in different ways. It could be accomplished by working out a mechanism for access. It could also be accomplished by minority participation in the ownership and the regulation of the media. Some citizen groups have been directing efforts toward that end. Black Efforts for Soul in Television (BEST) has tried, among other things, to widen the opportunities for black participation in the media. Their resistance to the Pastore bill with its effort to build a protected guild out of existing broadcasters stemmed from this objective.

William Wright of BEST has protested that "in the entire history of the Commission, no Commissioner has had the experience or sensitivity resulting from membership in one of the racial minorities in this country." He argues, "Minority participation in the Commission would be a necessary step toward this goal. The alternative is further division into separate, antagonistic societies." [12] (Now in Ben Hooks, the FCC has a black Commissioner at last.)

BEST, like the Citizens Communications Center, has been filing petitions to deny applications for renewal of television licenses. A project in which BEST joined with other blacks was an attack on the license renewal application of WMAL–TV in Washington, D.C. WMAL–TV, an ABC affiliate, is owned by a newspaper, the *Washington Evening Star*. BEST and its fellow petitioners contended that WMAL discriminated both by way of programming and in employment practices against the 70 percent of Washington's population which was black.

Although the sixteen blacks who brought the petition to deny renewal of WMAL's license represented such important organizations as the Black United Front and individuals like Walter E. Fauntroy, Democratic nominee for District of Columbia delegate to Congress, WMAL's opponents were no more successful than the cab driver in Salt Lake in getting the FCC to order an evidentiary hearing.[13]

WMAL filed an amendment to its application replete with information concerning the efforts it had made to ascertain community needs. As regards the media domination problem presented by the renewal of WMAL, the FCC observed that no one was actually competing for a license, exactly the excuse offered when it obstinately renewed WLBT in Jackson, Mississippi, over the protest of the United Church of Christ.

Only Nicholas Johnson dissented from the FCC decision dismissing the petition to deny WMAL's license. Johnson felt that the petitioners represented the black community and ought to have the opportunity to develop in a hearing their questions about whether WMAL had responded to and ascertained community needs. The present helplessness of citizen groups before the FCC, even when the attack is led by the leadership of a community, is bitterly illustrated by the adamant refusal of the FCC even to schedule hearings on community objections to the performance of a television licensee purportedly serving them.

When the FCC turned down the efforts of BEST and others to deny WMAL's license, the FCC specifically responded to the black community leaders' request that WMAL's programming should be broken down to ascertain how much of it was actually directed to the black audience. The FCC refused to order such a breakdown on the ground that it would frustrate television programming designed for the national audience.

But to break down the programming directed by a local network affiliate to minorities in the community is not necessarily to say that all programming must be directed to particular audiences. The FCC position and the network position are once again identical: since television is aimed at a mass audience, minority programming simply is not desirable.

A Problem of Accountability

The citizen group has turned to a kind of honorable black-mail, because it is clear that neither the channels of communication nor the regulatory process regulating those channels are open. The broadcaster says: let us do the representing for the viewing and listening public because no single unit in that public can represent the entire massive television audience. The activity of the citizen groups, said Jencks, is a kind of "vigilantism" which cannot appeal to the constituency of the whole community. He complained that the demands of citizen groups on radio and television stations "are rarely if ever concerned with any constituents other than their own."

But where is CBS' constituency? Where is the institutional check on CBS to make it accountable to its audience? CBS' constituency is its stockholders; the check on it is the annual statement of profits. Is that kind of a check any more stable a guide to the kind of programming a community should have than the demands of a radical black group for programming that will enhance the pride and the aspirations of the black community?

The basic dilemma in contemporary television policy is that there is no public mechanism to make the station accountable to the community served. In response, private power, represented by the under-class and those sections of the elite which are alienated, have combined to challenge corporate power in its classic private form. Jencks' is really the cry of man who is used to having the field to himself. But two can play and are now playing at the same game: making public policy without benefit of democratic or institutional authority.

Both the citizen groups and the broadcasters are private power groups. Neither is subject to effective public control and therefore neither is in any meaningful way accountable. Each has bred the other.

To be sure, many citizen groups do not reflect the desires of the broad base of the population of their metropolitan communities. But does contemporary television?

Is it not ironic that a CBS executive asks for public control of broadcasting because the pressure of private groups is not subject to constitutional restraint? Surely now the shoe is on the other foot. Perhaps, the broadcasting industry at last is beginning to comprehend the problems power presents when it is not subject to constitutional standards and its temperate exercise is dependent on the judgment—and the mercy—of its possessor.

Strengthening the Citizen Group

When a black citizen group alliance failed to defeat the renewal of WMAL–TV in Washington, D.C., William Wright of BEST was not surprised. Said Wright: "The only way to get justice is to go to the Court of Appeals and have the Commission overturned." [14] The federal courts, rather than the federal agency set up to regulate broadcasting, have become the forums where the citizen group has been able to secure recognition of public rights to broadcasting.

The new rights of access granted by the Supreme Court in the 1969 Red Lion decision are going to be meaningless unless the public gains access to the FCC, the tribunal which actually selects those who will operate American radio and television broadcasting. Since the licenses of the commercial VHF television stations in the big cities are already allocated, the key proceeding at the FCC is the so-called comparative hearing which is convened at renewal time when an incumbent applicant's license is sought by a competing applicant. The idea of the comparative hearing was to evaluate all applicants for either an original license or a license renewal together.

The comparative hearing device, as it existed before the

United Church of Christ case, was largely a farce. The proceedings were interminable and the conclusion foregone: the incumbent would win. If anyone really benefited from the comparative hearing procedure, it was the Washington, D.C., communications bar. The possibility of losing his license terrified the broadcaster and the existence of the comparative hearing kept that possibility alive. Communications law practice was something like the best medical specialties: the patients never died but they never really got better. Every three years there was a crisis.

When Warren Burger made it clear in the United Church of Christ case that the citizen group had a right to enter a comparative hearing, the cozy arrangement began to collapse. And when in WHDH an incumbent actually lost a big city television license, the sentimental attachment to the comparative hearing quickly disappeared.

As we have seen, the 1970 FCC Policy Statement on Renewals eviscerated the comparative hearing and undermined the 1966 United Church of Christ case which gives citizen groups the right to participate in them. The Policy Statement permitted what the Supreme Court in the famous Ashbacker case had denounced in 1946: granting an application for a license or a renewal without granting a hearing to other applicants for the same license.[15] In fact, the Policy Statement was worse than the pre-Ashbacker situation since there at least the FCC had intended to provide the losing applicant with a hearing. Under the Policy Statement if the FCC found that the incumbent was doing a good job, there would be no comparative hearing. For these reasons, the U.S. Court of Appeals found that the Policy Statement was a violation of the Supreme Court's Ashbacker requirement that there be comparative hearings when there are multiple applications for a new license or for a renewal.[16]

Nevertheless, the hard-won right of standing of a citizen

244

group to enter license renewal proceedings has been rendered fairly meaningless. If a television licensee is challenged by a competing applicant at renewal time, then at least there will be a hearing to appraise the incumbent's past performance and a citizen group has a right to participate in that hearing. But if a citizen group, lacking the financial means to compete for the license itself, petitions to deny the license of the incumbent, the FCC is not obligated to provide a hearing. Once again the representatives of the listening public find themselves with fewer procedural rights than the members of the industry. The promise of equality between the listening public and the broadcasting industry which has been offered to the public by the courts has been sabotaged where it counts, in the bureaucracy which administers the law.

The FCC desire to move away from evidentiary hearings open to citizen groups in broadcast renewal cases is understandable although hardly commendable. An FCC reaction to the petition to deny, now widely used by citizen groups, is illustrative. It says that it can deal with the volume of petitions only by deferring the applications for renewal. As a result, there is now a movement in the FCC to avoid citizen group requests for evidentiary hearings by following the type of motion for summary judgment procedure which is in use in federal civil litigation.[17]

In such cases, a party, usually the defendant, may request the deciding tribunal for summary judgment if there is no question of material fact. Such cases are denied on the basis of the papers supporting the motion. Recently, there has been a move to urge use of the summary judgment by administrative tribunals.[18] The Administrative Conference of the United States has made a recommendation for the adoption of procedures to implement summary decision in agency adjudication.

The use of summary judgment procedures is not a hopeful omen for citizen groups. Application of summary judgment procedures to petitions to deny license renewal applications could easily be used by an agency–industry alliance to kill off citizen groups. The advertised virtue of summary judgment procedures is that they will avoid long and costly evidentiary hearings. But the long and costly hearing is the only forum the public has to secure public exposure of a broadcast licensee's performance.

Having been unable to banish the citizen group from its formal proceedings, the agency is now planning to bury it in paper.

The ultimate decision that flows from an evidentiary hearing is more easily subject to scrutiny than one that comes out of a motion for summary judgment. An evidentiary hearing makes it possible for community groups to introduce in testimony the views of community leaders and to examine station staff concerning actual programming performance. These matters are likely to be far more vivid if developed in open hearing than if confined to documents to be read in a bureaucrat's office.

Broadcasters must file a license renewal application within three months of the expiration date of the license. There is therefore a three-month period before license renewal, an "open season" during which the public that has borne the broadcaster's programming for three years can put the broadcaster to three months' anxiety concerning whether a petition to deny will be filed.

There is now a proposal to require broadcasters to file renewal applications within four months of the expiration date. This will give the FCC time to get at the problem of deferred citizen group petitions to deny. It will also give citizen groups three months to negotiate with the station and to file petitions to deny. (Petitions to deny cannot be filed during the month immediately preceding license expirations.) The new time extension for license renewal applications indicates that the understaffed FCC is inclined to favor negotiation by citizen groups with television stations in their community.

A clear right to an evidentiary hearing by every citizen group which files a petition to deny on license renewal should be the standard procedure. In fairness, a broadcaster should be exposed to only one such hearing which all the protesting citizen groups should be required to join. The United Church of Christ case is authority for the proposition that entry to license renewal proceeding for citizen groups is particularly necessary where, as is often the case, there is no contesting license applicant.

Judge Burger remarked that if there was only one television outlet in a community, then the need to air community complaints was particularly great. If no one wants the license application on renewal, who else will protest? The citizen groups, in Burger's view, would often be the only, and therefore the necessary, objectors in the community.

The difference between having a right to file papers with a federal agency and the right actually to appear and participate in hearings before it in person was well appreciated by Judge Burger. Public participation in broadcasting, he said, cannot be "limited to writing letters to the Commissioner, to inspection of records, to the Commission's grace in considering listener claims, or to assure nonparticipating appearance at hearings."

It is true that Judge Burger did not require an evidentiary hearing whenever a citizen group files a petition to deny. But it is also true that his whole opinion assumes that some citizen groups would have that right. Yet the present prospect is that few will be given it.

The uncertainty as to whether a citizen group should have a right to a hearing after it files a petition to deny is robbing all such groups of that right. Burger reasonably suggested the citizen groups should have to show that they had representative status in the community in order to bring a case. The FCC has abandoned this requirement and instead has directed itself to reducing in absolute number the number of evidentiary hearings which citizen groups can demand. Nothing could be further from the intention of the United Church of Christ decision, which was designed to put an administrative weapon in the hands of citizen groups representing the public interest in broadcasting.

21 /

CATV: Instant Access

or Not?

THE ABILITY OF THE COMMUNITY ANTENNA TELEVISION SYSTEMS TO provide a multichannel service to every American community is now being pointed to as the technological answer to the media crisis. Certainly, there is a certain fitness in the idea that what crisis technology has wrought, technology should solve.

In conventional television broadcasting, the signal is radiated through space to the home. CATV (community antenna television) uses a powerful master antenna to pick up the signals of distant television stations and brings the pictures to the home receiver through cables or wires. The possible number of channels far exceeds what is available to commercial broadcasting—each house may easily receive at least twenty channels from the same system. In fact, systems with a capacity of fifty-four channels are now being built. Nicholas Johnson has suggested that the cables of the cable television systems should be treated like the lines of the telephone company. Channels should be made available to whoever wants them for television programming without any third-party restriction or interference. Just as a flat rate buys you a phone conversation, so a flat rate should buy you the opportunity for a television program.[1]

CATV is already a significant communication medium. According to the Nielsen rating firm, by the fall of 1970, 3.7 million American households were wired for cable.[2] This was 6 percent of the total. But cable, as it has developed, has not yet become the people's communications medium. Presently, CATV has been able only to reproduce what already exists, the offerings of the three major networks, plus the offerings of one or two local independents. Bringing twenty channels to subscribers as yet means multiplying the number of channels on which you can see the same thing. All the subscribers are being offered in many cases is the benefit of a clear picture and minor scheduling differences. Beyond that, CATV is today an underutilized medium with so many voices that it doesn't know what to say on them. CATV does some program origination now but program origination on CATV is a generous phrase: it includes devoting a channel to AP news, another to the weather, another to the time, still another to the stock market quotations, and perhaps a few hours to ancient movies or television series.

The information capacities of CATV are great, but it is still an unanswered question whether it can become a challenger to commercial and network broadcasting. That is why the FCC decision to require cable systems to do some origination of programming is so important.[3] If just one of the channels in every cable system offered original television programs, a massive infusion of variety and diversity in American television would be possible. It is an exciting prospect. But excitement at this point in CATV development is premature. It takes know-how, sophistication, and money to produce a program to match a network offering.

The potential of CATV as an originating source of television rests on a basic fact: A CATV system retransmits the signals of distant television stations to its subscribers without paying the originators of the programming. Nonnetwork television channels, particularly already financially weak UHF channels, were directly threatened by CATV. They had to pay for the programming which the CATV systems reproduced for free. Saving UHF from CATV became a major FCC goal during its early regulatory period. The FCC ordered CATV to keep out of the major one hundred markets where most of the UHF channels were. But even this limitation didn't solve the threat CATV presented to the existing economic and broadcasting patterns. Even exiling CATV to the remote mountain areas where its master antenna was the only means of offering isolated communities a variety of television programs and a clear picture presented problems. Suppose a CATV system in a West Virginia town imported signals from a score or more stations, what would be the effect on the one or two commercial VHF television stations which the town did have? CATV tends to break up the audience in such a community. As a result, the advertising dollar upon which the local VHF television station depends for its life is threatened. Furthermore, cable systems have been held not to violate the copyright law if they retransmit copyrighted material which is being carried by television stations.[4] This means that if a broadcaster wished to televise a movie, he must pay a royalty to the copyright owner of the movie. If a cable system operator, on the other hand, wishes to retransmit to his subscribers, he need not pay a royalty. To state the matter mildly, the situation has not enabled broadcasters to look kindly on the growth of cable. A detailed compromise proposal, worked out by Clay Whitehead of the White House's Office of Telecommunications Policy, has been received with approval by broadcast and cable groups.[5] It is designed to protect commercial television stations as well as copyright holders from CATV exploitation but still to stimulate CATV development. Nothing definitive on this problem, however, has been written into law.

On August 5, 1971 the FCC, in a now well-known Letter of

Intent, tried to set forth some guidelines for the future of cable television.[6] The FCC proposed to let CATV enter the nation's hundred top television markets. Under the proposed rule, a cable system would be allowed to carry two distant or out-of-town independent signals into urban markets in addition to local signals. This permission was designed to stimulate cable subscriptions and to enable cable to compete successfully with "free" television. This proposal made a great deal of sense. FCC Chairman Burch has pointed out the anomaly in the previous FCC rules, which expose the smaller and necessarily financially weaker small town television stations to CATV competition but protect commercial television in the lucrative big city markets from CATV competition.[7] Entry into the big cities, under the FCC proposal, would require compliance with some new preconditions: The cable systems would be obliged to use one of their twenty or more channels as a public access channel, open to anyone seeking access.

An unusual feature of an earlier proposal about cable, included in the FCC's June 1970 cable proposals, was that those CATV systems importing distant signals should pay 5 percent of their subscription revenues to noncommercial educational broadcasting; this idea was not repeated in the FCC Letter of Intent. The idea that cable help support ETV (educational television) had drawn some fire. BEST (Black Effort for Soul in Television) has argued that if 5 percent of CATV subscription revenues must go to the Corporation for Public Broadcasting, the real burden will be on the poor since CATV is financed by subscription fees.

Some of the optimism about CATV ignores the fact that UHF is presently the host to a noncommercial broadcasting system which *does* provide an alternative to commercial broadcasting—educational broadcasting. The effect that CATV may have on educational and UHF broadcasting is a real problem. The

Letter of Intent contained a provision designed to help UHF television: all cable systems "must carry the signals of all stations licensed to communities within 35 miles of the cable system".

In another recent move, the FCC required all cable television systems with more than 3,500 subscribers to originate programming beginning April 1, 1971.[8] (This requirement was later modified to require program origination only in systems with no less than 10,000 subscribers.)

How will CATV be able to originate programming on its own? How will a technology now selling a product it doesn't pay for (the television offerings of distant stations) be able to shift to program origination which would cost money? At a National Cable Television Association Convention, Ed Gray, a former McCann Erickson Agency executive, suggested that local CATV programming would only be possible through the creation of a national interconnected CATV network. Such a network of course would be able to sell national advertising.

Is program origination too big a task for independent cable systems without television network support which is not desired? Should CATV systems be owned and operated by public or educational entities as the Ford Foundation has proposed?

The CATV industry's willingness to make a sincere effort to develop program origination should not be overrated. Some cable operators have labeled a channel as their program origination channel and then leased the channel to a local radio broadcaster who then put his disc jockey shows on camera for the entire day. That is program origination? The FCC, somewhat despondently, said: We want program origination but we want it as an outlet for local expression. A day with the disc jockeys is not what was contemplated by a request for local expression.[9]

The FCC has ruled therefore that CATV systems should not enter into any arrangement which inhibits or prevents the sustained use of cable "for local programming designed to inform the public on issues of public importance."

Public Access on CATV

The tremendous channel capacity of CATV has attracted a good deal of speculation. CATV systems in the top markets may be permitted to carry two distant signals. But allowing two channels for importing distant signals still leaves many channels open. Hospitals, fire departments, police departments, cities and facsimile newspaper may use all or part of the time of a CATV channel. All this is novel enough. But CATV also has a science-fiction-come-to-life dimension. It would be possible to equip CATV subscribers for two-way communications which would make the cable an educator, bank, and security guard. Two-way communication, however, would require dual cable systems as well as "sophisticated electronics at both ends of the system—within the home and at the other terminal, be it the butcher shop, the police station, or the library." [10] These possibilities give a hint of the tremendous capacity for change in American life which CATV presents. In its August 5, 1971, Letter of Intent the FCC asked that new cable systems be obliged to have a two-way capacity.[11] Nevertheless, large scale two-way cable use is not an immediate prospect.

An intriguing possibility for immediate change that is within reach is that certain channels can now be set apart as complete public access channels. The FCC has asked the cable industry to give consideration to establishing public access channels on which individuals and groups within a community could express their opinions. Should every cable system have to pledge to maintain some public access channels? New York City in its cable system contract provides for two. A true public access channel would be a common carrier channel that would carry all the programming submitted. A charge could be made for the submissions. Yet there is a good argument that there is no need for a rate structure at all. CATV is so channel-rich that the overall subscription fee could underwrite at least one such common carrier channel.

Theodora Sklover, consultant on urban communications to the Bedford-Stuyvesant Restoration Corporation in New York City, has remarked on the need to distinguish between public access channels and common carrier channels. A public access channel still leaves legal responsibility with the cable system owner. Says Sklover, "If you are worried about obscenity, profanity, if you are worried about bringing in issues—Black Panthers, Jewish Defense League—the cable [operator] still is the guy who has to make the decision." [12]

Commercial broadcasting itself has had similar problems when broadcasters have been required to carry certain programming. In the equal time area, a broadcaster who sells time to X, a political candidate for U.S. Senator, is bound under the law to give an equal opportunity to reply to X's opponent, Y. Under the law the broadcaster could not exercise any right of prior review over what Y was going to say; yet, X could claim the station was legally responsible if he was libeled by Y. In a case involving such a problem the Supreme Court said the station should be given an absolute privilege, i.e. the station cannot be sued for libel.[13] A similar approach should be taken with regard to CATV. If the cable system operator is required to maintain some channels on an open-to-all-comers basis, then the minimum protection for such an obligation should be immunity to a libel suit.

The FCC by rule-making can interpret the "public interest" standards in the Federal Communications Act to provide guidelines for these problems. A final and yet very relevant factor is that since CATV systems are not licensed by the FCC, they may prove somewhat hardier in the defense of values of free expression than have commercial broadcasters. The fact that cable operators are not licensed by the FCC does not of course mean that the FCC cannot regulate cable. The Supreme Court has ruled that the FCC has jurisdiction over cable, at least insofar as cable affects broadcasting. The FCC, for its part, does claim power to regulate cable.[14]

The problem is illuminated by the FCC order of March 5, 1971, that radio broadcast licensees have the responsibility to review the lyrics of records before broadcasting them.[15] The FCC complained that some songs played tended to glorify marijuana or LSD. Whether a song actually did glorify drugs was a question for the licensee but the point was that it was his responsibility. The FCC said that radio broadcasters simply could not play records without someone in authority knowing what was in the lyrics. If the broadcaster fails to exercise control, the FCC warned darkly that it would have "serious questions as to whether continued operation of the station is in the public interest." This was interpreted by the radio industry as a plain English warning to stop playing drug culture records or risk losing their licenses.

A public access channel would place similar problems on the shoulders of CATV ownership or management, but surely, if the cable system operator is required to sell time on a common carrier basis, he ought not to be held legally responsible for what occurs on a cablecast over which he had no control.

The FCC's recent confrontation with the drug culture has more than one dimension for CATV. CATV can respond to the counter culture in a way that commercial radio cannot. Just as the underground press created an alternative press, so the channel abundance of CATV makes possible an alternative television. The problems are not beyond legal solution. Precise public interest standards issued before, and not after, the fact could advise cablecasters that the portrayal of language and conduct designed to encourage illegal action is not permissible. Flexibility should characterize such standards. Language which might not be tolerated after school at 5:30 p.m. may be entirely permissible at 11:30 p.m. What will not be satisfactory and what will paradoxically retard the full development of public access and common carrier channels is a rigid libertarian laissez-faire approach to speech. If no regulatory standards for programming on public access channels are provided, cable system operators will simply be frightened away from developing them.

Using Marshall McLuhan's apocalyptic approach, one can argue that at the very least constitutional distinctions should be made between the different media. Perhaps more freedom does and should inherently attach to the print media because its abstractness is a built-in social safety valve. The advocacy of print is necessarily more rational and less emotional in appeal and therefore needs fewer social controls. But the reality and concreteness of the human form and voice present on the television screen projects an immediacy to which classic constitutional laissez-faire concepts concerning freedom of expression are simply not responsive. Carefully drawn limitations on incitements to disobey the law, to riot, and to commit violence can be implemented by the FCC for cablecasting as well as broadcasting. The common carrier concept of CATV is only superficially like telephone service. Phone conversations, unfortunately, now do increasingly have unwanted auditors, private and public. But the enormous distinction between the phone conversation and public access or common carrier CATV is that CATV presupposes an audience. No matter how extensive the level of community participation in a public access CATV channel, no one wants the common carrier concept developed on CATV to the point that it becomes incompatible with the idea of an audience.

It is possible to have both public access channels and common carrier channels on the multi-channeled CATV system presently operating. Yet the idea of specific channels in a cable system directed to specific minority groups makes some observers nervous. Clay Whitehead of the United States Office of Telecommunications Policy told a group of elected black officials that he was opposed to "ghettoizing cable": "The hardware of communications should not be physically structured or divided up in time to enforce separate-but-equal service to minorities of any sort." Like Richard Jencks, who disapproves of specific citizen group demands for minority programming, Whitehead advised the black officials that they should be primarily interested in broadcasting which "ties us together as a people." [16]

Media critic Ben Bagdikian urges that if national cohesion is to be preserved "popular national media will be needed to provide commonly available news of reality and social values." [17] The national media are by definition not pluralistic in their appeal. A new communications scenario now appears: access and diversity are to find a home in CATV and the national commercial network programming will continue as before. The problem is that CATV, serving as a host for alternative cultures, may ignore the national media with their majoritarian concerns. Will the result be insufficient interaction among ideas, groups, and individuals?

The problem can be stated simply. On CATV it is possible for every local Marx, Rasputin, Voltaire, and Hitler to have his own show. If ever there was a participatory technology, it is CATV. The two franchise operators in the borough of Manhattan in New York City are obligated to subdivide their systems into subdistricts. Each subdistrict is to be given access for its community and the two cable systems (Manhattan Cable in lower Manhattan and Teleprompter in upper Manhattan) are bound to set up program origination facilities in each subdistrict. [18]

CATV: Instant Access or Not?

The dilemma is that each constituency wishes in the last analysis to do two things with the media: (1) to talk to each other and (2) to talk to the larger community. CATV certainly makes it possible to do the first in a way that commercial television does not. But if every group is to have his own channel, will it still be possible to reach the entire community? Richard Jencks of CBS said to me in sincere despair, "What our critics want is our audience for their ideas." He was right. Public access channels, the flourishing of the common carrier concept, are certainly part of the promise of CATV. But to reach the whole community will still require some legal mechanisms for access, reply, and diversity in those television media which will still attract a mass audience. On the other hand, the national media are jeopardized because of the fragmentation of the audience that may result when the multichannel capacity of CATV is actually in use.

We do not know whether the national mass media and the new individualized media promised by CATV can coexist. CATV makes possible electronics media which are not mass. Housing expert Roger Starr has commented on the ironies this presents to the counterculture celebrated by Theodore Roszak and Charles Reich. The dissenting magazine, he writes, is now commonplace in newsstands but mass magazines like the *Saturday Evening Post* are gone. New York daily newspapers are far less numerous today than they once were but weeklies, whether dissenting, radical, esthetic, or sexual, abound. The irony is that dissent abounds, but yet dissenters are still frustrated "not because they cannot speak, but because their fellow citizens do not follow." [19] This last observation is crucial. What will happen to dissent when at last it is given a forum but no one listens? If the millions are still watching "I Love Lucy," what will be the social consequences of that choice? People like Herbert Marcuse have already given us their answer—such a choice should not be permitted because it is not a rational choice. Most of us, however, are convinced that reason and our own choices are interchangeable terms.

Other media writers are concerned that the ultimate consequence of CATV may be merely the destruction of the large media audience which commercial television has created, with nothing left in its stead. It is hard at this point to think this is a danger.

We are at a watershed in CATV regulation. If all this abundance exists, why is there any need for federal regulation? CATV really highlights the anomalies in contemporary communications policy. In an odd way, the privileged status of the print medium has been underscored by CATV. The FCC was asked by the American Newspaper Publishers Association to make it clear that fairness, equal time, and sponsorship identification requirements would not apply to dissemination of newspapers. The FCC replied that the distribution of a newspaper by cable would not affect its legal status. But why not? CATV promises abundance in electronic communications, an area whose whole economic, legal, and constitutional milieu has been scarcity. The abundance in channel capacity which the CATV wire carries into a home will sooner or later reveal what has always been dormant in broadcast regulatory policy, that is, that the social basis or interest in broadcasting is the real reason for its regulation.

The FCC's successful claim of jurisdiction over CATV is a curious story. There was a real question whether cable television was "broadcasting" and therefore whether the FCC had any business regulating it. But the broadcast industry wanted CATV regulated. Despite its long record of protestations about the horrors of government regulation of broadcasting, the prospect of strangling the young CATV by an industry-dominated agency exhilarated the latter-day John Peter Zengers in the broadcast industry. For a long time, CATV's possibilities were confined to its first purpose—to bring clear reception to communities where ordinary TV reception was bad.

Cable system operators are not dependent on receiving an FCC license in order to enter the cable business; they must secure a franchise from the local municipal authorities. Cable in that respect is a boon to the cities. The franchise fees provide the hope of some needed and unexpected revenue. The FCC is proposing to limit municipal franchise fees to between 3 and 5 percent of the gross revenues; presently, about 5 percent of gross revenues are going to cities as a franchise fee.[20] The FCC is now proposing that no franchise be issued for more than fifteen years. At present, a cable system contract with a municipality can run from ten to twenty-four years. A question is open: without the famous "death penalty," the threat of denial at renewal time, how big will be the FCC clout? A CATV system operator or owner is not totally dependent like the commercial broadcaster on winning a renewal of his license every three years.

It would be wrong to think that the development of cable will immediately solve the access, fairness, and diversity problems that presently beset American radio and television. Commercial broadcasters have had an understandable tendency to ask that CATV keep out of entertainment and go in for public access and other innovative programming. Obviously, their interests would be served thereby. They will gladly assign the nonpaying controversial headaches to cable in perpetuity, just as they hope that the existence of common carrier channels will relieve them of the barrage of demands for access leveled at them by citizen groups. The FCC has wisely applied the same mechanisms for fairness and equal time to CATV which apply to commercial broadcasters. By the same token, the networks and the individual commercial broadcasters should not be relieved of their present obligation to make balanced presentations of controversial issues. CATV, as the technological answer to problems

2 6 1

of access to the media, is too untried to let its technology subvert existing communications policy.

In CATV, the promise of technology may be frustrated by legal controversies over jurisdiction and authority. A new roadblock in the endeavor to get cable systems into program origination is a 1971 ruling of the United States Court of Appeals for the Eighth Circuit that the FCC has no authority under the Federal Communications Act of 1934 to require cable systems to originate programming.[21] On June 8, 1972, the Supreme Court reversed the Court of Appeals on the question.

Whether original cablecasting becomes a major media reality or not, caution is in order; CATV is not yet the communications' messiah. The FCC wants the CATV industry to originate programming to provide an alternative to existing programming. In late 1969, cable operators were given permission to begin using their own commercials.[22] CATV systems now give the viewer a larger dose of old movies and new ball games than they would otherwise be able to obtain through regular TV transmission. Even at this level the CATV competitive threat to commercial television is a real one. Audiences are kept away from the networks. The advertiser stranglehold on network broadcasting will be undermined if the audience for network broadcasting is severely reduced. If nobody is there, no one will really care what happens.

It is something like the attitude of the daily newspaper industry to the so-called underground press. The daily press were first hostile; then it decided that the underground press was really quite a useful development. It represented no threat to the advertising dollar and, to the extent that it served the needs of the alienated, the young, and the disenchanted, the monopoly newspaper could say to the community, Look! now you have an alternative. It has at last dawned on the prestige monopoly press that they could do no better, even if they had arranged it, than to have as the community's newspaper alternative a bizarre pariah who had taken a vow of poverty.

Some have suggested that all television be cable television and that it be financed solely from subscriber fees, to prevent dependence on advertising again resulting in the homogenized blandness characteristic of present commercial television.[23] I think King Canute would have understood this wish—to wave a wand at the networks and to wish them dead. They will not go away.

The replacement of one technology by another will not solve media problems. It is not an either or proposition. Civility and balance, reasoned dialogue, rational decision-making—all the values which are represented by an access-oriented communications policy are not to be achieved by technology alone or by legal or constitutional changes. Putting too much expectation on technology is like putting too much emphasis on antiturst policy and concentration of ownership. Alternative technologies and division of control and ownership can weaken power aggregates but it is not clear that they have been very effective in the past or that they will be in the future. As is true of so much else in social policy, the first changes must be made at the level of ideas. When we finally recognize that freedom for the communicator is not necessarily freedom of expression for society, then antitrust policy or alternative technology will seem less panaceas and more just realistic means of access to the media.

CATV and the Other Media: Together or Apart?

Individual owners of television stations, newspapers, and radio stations have all heavily invested in CATV systems. This development has raised the question whether those with other media affiliation should be permitted to hold CATV systems. The FCC has rules to some degree restricting multiple ownership in the broadcast field. Presumably, such a policy is based on the premise that diversification of ownership will lead to diversification of ideas.

The theory may be flawed. Multiplicity of ideas will not inevitably flow from multiplicity of ownerships if all the ownerships are captives of the same economics—or think they are. If each broadcaster thinks lowest common denominator programming is the only way to economic health, it won't make much difference whether the station is owned by a broadcast chain, an individual, or a newspaper.

The whole structure of broadcast regulation is built on the idea that the individual broadcast licensee is the trustee for his programming. His promise to meet local service programming needs and his capacity to ascertain community needs is theoretically what wins him his license and his performance on this promise is what keeps his license. Despite the avowed emphasis on local service programming, VHF television licensees serve up programming supplied by the networks to which they are affiliated. The six o'clock and eleven o'clock news are "local" but even there much of the content is usually provided by the wire service and network film clips.

In such circumstances, just insisting on diversification of ownership is not enough. It is also necessary to insist on the development of mechanism for debate, access, and novelty within each broadcast outlet.

But CATV puts the whole question of diversification in a different light. Cable television of necessity must provide more local service programming than commercial television ever could. Commercial television is, technologically speaking, a limited access medium. The spectrum would not permit more than three or four VHF television stations in most communities. CATV changes all that. Most CATV systems functioning in the United States today have at least twelve channels; many will soon have twenty channels available for use, and forty channel cable systems are now planned for some communities.

With CATV, each district in a great metropolitan area can have its own cable system. In the New York area we have noted that it is already happening. Harlem has its own cable system, as does Inwood, New Jersey. If a particular metropolitan subdivision has a twenty channel system, it is hard to believe that a cable system would utilize all twelve channels for standard fare or deliberately leave the majority of its channels unutilized.

If a cable system management reserves channels for all the major networks, plus a channel for its own program origination, it will still have plenty of channels left for political, community, and public access programming. In such circumstances, is diversification of ownership important as a policy? Doesn't the technology of CATV *demand* diversity, no matter who owns it?

The answer to these questions, according to the FCC, is that the technology of CATV may never be fully utilized if cable is developed at the outset by broadcasters who have a tremendous investment in a threatened technology, broadcasting by transmitter. For this and other reasons, the FCC has prohibited a television station from operating a cable system in the same community it serves. Television networks have been banned from owning CATV systems anywhere in the United States. As for local television stations and networks which now own cable systems, the FCC has ordered them to divest themselves of those properties within three years. The FCC did permit multiple ownership of cable systems, but established, with some special restrictions for the hundred biggest population centers, a limit of fifty systems with a thousand or more subscribers as the maximum number of cable systems any one ownership could possess.[24]

The reluctance of the FCC to prohibit local radio stations from operating a cable system in the same community has been a special target for criticism. Berkeley law professor Stephen Barnett has urged that restrictions on crossownership of CATV systems and radio stations are necessary. The spectrum shortage in radio is less severe than in television. Of all.the dominant media (daily newspapers, radio stations, and television stations) there are more radio stations than anything else. As a consequence, local radio stations and cable systems are each technologically able to be more local than the many fewer network-fed "local" VHF television stations. Barnett urges therefore that cross-ownership between a radio station and a cable system serving the same community puts "under common control two local voices that might otherwise provide the community with the "diverse and antagonistic sources of information favored by the first amendment." [25]

A particularly strong consideration supporting this conclusion is that, although a cable system has an abundance of channels, the system operator is necessarily a monopolist. The ability of a cable system to serve a small section of a metropolitan area with a great number of channels is precisely what makes it economically impossible to have yet another twenty channel system serving the same community. In small communities especially, if the only, or one of the few, AM radio stations is operated by the same ownership as the cable system, the possibility of cable moving in new directions is unlikely. But if commercial considerations have replaced the ideological concerns of previous media lords, then it does not matter whether the media ownership is widely diffused or not.

Furthermore, the multiplicity of radio voices in some communities has been mentioned by the FCC as a factor arguing against the need for restrictions on common ownership in the case of CATV and radio. The FCC has invited comment on cross-ownership in the same market of a cable system and either a newspaper or a radio station. Barnett, writing when the rule against ownership by a local television station of a cable system in the same community was proposed, defended the concept of restriction against cross-ownership. Keeping the television broadcasters out of CATV would at least give CATV a chance to develop many different voices rather than merely provide an additional electronic means of expression "for the voices already dominant."

If public access may come to cable TV through the use of channels on a common carrier basis, why is ownership relevant? The key point, says diversification expert Barnett, is that public access channels are not required. That is still true. Public access is proposed. The common carrier concept has not even been proposed. Until channel leasing is required, ownership restriction is necessary. Moreover, since at least one channel for program origination is now required, diversification of control between the community cable system and the existing radio and VHF television voices in that community appears to be wise. An authentic new voice on the cable channel is most likely to result where those with vested interests in the community's existing media are not in control.

Cable can develop a right of access and free access at that, but the motivation must be there. For the black community it may well provide an entry not otherwise possible. The fact that every neighborhood can have its own cable system can provide the black-oriented programming which commercial television has stubbornly lacked. But cable television, it should be emphasized, merely presents a possibility for access; it does not represent a guaranty of entry to the media for those now excluded. For a big city ghetto dweller, cable fees are not cheap. William Wright of BEST has urged the District of Columbia City Council to consider as a requirement for franchise that a cable system will have to wire every home in the city free.

The typical cable system franchise contract with a municipality imposes on the owners little if any obligation concerning programming.

Cable television regulation is in a state of tension bred by the vagueness of cable's regulatory status. Cable policy makers are frustrated and bewildered by conflicting claims and consequent uncertainties engendered by local, state, and federal claims to regulation. The FCC has studied cable television, but it has preferred to proceed thus far more by proposal rather than by rule. As a result, cable development has been hampered.

Certainly the FCC has had some proposals under consideration which, if actually applied to cable, would radically transform American television. For example, the FCC has considered requiring all new cable systems to reserve one channel solely for local government uses. Local governments could use this channel without charge. Moreover, political candidates could use the channel for free political broadcasting at election time. Another proposal the FCC has considered is reserving a channel solely for local access purposes. The FCC defines a local access channel requirement as at least one channel made available "at no cost to local citizens and groups which are not engaged in programming for advertising revenue, but which desire to present views on matters of concern to them." [26] This will certainly go far to accelerate the common commercial television practice of not selling time for programs devoted to political and social controversy. In spring 1971, John Gardner, chairman of the new public interest lobby, Common Cause, wrote to the three major TV networks asking to buy a half-hour of prime time for prominent nonpolitical antiwar critics to rebut President Nixon's April 7 television address. The networks said they did not sell time for programs on controversial issues. Gardner turned to the independent TV stations around the country.[27] If cable burgeons in the seventies as expected, and if each cable system has a common carrier channel, the days of effective network restraint on public access may be over.

The FCC is also apparently ready to enhance both the public access and the common carrier concept. This is a sensible policy, since cable television is infinitely hospitable to a variety of approaches. Here again the FCC offered a good preview of how a common carrier channel would work. The FCC proposes that for each cable channel devoted to transmitting conventional television, another channel would be made available for facsimile printing, original programming, or leasing.[28] Third parties would lease time on a permanent or one-shot basis. What would be imperative on such a channel, of course, is that the arrangements for leasing be fair and nondiscriminatory.

It does seem reasonable that the innovative possibilities of cable are more likely to be realized if those in charge of it do not have other media affiliations. On the other hand, cable is so rich in its capacity for diversity that the suffocating sameness which characterizes common control in the media may not be quite as intense in cable.

In short, provision of a single public access channel on every cable system may not appear to be a great step forward. But it offers the promise of a great deal more television committed to community and public programming than is available in commercial television.

22 /

Access for What?

Obscenity on the Air

THE PROBLEM OF ACCESS TO THE MEDIA HAS LONG BEEN COMPLI-
cated by the need to keep race hatred and obscenity off the airwaves—a task now accomplished through voluntary efforts by
broadcasters. If a public right of entry not dependent on broadcaster permission is established, what protective shield will guard
the public from a barrage of obscenities and incitements to racial strife?

Network and station programming policies and judgments
often restrict freedom of expression far more than standards imposed by government would. Broadcasting, a medium of great
immediacy, has no control over the membership of its audience.
There is always a child in the house. Therefore, there is a consensus that some programming controls are necessary.

The danger that a right of access to broadcasting will wreck
the sensitive structure of private censorship is less an argument
against access than it is an illustration of the force of private censorship. The case for access must not be lost because a right of

access could be abused. To recognize access is not necessarily to provide access for everything.

Certainly the FCC should be able to delineate restrictions on some kinds of expression at early prime time hours without banning all questionable material across the board. Rules surely can be fashioned to cover the small radio station with a small late-night audience and the network television show with its massive early evening audience of children.

For the Supreme Court in the Red Lion case, the conclusive reason that the fairness doctrine was not unconstitutional was that the FCC's past cases provided a standard for compliance.[1] Where, however, there is an area of program content where either FCC rules and cases do not exist or else suggest no guidelines, the legitimacy of imposing FCC sanctions would of course be a different question. The FCC's past cases dealing with obscenity in broadcasting are an inconsistent and unreliable guide to future action. Unlike the situation of balanced presentation of controversial viewpoints, no real effort has been made to enunciate clear standards for regulation of obscenity in broadcasting. The problem is further aggravated because no full scale judicial consideration of the regulation of obscenity in broadcasting has yet been undertaken.

A tour of some of the recent FCC reactions to obscenity problems in broadcasting shows the ambiguity and uncertainty which characterize the regulatory role in this area.

WUHY–FM in Philadelphia broadcasts a weekly program, *Cycle II*, from 10:00 to 11:00 p.m. Designed for the "now" generation, the program uses the full range of the vocabulary of the youth culture. On January 4, 1970, Jerry Garcia, leader of a musical group called The Grateful Dead, was interviewed on the air from his hotel room. Garcia relied for emphasis on the two most famous four-letter Anglo-Saxon profanities. As a result, the FCC investigated WUHY.

The broadcaster thought the program could be justified for a number of reasons: "the time of the broadcast, the unlikelihood that children may be in the audience, and the necessity of continuing announcements to listeners in advance of disagreeable programming." The FCC did not agree and fined the station $100. There were some strange statements in its opinion. Primness was apparently going to become a regulatory standard:

> . . . it conveys no thought to begin some speech with "shit man. . ." or to use "fucking" as an adjective throughout the speech. We recognize that such speech is frequently used in some settings, but it is not employed in public ones.

Commissioners Bartley, Lee, and Wells, who decided the case, must not go to the theater very often. These three commissioners comprised a majority who agreed to notify WUHY–FM of liability for forfeiture of $100 because of "indecent" programming.[2]

In the opinion of the FCC, certain words further no debate and serve no social purpose. Such decisions, of course, illustrate the process of government censorship at its most rigid. A mechanistic approval to program controls which seizes on certain words, without considering the general context or the nature of the audience to whom it is presented, is antithetical to an access-oriented approach to communications policy. But giving the public entrance rights to broadcasting need not necessarily breed more government censorship. An access approach to communications and the process of censorship are natural antagonists.

Access is a means of securing entry to the media for some excluded groups and ideas. The criteria used to establish such entry cannot be used in reverse gear as arguments to justify the present hidden censorship of the media; that is, that a right of access will bring to the airwaves a flood of objectionable expression that will invite the clumsier censorship of government. Yet would it not be hard to equal the network bleep-bleep sound silencing the occasional heresy of the talk show raconteur?

Access and obscenity questions can sometimes coalesce. If a black playwright cannot get produced on television because the characters in his play do not use the language of Jane Austen, his access problem is more compelling because we need to hear and understand the contemporary vocabulary of anger and alienation, a language too intense and too disturbing for the commercial purposes of commercial broadcasting.

The small under-financed experimental stations have most often provoked the wrath of the regulators up to now. FCC antennae are somehow less sensitive to obscenity in the broadcasting of the great commercial networks. Even one or two individual complaints against a small station have been enough to invoke a regulatory inquiry.

An FCC investigation of a Seattle station, KRAB–FM, was set in motion on the basis of a single complaint. A Unitarian minister in Seattle, the Reverend Paul Sawyer, had prepared a thirty-hour "autobiographical novel for tape." The KRAB broadcaster decided to air it after he had listened to part of the tape, but on the Saturday morning of the broadcast, he heard some words on the tape he hadn't heard before. He ordered the broadcast terminated.

Despite the broadcaster's prompt action, this minor indiscretion on a high-brow Seattle FM radio station caused the FCC to renew its license for only a year, rather than the normal three-year period.[3] The broadcaster was punished on the theory that he had violated his own self-imposed program content standard that called for all material to be referred to the station manager for an audition before broadcasting.

Commissioner Kenneth Cox remarked pointedly that the FCC had received far more complaints concerning the *Smothers*

Brothers Comedy Hour or the *Rowan and Martin's Laugh-In* than had ever been received about any subscriber-financed station like KRAB. Yet, said Cox, he could not recall that any inquiries had ever been directed to CBS or NBC. (It should be remembered that it was CBS and not the FCC which finally purged the Smothers Brothers from broadcasting.)

The KRAB incident illustrates censorship of a special type. The government lets the station create a censorship procedure and then holds the station to do it. This cooperative arrangement appears to be an admirably intelligent compromise between private and public power. But actually this practice permits broadcasters and government to effect a degree of censorship which, as a matter of constitutional law, the government could not, either under the aegis of the FCC or through an Act of Congress, formally ordain. Sensitive tests worked out by the Supreme Court to regulate obscenity and at the same time to encourage as much expression as possible have been ignored.

Commissioner Nicholas Johnson, in dissent in the first KRAB ruling, protested the FCC's effort to make a dirty word test the guideline to obscenity regulation in broadcasting:

> The Commission can no more enforce a rule adopted by a licensee in violation of the First Amendment than it can enact one.[4]

The consequence of this policy, Johnson warned, would be to discourage stations from enunciating any programming policies at all.

The Seattle incident was not a great censorship case but it does illustrate use by government of a private censorship decision to enforce standards of censorship which would be unconstitutional if they flowed directly from the government.

What is the solution to the problem of obscenity in program

content in broadcasting? Kenneth Cox wants to see problems of obscenity on broadcasting subjected to general constitutional standards. Ultimately, this approach was at least attempted in the KRAB case. On petition for reconsideration of the short-term renewal order, the FCC offered KRAB a hearing on the matter. At the hearing the incident was approached by the hearing examiner with some effort to ascertain the standpoint of general constitutional law. He decided to renew the KRAB license for the full three year term.[5]

The legal materials the examiner had to decipher were ambiguous to say the least.

In the existing law on regulation of obscenity in broadcasting, the relevant federal statutes appear to be in open conflict, at least on the surface. Section 326 of the Federal Communications Act says that the FCC shall not censor:

> Nothing in this chapter shall be understood or construed to give the Commission the power of censorship over the radio communications or signals transmitted by any radio station, and no regulation or condition shall be promulgated or fixed by the Commission which shall interfere with the right of free speech by means of radio communication.[6]

Yet the liberalism of Section 326 is counterpoised by another federal statute which has a far sterner message:

> Whoever utters any obscene, indecent or profane language by means of radio communication shall be fined not more than $10,000 or imprisoned not more than two years, or both.[7]

The two statutes are actually less in conflict than appears. Regulation of obscenity is arguably not censorship if by censorship we mean a governmental restraint on expression which would violate the First Amendment. In a 1957 landmark de-

275

cision, *Roth v. United States,* the Supreme Court held that obscenity was not protected by the First Amendment.[8] If anything that was obscene was not protected by the First Amendment, the key question of course became: what was obscene? Summarizing the teaching of the Roth case and its progeny, the Court, nearly a decade later, defined obscenity as follows:

"Under the Roth definition of obscenity, as elaborated in subsequent cases, three elements must coalesce: it must be established that (a) the dominant theme of the material taken as a whole appeals to a prurient interest in sex; (b) the material is patently offensive because it affronts contemporary community standards relating to the description or representation of sexual matters; and (c) the material is utterly without redeeming social value." [9]

The hearing examiner in KRAB found the station guiltless of having committed obscenity.[10] In the course of the decision, the examiner relied on the WUHY case because there the FCC had attempted to set up guidelines "to steer a course between the censorship which the law forbids the Commission to exercise and the indecent obscene language which the law forbids the licensee to broadcast."

Unfortunately, in the WUHY case, the FCC ignored the concept of obscenity around which an entire case law had been built. Instead, the FCC made the operative concept the word *indecent* from 18 U.S.C. §1464, which prohibits the utterance in radio communication of "any obscene, indecent, or profane language." Yet in Roth, the Supreme Court had given a careful constitutional definition to the obscenity concept. Why the Commission chose to enforce a concept of indecency which had not received a limiting constitutional construction, rather than the concept of obscenity which had, is probably one of the less inscrutable mysteries of the regulatory process. The Commission probably thought that using a concept with which the Court had not concerned itself would provide greater room for maneuver. Relying on the indecency context nicely avoided submitting the problem to general and developing constitutional standards applicable to all other media where censorship for obscenity was involved. The oddity of enforcing the "indecency" idea was particularly highlighted by the FCC's defining it through a pale and devitalized version of the Supreme Court's test for obscenity:

> . . . we believe that the statutory term, 'indecent' should be applicable, and that in the broadcast field, the standard for its applicability should be that the material broadcast is (a) patently offensive by contemporary community standards, and (b) is utterly without redeeming social value.[11]

The Supreme Court's three-pronged definition of obscenity, however, summarized in the 1966 decision *Memoirs of a Woman of Pleasure* contained, besides the factors mentioned by the FCC, a requirement that to be judged obscene, it would be necessary to find that "the dominant theme of the material taken as a whole appeals to a prurient interest in sex." Clearly, satisfaction of this requirement is not easy and the difficulty in satisfying it is a fundamental protection for freedom of expression. An isolated salacious passage on a program would not contaminate the whole program under such an approach.

The FCC's standard for exclusion is patent offensiveness to contemporary standards. But what is the referent for patent offensiveness? It is not "appeal to the prurient interest" since the FCC excluded that. In a muddled way, the WUHY case, reaffirmed in KRAB, illustrates that the FCC is trying to compose a list of shock words that cannot be used in broadcasting.

This approach betrays intellectual poverty. The FCC failed even to mention the most recent work of the Supreme Court concerning printed matter marketed to children or minors, where state censorship was allowed greater scope. This omission is particularly irksome in broadcasting, where the possibility that a child will be in the audience so easily persuades both the FCC and the industry to encourage censorship far more restrictive than in other media. The FCC decision in WUHY, unfortunately, has not been challenged in the courts. The station preferred to pay the $100 fine and forget about it. As a result, a splendid opportunity for a thorough consideration of obscenity in broadcasting was lost.

Just as the development of the obscenity definition first set forth by the Supreme Court in the Roth case in 1957, has had the most profound social effect, in a libertarian sense, on the movies and on the print media, so a similar elaboration of standards with regard to obscenity on broadcasting ought to prove similarly beneficial. When the Supreme Court said that obscenity was not protected, the court's libertarian critics stammered and gagged: art and literature were in peril.

What had not been noticed was that the definition of what was not protected by the First Amendment was itself very restrictive. A single phrase, "utterly without redeeming social value," redeemed the decision on obscenity and made it the emancipator of literary and artistic freedom in the United States. If the standards which program content must meet are clear, it can only improve the opportunity for entry for much of what is now excluded from broadcasting.

Legal controls can only be justified, in the view of some, if an empirical basis clearly exists that shows that antisocial consequences will follow the use of objectionable expression. Does group defamation lead to racial strife and murder? Does pornography lead to antisocial or criminal behavior?

In September 1970, the celebrated Report of the President's Commission on Obscenity and Pornography was released.[12] The Report, after exhaustively summarizing and analyzing studies by social scientists, concluded that a relationship between exposure to pornography and antisocial and criminal behavior was, as the Scotch say, not proven. Therefore, the Report concluded, there was simply no basis for legislative regulation of obscenity. The 647-page Report fell on the body politic with a great thud. The President disavowed it. Some of the Commission members themselves dissented from it. Legislators denounced it. Why? Perhaps because the Report itself ignored the most important empirical fact of all: In a representative democracy, majority preferences are, and should be, a major social reality. An aspect of that social reality is the community consensus, reflected on state statute books throughout the land, that there should be some regulation of obscenity. The sensitivity of the public to the uncontrolled exploitation of obscene material is nowhere more likely to be greater than in the medium where impact on the public is most immediate and continuous, radio and television broadcasting.

- Academic discussion on obscenity sometimes exudes a certain air of self-righteous elitism. But despite the endless refrain: Down with obscenity legislation, legislatures stubbornly continue to enact antiobscenity legislation. The Supreme Court in its Roth decision proved to be far more politically astute than the President's Commission on Obscenity and Pornography. The Court did not say that there was no such category as obscenity nor even that if there were it could not be regulated. The Court said obscenity could be regulated but it gave a definition of obscenity which promised a greater measure of freedom of expression. That promise has largely been fulfilled in all media except broadcasting.

An idea the Supreme Court has made great use of, the concept of variable obscenity, is very relevant to broadcasting. Developed by Dean William Lockhart of the University of Minnesota Law School, it attempts to provide a definition of obscenity for use in law enforcement which will be especially sensitive to

279

how the material is used by its primary audience as well as how it is marketed. This concept can take account of the empirical reality of community concern about programs that might exploit sex in a way damaging to children, while also leaving room to encourage more adult programming. The lack of articulated standards now makes it easy for the networks and the broadcasters to evade their responsibilities to provide serious programming. Underscoring the pervasive lack of clarity concerning obscenity in broadcasting, Commissioner Nicholas Johnson asks an intensely practical question: "To put the problem bluntly, if *I Am Curious (Yellow)* is cleared by the Supreme Court for distribution in movie houses around the United States, how should the FCC react to a network proposal to show it on the 'Nine O'Clock Movie' to a potential audience of sixty million?" [13]

The question is a tough one. The answer depends not only on the time when such a movie would be telecast, but also on the nature of the community and whether it has one or two television channels or six or seven. The Supreme Court has endorsed not only the usefulness of a variable obscenity standard but also the idea that unwilling people ought not to have material they consider obscene thrust on them.[14] In 1970 the Supreme Court upheld a federal statute allowing a householder to insulate himself from advertisements that come through the mails offering "matter which the addressee in his sole definition believes to be provocative." In a sense, this decision is another facet of the variable obscenity idea. What one person finds indecent, another does not. The person upon whom unwanted material is thrust is protected. The freedom of expression of the communicator must yield to the equally important constitutional freedom of the individual—the right of privacy, the right to be let alone. For adults the validity of censorship, in a sense, depends upon consent.

But what is consent? Whether flicking the television switch

is voluntary to the same degree in our culture as buying a book or a magazine is not certain. For some, television is the sole source of entertainment. For others, it is a babysitter at hours long past the usual bedtime of middle-class babies.

The variable obscenity approach is likely to be the most useful one in tracing out all the subtle strands that make the obscenity problem in broadcasting the web it is. What can be considered obscene in broadcasting should depend upon a variety of factors, of which the content of the program is only one. Other factors should include the audience to whom the program is directed, the hour the program is broadcast, and the manner in which the program is marketed.

In a 1968 decision, *Ginsberg v. New York*, the Supreme Court insisted that a broader definition of obscenity could be employed when children were concerned, since the state had greater power to control the conduct of children.[15] The way to provide greater access to serious programming for adults on broadcasting in the form of movies, drama, and even politics may be by establishing standards that deny children access to such programming. Greater access for artistic freedom on television for adults depends on clarifying the more limited access rights of children. In the case which permitted the state of New York to prosecute one who sells magazines to children although the same magazines may be sold to adults, the Supreme Court quoted approvingly the formative work of Lockhart and McClure in this area:

> Variable obscenity furnishes a useful analytical tool for dealing with the problem of denying adolescents access to material aimed at a primary audience of sexually mature adults. For variable obscenity focuses attention upon the makeup of primary peripheral audiences in varying circumstances, and provides a reasonably satisfactory means for delineating the obscene in each circumstance.[16]

Yet, as we have seen, the FCC approach makes the suscepti-bilities of the child the standard for *all* broadcasting. The possi-bility that there might still be a peripheral audience of children at, say, 11 p.m., may now be used to deny the primary adult au-dience access to a film. The damage to freedom of expression which such an approach produces is, of course, the reason the Supreme Court specifically repudiated the test for obscenity em-ployed by the courts of Victorian England, which made the tastes of the pervert the measure of what a nation could read.[17]

An additional virtue of employing a variable obscenity test in broadcasting is that it is particularly compatible with the contin-uing technological change of the electronic media. When some Commissioners asked the FCC chairman's planning office whether creation of public access channels on cable television might not result in abuse, the response was that such abuse would be slight because the audience for the public access chan-nel would not be large. Moreover, the planning office consid-ered, audience attracted by the public access channels is unlikely to mind the use of obscenities.[18]

Certainly, the lack of audience reaction to the occasional ut-terance of an obscenity on small experimental radio stations sup-ports the planning office's estimate. If cable television ever re-places commercial television, the fragmentation of the audience among the many available channels may indeed lead to the civil libertarian's dream of a society whose media recognize no ob-scenity. Nothing could be legally called obscene if the primary audience to whom it is presented does not regard it as obscene.

In the WUHY case the FCC took only a partial and unsuc-cessful step to find the constitutional status of obscenity in broadcasting. The fact that obscenity depends upon the particu-lar media context was emphasized. But a clear endorsement of the applicability of the variable obscenity position to broadcast-ing would have done much to release programming from the present uncertainty, so frustrating to artistic expression, about just what program content is objectionable.

Sometimes the FCC itself has almost used a variable obscenity standard. In 1964 the subscriber-financed Pacifica Foundation, which operates FM radio in Los Angeles, Berkeley, and New York, applied to renew their licenses. Listener complaints against the programming of Pacifica stations were then reviewed by the FCC.

Pacifica station KPFK, Los Angeles, drew complaints because it had carried a reading of Edward Albee's *Zoo Story* and a program on the problems of homosexuals with eight homosexuals as panelists. Pacifica station KPFA in Berkeley drew criticism for readings of poems by Robert Creeley and Lawrence Ferlinghetti and for readings from an unfinished novel by Edward Pomerantz called *The Kid*.

Such programs are a sample of the kind of programming the commercial broadcasting public is missing. Broadcaster fear of FCC inquiry, along with a greedy desire to avoid adverse advertiser reaction, combine to block programming which might annoy or provoke the audience. Innovative programming is left to a small coterie of experimental noncommercial stations like the Pacifica group.

The FCC reaction to the complaints demonstrates how the agency deals with problems of obscenity. The FCC agreed with Pacifica that Americans living far from Broadway ought to have access to serious and provocative drama like *Zoo Story*. Pomerantz' *The Kid* was found to be in the "public interest"—an odd accolade for a novel.

With regard to poets Ferlinghetti and Creeley, Pacifica itself conceded that passages from the poems did not meet the stations' own standards. Accordingly, Pacifica made the familiar promise with which we are by now familiar: we will censor better in the future. Pacifica's *mea culpa* concerning the attack on

Creeley was amusing. Creeley's voice, mourned the station, is a monotone. Since Creeley read eighteen "perfectly acceptable" poems in this monotone, the station's editor had become so lulled that he failed to catch a "few offensive words in the nineteenth poem."

The controversial Pacifica discussion of the problems of homosexuals, however, was considered to be "well within the licensee's judgment under the public interest standard."

One Commissioner, Robert E. Lee, disagreed on the assessment of the homosexual program. In Lee's view, the panel show of eight homosexuals was "nothing but sensationalism." He said that if physicians and sociologists discussed homosexuality as a problem, such a program might benefit the public, "But a panel of eight homosexuals discussing their experiences and past history does not approach the treatment of a delicate subject one would expect by a responsible broadcaster. A microphone in a bordello, during slack hours, would give us similar information on a related subject."

Commissioner Lee was trying to use a public interest standard to judge allegedly obscene programming. But surely such a standard is hopelessly vague, bound to give the subjectively predetermined result.

The FCC concluded there was no basis in the complaints for denying the renewal applications of the Pacifica stations. All that was involved, said the Commission, was the application of the licensee's own programming standards.[19]

This approach exemplifies a flight from responsibility by the regulatory agency and an infringement on the access rights of the public. The FCC professed to be concerned about the danger of imposing sanctions on broadcasters for carrying provocative programs. Certainly, listener complaints cannot be the measure of suitable programming. The Commission itself rightly observed: "Were this the case, only the wholly inoffensive, the bland, could gain access to the radio microphone or TV camera." Standards of program content in the obscenity area should be developed by the regulatory agency set up by Congress. Government must make it clear that it will not enforce licensee program content standards which are more restrictive than those that could constitutionally be established by the FCC.

The Pacifica case does show that a contextual approach to obscenity, using a variable definition of obscenity, is workable and can be enforced. The difficulty is that adhering to a variable obscenity standard at present depends entirely on the desires of the individual broadcaster. The FCC made this clear in its Pacifica decision: "Pacifica states that it is 'sensitive to its responsibilities to its listening audience and carefully schedules for late night broadcasts those programs which may not be understood by children although thoroughly acceptable to an adult audience.'"

This approach does far less to encourage creative, experimental programming than would be the case if FCC guidelines or rules actually stated a variable obscenity standard which would make it clear that complaints against a program broadcast after a certain hour would not be entertained and that complaints against programming satisfying a variable obscenity standard would not be used against a station in renewal proceedings.

Even in past FCC decisions, there are glimpses of how a variable obscenity standard in broadcasting could work. In a 1962 case, Palmetto Broadcasting Co.,[20] the license of a Kingstree, South Carolina, radio station owned by Hollywood actor Edward G. Robinson, Jr., was denied renewal. Among the grounds for the denial was a disc jockey show featuring Charlie Walker. The program, heavy on off-color jokes and commentary, occupied a substantial portion of each broadcast day.

The program, said the FCC, was "coarse, vulgar, suggestive, and susceptible of indecent double meaning." The FCC said it reached this conclusion by way of a public interest standard and not by relying on the statutory language of 18 U.S.C. §1464 ("obscene, indecent, or profane"). The suggestion was that in a broadcast context what is obscene may be different than if a criminal statute were employed. The FCC's position appears to be that a broadcaster is given a license to perform in the public interest and a substantial segment of "coarse" and "vulgar" programming is not in the public interest. A program record which would justify not renewing a broadcaster's license might not justify bringing a criminal prosecution against him.

Similarly, in Pacifica, the FCC compared the sporadic complaints made "years apart," against two experimental poets with the situation in the Palmetto case where "we found that the patently offensive material was broadcast for a substantial period of the station's broadcast day for many years."

The FCC in Palmetto did not avowedly employ a variable obscenity approach any more than it did in Pacifica. Indeed, in Palmetto the FCC sought to avoid the larger constitutional issues. Apparently, if problems of obscenity were called problems of "coarseness and indecency," it was less necessary to cleave to the general principles of obscenity law. This kind of nominalism, indulged in by the FCC again in WUHY in 1970, is self-defeating and has a directly debilitating effect on the quality of broadcast programming.

The FCC's aversion to a systematic approach to obscenity problems in broadcasting is not unique. The federal courts have also been anxious to stay out of the area. In the Palmetto case, the Federal Court of Appeals affirmed the FCC decision not to renew WDKD's license, but only on the basis that the owner of the station had misrepresented facts in his renewal applications: the court said, "We intimate no views on whether the Commission could have denied the application if Robinson had been truthful." [21]

The basic regulatory assumption in obscenity as in other aspects of programming comes through in the Pacifica decision: programming is a matter of licensee discretion. Proving abuse, in the judgment of the FCC, is best done by showing that the licensee violates its own programming standards. All of which tends to perpetuate the blandness and the inanity of today's commercial "entertainment" programming.

The trouble with making industry censorship the norm is that so little public attention has been given to what actual broadcast censorship practices are. Why are movies on television cut? Because of "blue" passages? Or because of the need for a specified amount of time for commercials? Neither the public nor the FCC has ever really been told. Both those reasons are obviously major considerations, but there are no published standards. At least in regard to obscenity problems, there are the FCC standards. For the rest, what we have now is censorship in the dark.

The regulation of obscenity in broadcasting has been obscured because the FCC has taken it upon itself to modify the general constitutional approach to such problems in the case of broadcasting rather than to comply with the particularized definition set forth by the Supreme Court. No court has approved this policy. To make matters worse, the FCC itself has established no regulatory standards defining what is obscene in a broadcast context. What is needed is an FCC Report on Obscenity in Broadcasting as comprehensive and thorough as the 1949 Report on Editorializing that gave birth to the fairness doctrine. Then perhaps it would be possible to obtain from the courts a statement of the constitutional parameters of FCC and obscenity censorship as practiced by the FCC and the industry.

Enforcement of a right of access to broadcasting is not designed to broaden exposure to the obscene, or to lessen it, for that matter. Access as a right is dependent to some extent on the establishment of program content standards dealing with obscenity. The paradox, therefore, is that a larger access is dependent on censorship, a minimal censorship to be sure, but nonetheless censorship. But the censorship must be one whose standards are public, and whose criteria will be constitutional instead of submerged, private, extra-constitutional and eccentric as are the censorship standards now in actual use in American broadcasting.

The threat of abuse of access to broadcasting is now a barrier to its emergence as a right. It will continue to loom large unless it is made very clear that a right of access does not compel the broadcast media to transmit all material submitted no matter how obscene, or socially corrosive. Right now, both access and obscenity are in limbo because uncertainty concerning both causes the FCC and the industry not to do anything in either area.

Access for Hate?

Richard Jencks of CBS has criticized those who seek access for dissident and minority groups to speak directly to the public on television. Said Jencks: "It is characteristic of those who hold this view that the examples they choose of groups who need this direct access rarely include the Ku Klux Klan, the Birch Society or other elements of the extremist right wing groups which nonetheless would be quick to claim such a right." [22]

Jencks' comments are designed to defend private censorship on grounds unsettling to liberals, but his claim that access for the left must inevitably mean access for the right should not be allowed its intended *in terrorem* effect. The answer instead is that it is indeed the neutrality and even-handedness of the access principle that makes it implement democratic values like freedom of the press.

The question "Access for what?" does raise a serious problem. Simply put, it is this: Is there to be access for hate? Clifton Daniel, speaking about this problem in the print media, has posed the question more sharply:

> Nowhere in the literature on access to the press do I find any conspicuous mention of the hate groups. Does this newfangled interpretation of freedom of the press mean that an editor would be obliged to give space to ideas that are hateful to him? Must he give space to advertisements that are offensive to his particular readers? Must a Negro editor give space to the Ku Klux Klan? [23]

The problem of whether the media, print or electronic, may intentionally be used to sow racial hatred and discord is much less resolved than the problem of obscenity. The Supreme Court's 1957 Roth case, and its later additions and corrections, have at least sketched in an approach to dealing with obscenity in print, if not in broadcasting.[24]

The problem of the use of the media in regard to expressing racial hatred is much more muddled. The continuing uncertainty is strange, since in the matter of group defamation, as in obscenity, we have a landmark Supreme Court case. In 1952 the Supreme Court upheld a 1917 Illinois statute which applied criminal sanctions for "manufacturing, publishing, or exhibition" in a public place of certain publications.[25] The prohibited publications were those which ascribed "depravity, criminality, unchastity or lack of virtue" to a class of citizens, or which exposed persons "of any race, color, creed or religion to contempt, derision or obloquy." Finally, the statute prohibited publications which were "productive of breach of peace or riots."

The case grew out of the activities of Joseph Beauharnais, president of the White Circle League, who organized the distribution of leaflets on Chicago streetcorners. The leaflets called on the mayor to halt the Negro "invasion" of white neighborhoods. The pamphlet warned that if "the need to prevent the white race from becoming mongrelized by the Negro will not unite us, then the aggressions . . . rapes, robberies, knives, guns and marijuana of the Negro surely will." Beauharnais was convicted of having violated the statute and the Supreme Court of the United States affirmed the conviction.

The case was a first cousin to the Supreme Court's great obscenity decision five years later. Group defamation, like obscenity, was simply not within the range of protection as freedom of expression. But the parallel between Roth and Beauharnais is only superficial. The Supreme Court's obscenity decisions have generated a whole new freedom in books and movies, but the 1952 Beauharnais case has gone nowhere. It stands isolated among the decisions of the United States Supreme Court; later decisions have neither expanded nor reversed it. The Illinois legislature subsequently repealed the statute which the Supreme Court affirmed. Therefore, it is a technical lawyer's matter, as Justice Frankfurter said in his opinion, that "libelous utterances" were not within "the area of constitutionally protected speech." Therefore, he reasoned that it was unnecessary to apply First Amendment standards such as the clear and present danger test:

> Certainly no one would contend that obscene speech, for example, may be punished only upon a showing of such circumstances.

The lawyers for Beauharnais argued that a law which made group libel punishable might be used against political groups. Frankfurter said the Illinois statute has no such intent: "The rubric 'race, color, creed or religion' which describes the type of group libel which is punishable, has attained too fixed a meaning to permit political groups to be brought within it." Frankfurter thus anticipated the 1964 Supreme Court decision which made public libel, or criticism of government, protected speech.

The Supreme Court's decision in Beauharnais involved the law of criminal libel, which is concerned with preventing breaches of the peace. Civil libel law, on the other hand, is concerned with protecting the interest in reputation. Frankfurter relied on the relationship of criminal libel to maintaining the public order in his decision: "Illinois did not have to look beyond her own borders or await the tragic experience of the last three decades to conclude that willful purveyors of falsehood concerning racial and religious groups promote strife and tend powerfully to obstruct the manifold adjustments required for free, ordered life in a metropolitan, polyglot community."

The Supreme Court ruled therefore that an American state legislature might rationally conclude that there was a basis for enacting group libel legislation: that the status of individuals in society is related to the status of the group into which he is born.

The Beauharnais group libel case was a 5–4 decision. Justice Black, who dissented from the majority opinion, said that if minority groups took comfort from the validation of a group libel statute, they should reflect on some ancient wisdom: " 'Another such victory and I am undone.' "

Justice Douglas tried in another dissent to insure that resolution of intergroup hostilities was not hindered by the Constitution:

Hitler and his Nazis showed how evil a conspiracy could be which was aimed at destroying a race by exposing it to contempt, derision and obloquy. I would be willing to concede that such conduct directed at a race or group in this country could be made an indictable offense. For such a project would be more than the exercise of free speech. Like picketing it would be free speech plus.

But, such a constitutional analysis is not much help. Of course, Hitler showed how ugly group libel could be. Hitler and the Nazis also showed how easy it is to use group defamation to spring to political power. Use of the media in the United States to stir intra-group hostilities is not without precedent. The political influence of the anti-Semitic priest of the 1930s, Father Charles E. Coughlin, was made possible by radio. Fortunately, another radio voice upstaged him, that of Franklin D. Roosevelt. Douglas suggests using the clear and present danger approach to group defamation problems. It is too clumsy a tool to measure the effects of something at once direct, subtle, and cumulative like group defamation broadcasts. The clear and present danger test would by its very structure acquit many programs or remarks devoted to racial libels. To this criticism, the traditional civil libertarian response is that acquittal in the name of free speech is the assigned function of the clear and present danger. Unless there is imminent danger of some substantive evil, the objectionable expression should stand. But what about a station which programs a substantial percentage of attacks on racial groups? Can such programming be attacked collectively? Presently, such situations are attacked obliquely by treating them as fairness doctrine problems and requiring a roughly equivalent amount of reply time. But is the damage done by group defamation healed by such a remedy? How should the problem of the racial slur, of the defamation of whole racial and religious groups, be handled?

If one believes in access to the media, it certainly can be argued that the libertarian heart of the access concept invites—in fact, commands—hospitality to appeals to racial hatred and even to genocide.

There is no question that the Anglo-American civil law has been continuously hostile to legal recognition for the claims of members of religious and racial groups on the basis of their membership in the group. There are two reasons: (1) the excessive individualism of the common law tradition was antagonistic to legal recognition of the status and vicissitudes of groups, and (2) the marketplace of ideas theory of truth permits entry for the racial slur in the confidence that the hate merchant would not triumph. The social cement which justifies such confidence has in the main held fast. But by the late 1960s no less a civil libertarian than John Pemberton, the executive director of the American Civil Liberties Union, was warning of a discouraging increase in intergroup hostilities in the United States and concluding that defamation has once again become a major problem.[26]

. . . .
You pale faced Jew boy—I wish you were dead
. . . .
I got a scoop on you—yeh, you gonna die
. . . .
Then you came to America, land of the free
And took over the school system to perpetuate white supremacy
Guess you know, Jew boy, there's only one reason you made it
You had a clean white face, colorless and faded
I hated you Jew boy, because your hangup was the Torah
And my only hangup was my color.

On December 26, 1968, this poem, aptly named "Anti-Semitism" was broadcast on New York radio station WBAI's *Julius Lester* show.

The poem was read by Lester Campbell, who had been a history teacher at Junior High School No. 271 in New York. The poem was one of several mentioned by Campbell composed by a young black poet, Thea Bahran. The sentiments in the poem and its reading by a black teacher reflect intergroup hostilities between New York City Jews and blacks. The dispute resulted from the bitter controversy over "community control" between the black community in the Ocean Hill–Brownsville section of Brooklyn and the United Teachers Federation, many of whose members were Jews. Thea Bahran's poem was "dedicated" to Albert Shanker, United Teachers Federation President, who is Jewish.

WBAI in New York City is a Pacifica radio station. Like the other Pacifica Foundation radio stations in Los Angeles and in Berkeley, it is not commercially sponsored. Pacifica operations derive their support from the contributions of their listeners. The Foundation states in its articles of incorporation that its objectives include promoting "the full distribution of public information" and obtaining "access to the sources of news not commonly brought together in the same medium." Also listed as one of its objectives is contributing "to a lasting understanding . . . between the individuals of all nations, races, creeds, and colors" and studying "the causes of religious, philosophical, and racial antagonisms." The poem read by Lester Campbell reveals that these goals are not necessarily harmonious. On the January 23, 1969, *Julius Lester* show, black reactions to the poem and to the issue of anti-Semitism were discussed. One of the guests was Tyrone Powers, representing the black parents and students of the Bedford–Stuyvesant section in Brooklyn. Although not all the comments made on this program were anti-Semitic, Tyrone Powers did say, "As far as I am concerned more power to Hitler. Hitler didn't make enough lampshades out of them. He didn't make enough belts out of them." The host of the show, Julius Lester, said in reply that it would be a "dead-end street if we get too involved in that hate thing." Protests immediately ensued.

WBAI president Robert Goodman refused to respond to requests to silence Julius Lester: "Our answer is that the practice of freedom of expression, the process of full discussion, open to all, involves some risks to the society that practices it but the rewards are high and the risks must be run." WBAI also attempted to point out that past programs had attempted to stimulate better relations between Negroes and Jews.

The United Federation of Teachers filed a complaint with the FCC asking investigation of the conduct of WBAI–FM because of the two *Julius Lester* programs with their anti-Semitic subject matter. The FCC, in a long letter of reply, refused to make any investigation or to take any action in the case.[27] While mentioning that the FCC is prohibited by law from taking action that would restrict free speech, the FCC did suggest that government intervention in this area would not in all cases be precluded, that there are some situations in which speech is so interconnected with "burgeoning violence" that remedial action would be necessary.

The FCC gave as an example a broadcast licensee who repeatedly appealed to listeners to assemble at the University of Mississippi on the day of rioting there over the enrollment of James Meredith at the university.

The FCC said that its concern was limited to whether WBAI had fulfilled its obligation to afford reasonable opportunity for the presentation of conflicting viewpoints. Since WBAI had fulfilled this obligation, the Commission said its responsibility was exhausted.

How satisfactory is this analysis? Whether expression can be restricted on broadcasting apparently depends on the extent to which speech is interlaced with burgeoning violence. How literally is this to be interpreted? Must the likelihood be that the broadcasts will lead to immediate violence? As the constitutional lawyers put it, must there be a clear and present danger?

Application of such a test—speech brigaded with violence—is no easy matter. But any approach which focuses on the likelihood of immediate violence is obviously unable to deal with the cumulative effect of continued appeals to racial violence.

Nicholas Johnson relies on the access concept in his long

opinion in WBAI. For him it is clear that access for programs like that *Julius Lester* show is an illustration of the full meaning of access to the media. In the last analysis, I suppose Nicholas Johnson is right. The right of access must mean the broadcasting of an occasional hateful interview. The hope is that access will be the preferable and the practical remedy for group defamation. The occasional hate broadcast is, unhappily, the measure of authenticity and honesty in broadcasting. Diversity of ideas can never be a reality in broadcasting unless the truly angry debate has a place.

In appreciating the impact of economic structure on public opportunities for expression in the electronic media, Commissioner Johnson is sophisticated and realistic. What I think he does not fully recognize is that the opinion-making progress implicit in the marketplace of ideas theory may be completely romantic, not only with regard to entry to the media but in connection with the impact of ideas on the public. The liberal optimism behind every line of Commissioner Johnson's opinion in the WBAI case is surely based on the confidence that if free opportunity fully to voice appeals to racial hatred is provided, the only counterpoise necessary is that the racial or religious groups attacked also have their day in broadcasting. For Johnson, the meaning of free speech in the media is a right of access which imposes no restriction on program content. He argues for the long-term desirability of the full airing of individual and group beliefs and hostilities, no matter how socially corrosive that ventilation may be in the short run.

Yet it is a rare person who is willing to tolerate the dissemination of all ideas on television, given the intimacy, the impact, and ultimately the power of the medium. Every one has a certain threshold of pain with regard to media assaults on things he holds precious. For example, Commissioner Johnson believes that cigarette advertising should not be seen on television because to sell cigarettes is to sell death. And so some Jews in Brooklyn think that to advocate anti-Semitism on radio is the equivalent of selling death. It is a harsh analogy but I think it is an honest one.

Certainly, it is the promise of the access principle that ethnic groups in our society will be afforded a legal handle by which to force entry to the media so that the eyes of the whole community may see their separate worlds in an authentic light. The access theory is leading Mexican-Americans, Puerto Ricans, Italian-Americans and Negroes to seek direct representation in broadcasting. The chance to present the case for the group whose vicissitudes one shares ought to be far more effective than merely being allowed to answer a hate broadcast. Access on television for the various polyglot constituencies in the television audiences may be far more effective for tolerance and diversity than a grudging and mechanical award of reply time to a broadcaster-selected "establishment" minority group.

The effect of access in television in this context is really to give voice to pluralism. It is at war with the concept of a homogenized national audience which has been the ideal of the broadcast media. The emergence of access in this connection does have its perils. The effort to make the marketplace of ideas work may fail. The emergence of some racial hatred in broadcasting may prove alluring to the public. There is a question as to whether Archie Bunker is a figure of admiration or ridicule. If television begins to reflect the diversity of our population, the majority may begin to resent actively the reality of the diversity which is now suppressed. Access theory offers an opportunity to remedy the problem of group libel, but it is also a risk. Nowhere in the media is application of an access principle more of an experiment than in interracial conflict. We now have network taboos; they could be replaced by government prohibitions on group libel. The Supreme Court's 1962 decision still stands ready to justify such a venture. But the whole point of assuring access to the media is to revitalize the concept of the market-place of ideas. Access is a last desperate effort to act out the phi-losophy of the eighteenth-century enlightenment on which the First Amendment is based, that freedom justifies itself.

An example of group libel on radio in 1968 illustrates how hard it is for an offer of reply time to counteract hate broad-casts.[28] The license of Station KTYM, Inglewood, California, came up for renewal. The Anti-Defamation League of the B'nai B'rith (ADL) opposed renewal, claiming that the commentary of Richard Cotten, carried by the station, had contained anti-Se-mitic material. The FCC agreed with the ADL that Cotten had made offensive remarks about persons of Jewish faith, and that he had equated Judaism with socialism and socialism with Com-munism. The station offered the ADL free equal time to re-spond to Cotten's broadcasts in any way it chose. The League told the FCC that it did not want to accept the offer. It essen-tially argued that Cotten's broadcast utterances were so contrary to the public interest that a radio station carrying them should not have its license renewed. The FCC permitted KTYM to keep its license, and the ADL went to the courts to challenge the order. Warren Burger, now Chief Justice, wrote the opinion and went out of his way to quote with approval the concurring remarks of FCC Commissioner Lee Loevinger.

Loevinger has long argued, both on and off the FCC, against any programming standards at all on the basis that programming standards, insofar as they seek to control the judgment of the station owner or his staff, constitute censorship. He asserted that no one could even agree on what a religion was, never mind on what was a libel of a religious group. He sharply disagreed with the ADL contention that "appeals to racial or religious preju-dice" are to be classed with hard-core obscenity, declaring that under such an approach, only the views the ADL holds or finds

298

acceptable can be broadcast. To classify racial and religious speech as unprotected, Loevinger said, was "irreconcilable with either the fairness doctrine or the right of free speech."

This laissez-faire view of freedom of expression is certainly the dominant one. It is an application of a romantic theory of freedom of the press and of free expression in broadcasting. In this classic libertarian view, all the FCC can do is to see that the opportunity is kept open for the "presentation of all points of view." But isn't the principle of even-handedness here somewhat simple-minded? A radio spokesman says that the blacks should be sent to Africa or Jews should be killed. Is the adequate remedy for this to guarantee the defamed groups time to reply? What is to be the content of the reply? That the Jews should not be killed? That the blacks should not be deported to Africa?

It is the libertarian ideal that all ideas are debatable. But the power of electronically disseminated hate is a reality. What is the resolution of the conflict between the real and the ideal?

The ADL in the Inglewood case did not accept reply time. It was not interested in an opportunity to discuss the idea that Jews are Communists. The charge was untrue, and to debate it would publicize it. That was exactly what the ADL was in business to prevent.

The Cotten programs, as well as impugning Jews, had also specifically attacked Arnold Forster, General Counsel of the Anti-Defamation League of B'nai B'rith. In a separate opinion in the case, Judge J. Skelly Wright pointed out that libelling an individual and attacking a group were separate problems and required different approaches.

He saw that the problem of replying to group hatred reveals "a substantial flaw in the theory of the fairness doctrine." The offer of reply time was legally sufficient, but it was not surprising that the ADL did not wish to "dignify or exacerbate the attack" by replying.

299

Basically, Judge Wright suggests that the station go out and find those who will take advantage of reply time to respond to group defamation so that racial libel does not go unanswered. Wright also indicated that consistent slanting of an issue may result in denial of license renewal, even if the mechanical offer of reply time is made, as happened with Carl McIntire's station WXUR in Media, Pennsylvania. But, certainly, the most trenchant thing Judge Wright says is that the group libel dilemma exposes a flaw in the fairness doctrine. There are some issues that do not respond to "balanced presentation."

Conclusion

The idea that some subjects are too "hot" (in McLuhan's concept) to be usefully presented in some media is a great challenge to the romantic notion that all ideas should compete in the marketplace of ideas. Perhaps in the immediacy and intimacy of television some subjects will invariably so inflame the emotions of the viewers that no balanced presentation, no reasonable consideration, will be possible. If so, the need to develop legal concepts to regulate the airing of such matters will run counter to the whole trend of American constitutional theory that the government should not intervene in problems of free expression.

A right of access to the print and broadcast media for minorities whose ideas or ways of life have hitherto been underrepresented is one way of grappling with both the enormous power of the mass media and the difficulty of mass participation in it. To the extent that a right of direct, unsupervised, unedited public participation in the media is recognized, the present system of precensorship will be displaced. This system, with its taboos on defamation of race or religion, has made overt group libel rare in the press and broadcasting, particularly network broadcasting.

But it has also made the showing of living minority cultures a television taboo: in comedies, dramas, and adventure thrillers, in news and discussion programs, and in the repeated commercials, the dominant WASP culture is seen as the only culture, unless Italian- or Mexican-Americans are used for comic effect. Public access to media is a challenge by the pluralistic reality of America to the myth of cultural and ethnic homogeneity continuously depicted in American commercial broadcasting.

To challenge the myth and displace an effective system of censorship will undoubtedly create problems. But these problems arise out of an effort to give authenticity and reality to the media, as well as a sense of public participation which is presently lacking.

A right of access enables minority groups, who are the usual targets of group defamation, to portray themselves as they see themselves. It may be that, given access, such groups will merely display their own ethnocentricities and lack of tolerance for other cultures. We return then to the question with which we began: if the right of access comes, must there also be access for hate? My reluctant answer is Yes. The clear and present danger doctrine is no real barrier. It is meant to prohibit incitement to bloodshed during civil disturbances as well as incitements to create such disturbances. But the group defamation issue is too subtle and too deep to respond to tests created to preserve the security of the state. None of the examples of group defamation in the broadcast media mentioned in this chapter would be prohibited, in my judgment, by the clear and present danger doctrine, for none of them revealed any imminent calamity. The clear and present danger doctrine is a constitutional tool designed to deal with apocalyptic events rather than the dreary content of routine prejudice.

In the last analysis, prohibition of group defamation and a right of access are not basically compatible. Too much of the

301

rage of the underclasses in America—of the blue-collar ethnic minorities, the blacks, the Chicanos, the Puerto Ricans—tends to express itself in a racial vein. Constitutional doctrine simply is not up to the task of disentangling racial libels from political and social controversy.

Changes in the way public opinion is formed have created pressures to require new approaches to the opinion-making media. Before changes can be made, the traditional approaches to free expression problems must be rethought if we are to correct imbalances in communicating power. Enlarging opportunities for entry to the media for minority groups, as well as providing reply time, must be the means by which intergroup conflict is resolved.

The classic libertarian position says in essence that in the world of ideas, sorting the wheat from the chaff is hopeless. Any sorting usually loses more wheat than chaff. But the media are willing to try. Indeed, they warn that if the present media gatekeepers are replaced or forced to submit to some principle of nondiscriminatory access, an appalling traffic consisting of the xenophobe, the purveyor of the obscene, the racist, and the socially destructive, will rush through the tube and overwhelm us. This is really what Richard Jencks and Clifton Daniel mean when they speak, no doubt sincerely, about the menace of the hate-mongers.

It is the risk of retaining chaff and worse that an access principle presents. But is not a new dilemma. Brandeis believed that in the opportunity for freedom of expression, and in the integrity of national debate, were found the best guarantors of the public order.[29] Years later, Justice Douglas wrote that the very point of free speech was to invite dispute, anger, and disquiet.[30] The point of having a debate is to give people information on which to base a decision. If like Marcuse or Hitler or Lenin, one has an entirely preconceived vision of a just society, then the media will seem to exist only to usher it in. Then, of course, access will not have furthered the democratic way of making decisions but will only have accelerated its decline. But if the future is open and our pluralistic society is developing toward a many-faceted culture whose shape we cannot now foresee, then upon securing access to the larger public, each of the many bitter and troubled communities may diminish in anger and increase in willingness to accept the democratic consensus. The conclusion in this matter is not in the least foregone.

A right of entry to the media is merely an up-dating of liberal humanism. In the end, liberalism may not be enough. In the meantime, it is worth an experiment. There is a line in the work of Isaac Bashevis Singer where someone says that the wicked make noise and the just sleep. It is time for the law to insist that the just speak.

23 /

The Media Look at Access

ALTHOUGH USUALLY CRITICAL, JOURNALISTS HAVE BEEN FASCI-
nated by the suggestion that their readers, listeners, and viewers
might be allowed to talk back. When students are asking a voice
in running the schoolhouse, when consumers are asking a say in
the manufacture and the terms of purchase of the goods they
buy, newsmen are increasingly sensitive to and intrigued by the
suggestion that the public might have rights in the media.

Journalists have given the access idea a mixed press. One of
the better-known spokesmen for the responsible press is Ben
Bagdikian. (A responsible press is a publisher's code phrase: it
means, Leave us alone; we'll be good.) Ben Bagdikian, longtime
newspaperman and writer on problems of journalism, recently
on the staff of the *Washington Post*, wrote a paper for the *Columbia Journalism Review*, having some fun with the access
idea, mostly in order to demonstrate its impracticality:

> *Editor & Publisher,* the Old Testament of newspaper
> printing, might be ordered by a court to feature the latest re-

3 0 4

lease from the National Association of Broadcasters claiming television to be a superior medium of advertising. *Broadcasting*, the weekly encyclical of electronic movie-attendance, would be forced to give equal space to FCC Commissioner Nicholas Johnson. It would take ten full issues of the magazine to let Johnson catch up, by which time the Tobacco Institute would have sued *Broadcasting* for letting this period go by without quoting in full a speech by Senator Ervin on how much the tobacco industry has done for the economy of North Carolina.[1]

Bagdikian's examples of the difficulty in implementing access deal with magazines rather than newspapers, where the access problem is most critical. Most American cities are one newspaper cities. If a public issue or a citizen group or a political candidate is shut out from a community's only daily newspaper, the loss to that community is really irreparable. On the local level and on the most personal human level, a community depends on newspapers in a way that no other print media can rival and which broadcast media cannot duplicate. One can amuse oneself by asking if the official magazine of the Seventh Day Adventists has to take advertisements for Sunday worship. But the crucial distinguishing factor about a city's daily newspaper is that it is read by the black and the white, the Seventh Day Adventist, the atheist, the Roman Catholic and the Orthodox Jew. Reality in such order as it is able to manifest itself comes across the breakfast table or the dinner table through a community's daily newspaper. Precisely because of the catholicity of the newspaper audience, the interchange of ideas in a literate and reasonable way is immensely important. Obviously many people read and subscribe to special magazines where they can talk to themselves according to the myths, beliefs, and argot of their various special causes and sects. However, it is because all of us share the daily newspaper that access to its columns must be approached as a more serious and deeply felt goal.

In Bagdikian's examples, someone wants to oppose the known editorial slant of a publication. He says the access concept would apply to newspaper news content that which is already true for advertising: "The courts have made plain that they will not permit arbitrary denial of advertising space in a monopoly or near-monopoly medium." Unfortunately, that is not true. Arbitrary denial of advertising space by privately-owned daily newspapers in monopoly and near-monopoly situations is a continuing reality across the country and the courts still, unfortunately, refuse to prohibit it.

Some journalists tend to agree that advertising should be an open house. Publishers don't, and as we have seen, the courts have sustained the publishers. Some journalists, like Ben Bagdikian, believe to their credit that newspaper advertising should be open but balk at having news content tampered with. But in law and practice neither is open.

Instead of access, Bagdikian proposes a more modest approach. He suggests to the press four methods "to win back public confidence and meet urgent social need": (1) Newspapers should include a full page which carries six or seven ideas of the experts themselves (The *New York Times* has in fact taken up this suggestion); (2) A full page should be devoted to letters to the editor; (3) A troubleshooter or ombudsman should be appointed by the paper to follow up public response to the organization's judgment and performance; and (4) A local press council of community representatives should sit down monthly with each publisher.

Bagdikian's suggestions are certainly useful but they don't have many teeth. We are not dealing with genial old publishers who have only to be gently nudged to represent more fully the real spectrum of opinion within their communities. Many American newspapers are absentee properties of newspaper chains whose main concern is the profit-loss ledger. Their primary interest is commercial advertising and they have little concern with the social and political problems of the particular community. For many papers across the country, wire service news, advertisements, syndicated material, and a fairly superficial coverage of local news comprises the news diet. It is the nonmetropolitan one newspaper city that needs entry as a right for both the editorial advertisement and for rejoinder for excluded ideas.

For liberals, criticism of the American press is often muted by the thought that there is always the *New York Times* and CBS news. On the other hand, the major conservative critic of the American press, Spiro Agnew, has attacked the Eastern metropolitan press. Agnew criticizes the press for its unrepresentative coverage, its disinterest in investigative journalism, its movement toward a new journalism of commitment without acknowledging its departure from the older journalism of detachment. As a general proposition, these criticisms expose genuine problems that presently trouble the American press. If they were broad-based criticism, his remarks should have evoked concern in all quarters. The reason they evoke bitter partisanship, however, is that they were made with deliberate political targets in mind. Continual targets for Agnew are the liberal Democratic *Washington Post* and *New York Times*. The intellectual emptiness of a paper like the *Albuquerque Star* has never troubled him, nor has the narrow conservative partisanship of the *Indianapolis Star* or the *Manchester Union Leader*. It is a pity that Agnew's media criticism has rendered itself suspect, because his concern about concentration of ownership, about newspaper chains and network power, is basically right on the bull's-eye.

The usual journalistic reaction to the idea of a right of access to the press has been hostility. Robert U. Brown of *Editor & Publisher*, the prestigious trade journal, discussed the idea under the heading, "Compulsory Publication." For Brown, there were two things wrong. To begin with, there was simply no access problem: "First of all, we are not aware of any minority views not being expressed in print today." Secondly, "The theory of a guarantee against government intervention as to what is printed is completely incompatible with any legislated or judicially regulated publications." [2]

Here Brown is on firmer ground. There is no question that the future of access will be decided at the level of constitutional theory. Success for recognition of access to the press depends on whether courts can be persuaded that a contemporary interpretation of the First Amendment permits imposing affirmative duties on the press. It depends also on being able to convince the courts that the only newspaper in a city is really a private government whose activities must be constitutionalized.

But to say that media power must be constitutionalized is easier than saying how it should be constitutionalized. Two journalism professors at the University of Missouri, Dennis Brown and John Merrill, have criticized the right of access on just this score.[3] If publishing decisions are taken away from editors and publishers, they ask, who will make them? Will it be a Federal Press Agency organized like the Federal Communications Commission? If minority views are to have a right of access, which spokesmen for a minority will exercise it? Brown and Merrill accurately point out that "undoubtedly, there is a pluralism in minority opinions even on a simple issue."

Another problem foreseen by Brown and Merrill in enforcing pluralism in the press is the issue of "proper emphasis." Would the space or emphasis given a particular minority view be decided by the proportion of the total population which the minority comprised? If not, they ask, would emphasis given a minority view be decided on an estimate of social importance of the particular view seeking entry?

These questions are designed to show that the process of editorial decision cannot really be submitted to any rational process: the issues are too complex, the decisions too subtle, to be directed by any kind of mechanistic federal regulation.

These are all worthy objections, but they are objections to a proposal that no one has made. No one has suggested that the entire process of editorial decision-making be submitted to some external decision-maker.

The access idea is at its simplest operational level an effort to make the traditionally open sections of the newspaper open in fact. If a paper carries advertisements, the right of access would impose a duty to sell to all who wished to advertise. If a paper carries letters to the editor, a right of access would make it possible to inquire whether the column was fairly administered. If an editorial attacked a group or individual, a right of access would also insure a right of reply. Surely these are moderate suggestions, a necessary correction of the imbalance between the communicator and his audience. The decision as to which story goes on page one will still be an editorial decision. The news columns will remain a matter of the in-house judgment of the paper's staff and publisher. Access will open up only those parts of the newspaper which maintain the pretense of openness. As to the requirement of reply space for persons or groups attacked in an editorial, access only implements that debate which presumably freedom of the press exists to assure.

I have mentioned the discussion of access featured on the program, *News in Perspective*, produced under the auspices of the *New York Times* and televised on September 17, 1969, over the National Educational Television Network. Under the heading, "The Right of Reply," James Reston, vice-president of the *New York Times*, Richard Jencks, president of the CBS Broadcast Group of the Columbia Broadcasting System, and moderator Clifton Daniel, associate editor of the *New York Times*, jointly grilled me on the wisdom of access to the media. I presented the following view: Freedom of the press presently means freedom of the publisher, freedom of the television network, freedom for the station owner; but the interest of the reader, the viewer, the audience as a whole, is not considered. Freedom of the press should be interpreted in light of its primary purpose to inform society sufficiently so that it is capable of undertaking the task of democratic government. Freedom of the press needs to be rethought in order that it may protect and reach a broader class of the public. Finally, I urged that the communications media be considered by their responsibilities rather than by their privileges.

Clifton Daniel asked Reston whether he would agree that there is a right of access of the press and that it should be enforced by law. Reston responded that obviously there had to be access "but if you are asking whether I favor turning over the editing process to cops and judges, the answer is certainly not."

The question is rather whether there ought to be press accountability. The traditional conception of freedom of the press has had no place for press accountability. The press made government accountable to the public, a task best accomplished, it is argued, if the press is accountable to no one. This is a conception which it seems to me is now difficult to maintain. First of all, the press is itself an obviously powerful private government, increasingly centralized in ever fewer hands. Secondly, as a legal matter, press accountability has long existed in English-speaking countries through the law of obscenity and libel. But requiring access for an unpopular idea works differently and is more compatible with freedom of the press than the law of libel. Obscenity statutes criminally punish expression. Libel laws through the civil courts can attach heavy damages to offending expressions. Access laws on the other hand provide that more expression be required. This is a vital distinction.

Assuming for a moment that enforcement of a right of access in the courts is not a sinister development, the question arises: Is a right of access necessary? James Reston believes that there must be access but that law is not needed to provide it. In his view, newspapers would not be tolerated if they failed to provide it.

Richard Jencks of CBS News thought there essentially was no access problem nor did he agree that the networks ever impose their own prejudices and predilections on public affairs in broadcasting. Reston said, however, "I would not want to see us get too holy in defense of the press, radio, and television." He thought that many who were criticized in the press were not dealt with fairly and that corrections were often given grudgingly. But outside solutions to the problem seemed to him unnecessary because the newspaper readership and the broadcast audience will call the media to account. Their dissatisfaction will force correction. But how? What pressures can readers or viewers, particularly minority ones, apply? There is simply not enough choice available to force the media to make fundamental changes for the better on their own.

Media unfairness is not the result of any conspiracy. Obviously, network presidents do not get together to decide the thought patterns they will impose on two hundred million Americans. The process is far subtler. In the Soviet Union the media are organized to sell an ideology, and to that task they set themselves unswervingly. In the United States the media are organized to sell products. Between fanaticism and commercialism, I suppose I prefer commercialism. But it is not an attractive choice. The political scientist V. O. Key said incisively that newspapers are essentially people who sell white space to advertisers. Broadcasters are essentially people who sell time to advertisers.

Decisions in the press and broadcasting are made frequently by people who have no concern for ideas one way or the other. The only way the media can combine making money and talking about ideas is to talk about only those ideas that are not too controversial. They ignore those controversies which most of us are not willing to accept as tolerable because those issues might anger audiences and dislocate broadcasting's commercial purposes. This attitude toward controversy, in my judgment, has created the need for access to the media.

Jencks' reaction to the contention that there was a need for public access to broadcasting was to doubt that the charge could be documented.

One of the most perplexing obstacles to the right of access is the media insistence that there is no access problem, or, alternatively, if there is one it is the critic's responsibility to document it. For example, I remarked on the *News in Perspective* television show that media coverage of protest against the Vietnam war did not seem to me very substantial until Senator Eugene McCarthy was able to demonstrate in 1968 that 40 percent of the Democratic voters "in so unsubversive a state as New Hampshire" were disenchanted with the war. Richard Jencks challenged this observation, remarking that it was media coverage of the war and the protest that enabled McCarthy to attract the support he did. Reston added that the television camera on the battlefield and news reporting on the war were what stimulated protest to the war. Then the representatives of the CBS television network and the *New York Times* turned to me and asked me to document, immediately and over the air, denials of access to the media. My response was that it would be easy for them to document the need for access but not for me.

The critic cannot know what is not admitted to the media. Critics of all other institutions have the media to aid them in their inquiry, but not so the media critic. Since the colloquy about media coverage of the Vietnam war before 1968, the former *Times* man, James Aronson, has published a book which argues that during the formative stage of American involvement in Vietnam the American press served as a willing arm of government.[4] He chronicles how little press coverage was given to South Vietnamese resentment against Diem. He emphasizes how major American newspapers accommodated themselves to government policy. Significant, for Aronson, of the long-standing American press support for the administration position on Vietnam was press reluctance to publish anything reflecting badly on Nguyen Cao Ky, the new premier of South Vietnam. Ky was quoted in the *London Daily Mirror* as saying that he had only one hero, Hitler. One would have thought that this would be news. Yet, observes Aronson, no representative of any American newspaper in Europe picked up the story nor did any American wire service: the story eventually appeared in the American press only after readers inquired about it. Aronson is a bitter critic of James Reston: "Reston and less prominent but no less acquiescent journalists were in effect acting as propaganda agents for the State and Defense Departments in distorting and confusing the facts." Aronson says that such journalists "kept from the American public information it needed to weigh and form opinions on the war in Vietnam." Yet, although Aronson is overly and unfairly critical of Reston, he joins Reston in decrying a right of access for opposing views in the press. Like Reston, he believes that access presents more dangers than benefits. His answer to unfairness in the press is the alternative press, the underground press. Perhaps it is not surprising that Aronson sees the remedy for press failings in the new radical press of which he is a part and that Reston finds the salvation for press problems in voluntary redemption by the establishment press of which he is a most distinguished representative.

The problem Aronson is writing about is real: the attraction power aggregations have for each other. No one has written more thoughtfully and with more troubled sincerity than James Reston on the adeptness of presidents in coopting influential journalists.[5] The *New York Times* is itself a private government of not inconsiderable power. It has a natural tendency to reflect the establishment position in spite of itself. And now that the establishment has fled from support of American involvement in the Vietnam war, it is no surprise that the prestige press have also fled from it.

The press as relentless critic of government, forever holding a merciless searchlight on the performance of public men, is a picture often used as support for claiming that the freedom of publishers is essentially the freedom of the people. But we cannot depend on publishers alone to assure the kind of debate and discussion which is necessary to continually renew the nation's institutions, to keep them responsive to change, and sensitive to discontent.

My criticism that the media is in large part commercially motivated has rankled the industry. It is, said Jencks, a "reckless charge" and "substantially false"—which comfortingly implies that my description is at least partially true. Reston's response was more incisive and profound. In his view, a more valid criticism of the media might be that they tell us too much rather than too little. A good case can be made for this view. When has the restlessness in society, the ugliness between groups, the crisis in authority, and the general fury and anger which characterizes so much of our national life ever been so intensely vivid and immediate as now? And who, if not the media, has brought the intensity of our problems home to us?

If we are to understand the kind of media exposure which our social problems presently receive, we must go back to the commercial orientation of the media. News is paid for by advertisers. News is sold to viewers to expose them to the advertiser's sales messages and because news is part of the network's idea of its public service obligation to its audience. I do not discount the depth of concern for the latter in broadcasting circles. But the broadcast audience is attracted primarily by packaging news as entertainment. News in broadcasting is seen both as reality and diversion.

Perhaps that is why some bizarre disorder enjoys a different level of access to network news shows than does a point of view which is presented in a rational, coherent way. In May 1971, Vietnam war veteran and antiwar hero John Kerry was asked on a network show why the veterans who demonstrated in front of the U.S. Capitol in Washington threw away their medals. How else, Kerry asked, were they to attract the attention of the public? The Vietnam Veterans Against the War had scheduled news conferences but the media had not been interested: they had gone too often to the well of war protest.

Successful protest in America demands the instincts of P. T. Barnum and the agility of Harry Houdini. The dramatic jolts to tradition and institutions depicted nightly on television are in fact occasioned by television's need to depict something unsettling nightly on television.

If a group burns its draft cards in a public square and attracts a crowd, its opportunity for free broadcast time and newspaper coverage is much increased. Such conduct certainly has chance of making the local television news and perhaps the national news as well. If an antiwar group descends upon the offices of a chemical company making napalm, its opportunity for free time is also enhanced. Free media access for antiwar and antidraft views using more rational presentations is far more restricted. Without the drama there would be no admission.

After the President's speech announcing the intervention in Cambodia, antiwar Senators were denied time by all but one network and that one charged such a price that one of the dissenters, Senator McGovern, considered mortgaging his house to pay for the broadcast. But a massive protest and unprecedented strike—the furious response of the American college students to the Cambodian intervention—captured the news media without the students' paying a single penny. The network and newspaper coverage of the student protest forced the President to reply in the guise of press conference.

But in the beginning, the students had neither asked nor been granted broadcast time. They had by the form of their protest, by the act of closing over four hundred universities, acquired the broadcast time which otherwise would have been denied them. In this sense, Reston is right: there *is* access to the media. He did not mention its incalculable social cost.

Not all the media reactions to the access idea have been unsympathetic. Richard L. Tobin of the *Saturday Review*, writing on "The Omnipotence of the Majority," discusses the crisis in the American opinion process by remembering the fundamental criticism of American society voiced by de Tocqueville more than a century ago: dissent had no place to turn. Public opinion is the expression of the majority, and the legislature and the executive do their bidding. The consequence for a minority position, no matter how deeply felt, is submission.[6] Tobin believes that establishing access to the media may serve as a counterbalance to the "overpowering omnipotence of the majority." Entry to the media offers hope of actually changing public opinion.

Sometimes it is said that dissent in America has been too shrill. President Nixon during the Cambodian crisis complained that the young speak so loud that they are hard to hear. That this may be true, however, reveals the fundamental difficulties involved in a majoritarian approach to public opinion. Intensity of conviction in a society is worthy of respect, even though it is a minority conviction. The reality and the importance of dissent should not be downgraded because public opinion polls show that the majority supports another policy. Majority but passive support for a policy may justifiably inspire dissenters to seek access to that majority in order to change their minds. Legitimizing entry into the media will make it less necessary to get the majority's attention by means of bizarre, shrill, and even violent protest.

Richard Tobin says that establishing a right of access to the media may serve as a necessary antidote to the tyranny of a majority. But what may happen when the novel, the heretical, and the antiestablishment point of view is aired by right and still the nation's power centers refuse to respond because the majority is not sufficiently stirred? To put it another way, is the crisis in the American system a problem of lack of access for ideas, or rather a confrontation between a determined but silent majority and an angry and convinced minority?

First Amendment theory is predicated on the idea that opportunity for expression, in a phrase of Justice Brandeis, is the "path of safety." The health of the social order bears a real relationship to the extent to which its members consider it to be responsive to their wishes.

Freedom of expression is supposed to frustrate government repression and private rebellion. But suppose it does not? Obviously angry minorities do create revolutions. America has not signed any treaty with history that immunizes it from violent revolution. Yet our society expects that dissenters will wait patiently, and that their anger will be tempered by the hope that they may yet prevail. What is necessary is to make that expectation more than chimerical.

A distinguished scholar, Charles McIlwain, has described the basic concept of constitutionalism to be the limitation of the power of the majority. Opportunity to reach the majority allows dissent to participate normally in the processes of opinion. To approach freedom of the press as basically an antimajoritarian idea is far more fruitful than to approach it solely as a restraint on government. To take the latter approach deprives the whole concept of freedom of the press of contemporary meaning and relevance.

American journalism has lost its individualistic character.

Freedom of the Press for Whom?

Newspapers are now owned by corporations. The Hearsts or Pulitzers with their various causes, noble and venal, are rarities today. It is an unusual publisher, like Katherine Graham of the *Washington Post* or Eugene Pulliam of the *Indianapolis Star*, who is noted for his or her social and political opinions. For this reason, it is pollyannish to expect that the newspaper chains which benefit from blandness and indifferentism will seek out opportunities to ventilate the searing social problems of our time. It is like Mark Twain's critique of his wife's swearing: the words might be there but they wouldn't have the tune. The need is for normal representation of all the segments of community opinion in the daily press, and a good share of it must be in the voice and the idiom of the group represented.

24 /

The Future of Access to

the Media

Romance and Realism about Freedom of the Press

FREEDOM OF THE PRESS IS ONE OF THE MORE ATTRACTIVE PHRASES in American life, law, and myth. What does it mean? Why is it an important value in our society? Minimally it promises that newspapers cannot be restrained or intimidated by government for what they allow to be printed in their pages. The First Amendment to the U.S. Constitution states: "Congress shall make no law abridging freedom of speech or of the press." It says nothing about the actions of state legislatures. From 1791 until 1925 the First Amendment was thought to apply only to the federal government. In 1925, in a nearly forgotten case, the Supreme Court casually observed that "freedom of speech and of the press . . . are among the fundamental personal rights and 'liberties' protected by the due process clause of the Fourteenth Amendment from impairment by the States." [1]

Thus our present constitutional law of freedom of the press is only a little more than forty years old. Although the doctrine itself is far older, its usefulness as a practical safeguard is a twentieth-century phenomenon.

Changes in our approach to freedom of the press are bitterly resisted. Now an access-oriented approach is attacked as a violation of the concept because, it is urged, the Constitution speaks only to government and not to private power groups. But the law of freedom of the press was extended from the national to the state governments in the past without constitutional amendment. The Supreme Court said the word "liberty" in the Fourteenth Amendment ("No state shall deprive any person of life, liberty, or property without due process of law") was a concept sufficiently broad to warrant the conclusion that it obligated the states to respect freedom of the press. I believe that the reference to freedom of the press in the First Amendment itself permits an interpretation today which will make the concept continuingly vital and meaningful. Such an interpretation would permit governmental action to provide for positive expression.

Our approach to freedom of the press has operated in the service of a romantic illusion: the illusion that the marketplace of ideas is freely accessible.

After the first World War, in a case involving a socialist who was prosecuted for distributing leaflets which were allegedly designed to "cripple or hinder the United States in the prosecution of the (first) World War," Justice Oliver Holmes wrote a memorable opinion:

> But when men have realized that time has upset many fighting faiths, they may come to believe even more than they believe the very foundations of their own conduct that the ultimate good desired is better reached by free trade in ideas— that the best test of truth is the power of the thought to get itself accepted in the competition of the market, and that truth is the only ground upon which their wishes can safely be carried out.[2]

A half a century later, Holmes' eloquent description of the free marketplace of ideas depicts an ideal, not a reality. There *are* enormous limitations on the "power of thought to get itself accepted in the competition of the market." In Holmes' concept of the marketplace of ideas the only limitation on the currency of ideas is an intellectual one. But there is no free trade in ideas. Ideas in a mass society are transmitted in the mass communications media of television, radio, and the press. Admission to them assures notoriety and public response. Denial assures obscurity and, apparently, frustration.

We assume that the only obstacles to debate and discussion are the penalties that the state may apply to unpopular debate and provocative discussion. Our law of freedom of expression, however, has done very little to insure opportunity for freedom of expression.

The traditional liberal position on ideas is essentially Darwinian. Ideas engage in a life of mortal combat and the fittest survive. In this struggle, the continuing menace has been seen to be government. That private power might so control the struggle of ideas as to predetermine the victor has not been considered. But, increasingly, private censorship serves to suppress ideas as thoroughly and as rigidly as the worst government censor.

Publishers are not the only private censors. Printers in a number of cases have refused to set in type copy submitted to them. Some printers have refused to work for underground papers. These papers have sometimes had to be printed far from the community in which they are distributed. The November 1970 issue of *Scanlan's Monthly* was rejected by fifty or sixty printing companies because of an article on guerilla warfare in the U.S. The legal director of the American Civil Liberties Union, Melvin Wulf, was quoted in the *Wall Street Journal* as saying that repetitions of the Scanlan situation could destroy freedom of the press.[3]

But although the ACLU was very critical of private censorship in the Scanlan incident it has been ambivalent to the proposal for a right of access to the press. It held to the old liberal suspicion of government intervention and faith in the market-place of ideas. The 1968 ACLU biennial conference in Ann Arbor, however, revealed deep disenchantment with the closed quality of the mass media. There was evidence of new sympathy for means of broadening public participation in the media, as in other powerful social institutions.

The ACLU Biennial Session recommended that the ACLU bring law suits to challenge the discriminatory refusal of advertisements and notices in publications. It was also suggested that the Communications Media Committee consider supporting media challenges when individuals and organizations are subjected to a pattern of derogatory treatment. In essence, this recommendation supported a right of reply. Finally, the establishment of a permanent citizens' advisory commission to audit and report on media performance on a national basis was recommended.

At a meeting after the Biennial Session, the Communications Media Committee offered a revised version of the recommendation to the National Board:

> That the ACLU bring selective lawsuits challenging the discriminatory refusal of non-commercial advertisements and notices in publications of general circulation on grounds of race, creed or color.

Neither the original nor the revision was approved.

Perhaps it was felt that commercial advertising has a lesser claim to First Amendment protection, but if the right is given only to noncommercial advertisements, the resulting public access to advertising would be fairly slender.

The ACLU proposal to include public notices about meetings as well as to permit advertisements is necessary. Many groups feel excluded from the daily press. Lack of publicity for their meetings and activities severely limit their opportunities to grow in status or influence in their communities.

Practically speaking, a right of reply is easy to implement because it is triggered by a newspaper attack. But suppose a newspaper does not attack but merely ignores? What then? Should the paper be compelled to provide so many pages to various groups in the community to do with what they choose? Commandeering of newspaper space would be a rather radical alternative. What the ACLU suggests is that, in view of the complete dependence of a community on its newspaper for notices of public events and meetings, at least there ought to be a way to compel their publication. It would be very similar to the legal notice advertising which most newspapers are now compelled to take under the law of most of the states.

The need for further development of cumulative remedies to provide access to the press is shown in recent cases where the black community was forced to pay for the most elementary kind of press recognition, while whites received it as a matter of course.

In the late 1960s, a protest was directed to the long-established refusal of the Lynchburg, Virginia, daily newspapers to publish the obituary notices of members of the Negro community. If a black man died, his family could tell the rest of the community about it only by purchasing a commercial advertisement.

Another situation arose in Montgomery, Alabama. The same company owns and publishes both the morning paper, the *Advertiser,* and the evening newspaper, the *Journal.* The company also publishes Montgomery's only Sunday newspaper, the *Advertiser-Journal.* That the same company owns the entire daily press in Montgomery is not surprising: the pattern is standard across the country. But the evils of monopoly are not usually so readily discernible. No Negro social announcements had ever graced the society pages of Montgomery newspapers: instead, the papers all had separate Negro social pages.

A group of Montgomery Negroes finally filed suit against the papers on June 15, 1971, in the federal district court. They said that the policy of the newspapers was an arbitrary denial, based solely on race. The argument was that refusal to publish Negro bridal announcements in the society section of daily newspapers violated the due process and equal protection clauses. They asked that private power groups be subjected to constitutional standards when they exercised "monopoly control in an area of vital public concern."

The court said it found this argument quite appealing, but it could not accept it.[4] Basically the case fell on the Achilles heel of the access to the press concept—the state action doctrine. The court relied on the Seventh Circuit's decision in the Chicago newspaper case, discussed in Chapter 2.[5]

Placing Negro social announcements on a separate Negro news page is an imitation in the media of the community social system. But segregation in public facilities has been found unconstitutional. The shibboleth that perpetuates a media-supported social system of racial discrimination is that newspaper action is private action and is therefore constitutionally immune. When voluntary continuation of a discriminatory policy by private newspapers is judicially enforced, then the discriminatory treatment should be considered state action. In Montgomery, an irrelevant confusion between freedom of the press and press absolutism has resulted in the federal court's continuing the now outmoded and romantic view that freedom for newspaper publishers is freedom of the press. This is an idea that dies hard. At that ACLU Biennial Session, some members were shocked by the suggestion that newspapers should be required to carry material and advertising opposing the basic editorial policy of the newspaper. This attachment to the rights of property is characteristic of the classic liberal position. What it ignores, however, is that as early as the late nineteenth century very conservative judges were persuaded to accept the idea that restricting the use of property was appropriate when the property owner had a monopoly in a business which clearly had a public interest.

No one thinks that the Board of Directors of AT&T approves of every conversation that goes along its telephone lines. The daily newspaper could never be treated as a common carrier to the same extent as the phone company, but community dependence on the daily press gives it something of a common carrier role, although the press has no reciprocal responsibilities to its readership.

But application of the law to the press is not forbidden. Although the press once vigorously argued to the contrary, it is now unmistakably clear that the antitrust laws, for example, apply to newspapers as well as to other businesses. In fact, one of the paradoxes in any discussion of press responsibility is that the press has not been slow to invite, in fact demand, government intervention where it is to the financial advantage of the press. Special mailing rates are provided by federal statute, for example. Some sections of the press have waged an energetic, insistent, and successful campaign for legislation to allow newspers to share facilities in a given city.[6]

There is inequality in capacity to communicate ideas just as there is inequality in economic bargaining power. Indeed inequality of power to communicate is usually one aspect of inequality in general economic bargaining power. In the broadcast media, the VHF television outlets are almost completely in the hands of network affiliated stations, and possess the mass audience. The licenses of these stations are almost invariably renewed by the Federal Communications Commission at three-year intervals. The unregulated daily newspaper industry is equally unfriendly territory for new entrants and new voices. The cost of establishing a competitive daily newspaper is all but absolutely prohibitive.

Inequality in the ability to communicate ideas is so clear that few would dispute it. What is disputed is that the situation is a problem and that, as a constitutional matter, anything can be done about it.

As a result of new court decisions like the Democratic National Committee case, the power of the media barons, as Nicholas Johnson has well styled them, has been challenged as never before.[7] The play of ideas, and the initiative to express them, is now out of the cozy familiar hands of broadcaster and bureaucrat. Propaganda may now be issued by any group able to purchase broadcasting time. The ability to propagandize is no longer limited to the commercial advertisers.

Counsel for the FCC and the industry argued against the use of spot advertising for public or political issues. The onesidedness, the brevity of spot editorial announcements, it was alleged, could only distort information. Opening the spots to the public for noncommercial purposes would confuse and oversimplify complex issues. Wright's answer was a constitutional one. The First Amendment protected "many forms of misleading and overly simplified political expression in order to ensure robust, wide-open debate." He might have added that democratic political debate has never had to meet a Socratic standard of dialogue.

Although the Federal Court of Appeals daringly set aside a broadcaster-imposed and bureaucrat-supported ban on editorial advertising, it was very sensitive to the fact that the lack of state action in the newspaper cases had inhibited a number of federal courts from imposing a similar ban on discrimination in the sale of editorial advertising in the press. Judge Wright distinguished the situation of broadcasting: "Almost no other private business —almost no other regulated private business—is so intimately bound up to government and to service to the commercial." The court then referred to a Los Angeles movie ad case[8] and the Chicago newspaper case[9] where requests for access for ads for movies and a union labor dispute respectively were rejected. Then, somewhat cautiously, Judge Wright said:

> While the governmental involvement in and public character of newspapers is surely less than that of broadcasting, we of course need express neither agreement nor disagreement with the cited decisions here.

One little wrinkle in Judge Wright's opinion is intriguing. Older broadcast cases, involving suits directly lodged against the broadcasters, treated broadcast companies as private corporations immune from First Amendment obligations. But in this case the FCC had approved the industry practice of rejecting the sale of advertising time for noncommercial purposes. Governmental approval of or acquiescence in action by private broadcasters therefore transformed private action into state action. For support, Wright relied on the Supreme Court's determination that racially discriminatory restrictive covenants cannot be judicially enforced since the action of judicial officers would be regarded as the action of the state.[10]

Here is reasoning with radical possibilities for change. If government support of private corporate action makes such activity state action, then judicial approval of denial of access to editorial advertising also transforms the action of private newspaper publishers and makes it public or governmental.

Although the Democratic National Committee case professes to take no position on the right of access issue, the theory that governmental approval of broadcaster action is state action readily lends itself to solution of the state action problem in regard to the press. But the case cuts an even broader path for the future. The scope of First Amendment protection, the court quite properly says, should not depend on " 'public–private' technicalities." The analysis should be functional. The two questions should be, What is the government involvement in or public character of an enterprise? and What is the importance or suitability of that enterprise for the communication of ideas?

If, for First Amendment purposes, what is public depends on its importance to the communication of ideas, then broadcasting is a public forum. But does not this test also describe the situation and function of the daily press? Judge Wright wrote of the broadcast media in the landmark Democratic National Committee decision as follows: "In a populous democracy the only means of truly mass communication must play an absolutely crucial role in the processes of self-government and free expression, so central to the First Amendment. That can be said of almost no other 'private' enterprise." These remarks are almost true—almost because there is another 'private' enterprise that is as important a forum for communication as broadcasting —the newspaper press.

Access and Propaganda

In contemporary protest on both the Left and the Right, propaganda seems to be increasingly preferred over discussion and the approach of reason. When a federal court of appeals declared in 1971 that the FCC-supported ban on the sale of advertising time for controversial social or political purposes violated the First Amendment, *Broadcasting* said the ruling would prohibit broadcasters from rejecting "paid propaganda." [11]

Will then the rise of access to the media be finally a victory for propaganda? Jacques Ellul has written that there are two kinds of propaganda: agitation propaganda and integration propaganda.[12] Integration propaganda is aimed at adjustment. Agitation propaganda aims to turn resentment to rebellion. He thinks the United States offers the most important examples of the use of integration propaganda. Perhaps the primary problem in the United States is that protest is essentially agitation propaganda but the media has habituated the public to integration propaganda. Ellul's analysis helps us to appraise both the past consequences of lack of access to the media and to estimate the possible consequences of providing that access in the future.

Entry to the means of communication must necessarily, I think, take the edge off social anger. But, it is difficult to say whether the new access for paid ideological spots on broadcasting will be used for agitation or integration propaganda. The chief distributors of agitation propaganda in the United States today are unintentionally the broadcast media. By just providing news of the activities of those engaging in social rebellion, they spread agitation propaganda. Reporting and dramatizing protest feeds the protest movement.

At the present time, access to the media is obtained through applying external pressure rather than by obtaining formal permission.

A measure of the jaded standards of the media is that when protest leaves the level of reason, broadcast time and newspaper space become abundantly available. The "sit-in", the campus protest, the draft card burning, the flag burning, and the ghetto riot are all communications media in default. But not everything worth saying can be said in that way, or at least, not without grave risk of damage to the social order.

To confront the mass audience suddenly with agitation propaganda, when it is accustomed to a diet of integration propaganda, produces rage and disorientation. People see the electronic reality, but the truth makes them angry. They cannot believe in the reality of something that seems deliberately bi-

329

zarre. They hope, and so partly believe, that the television portrayal of reality is staged and false. Surely, the youth posed with the clenched fist, the person spitting on the flag, would not exist if the television cameras were not turned on them.

For the protestor, media coverage enhances the credibility of his protest. Coverage reinforces the sense of outrage in sympathetic viewers by reassuring them that there are many like-minded spirits.

Some events are too massive, involve too many participants and too much violence, to have their authenticity doubted. An example was the 1968 racial disturbance which followed the death of Martin Luther King. Television coverage of the actual disturbances was actually muted in order not to incite others.

An important illustration of public skepticism about television was the popular reaction to television coverage of the Democratic National Convention in 1968. People refused to believe what they saw. They saw on their television screens police beating students and demonstrators on the head. They heard Senator Ribicoff speak out in indignation. They saw Mayor Daley shout back in anger at Ribicoff's charges. But the viewer reaction, measured by the letters received by the major networks, was overwhelmingly critical of television performance. Why? Because the barrage of agitation propaganda let loose on an unprepared public contradicted the world order which had been implanted in its mind through integration propaganda. People criticized the networks, claiming that the police response was shown but not the crowds' provocation. The integration propaganda, the myth, was that police do not punish political dissenters, only law-breakers. Since no law-breaking provocation had been shown, the assumption was made that the networks had conspiratorially refused to show the provocation in order to stimulate criticism of the Johnson Administration, Mayor Daley, and law and order in general.

We do not lack for examples in recent social history of unin-

330

tentional media distribution of agitation propaganda. The student general strike of May 4–8, 1970, over the Cambodian incursion offered a challenge to the received myth of freedom of expression in the United States. The strike succeeded. The media reported the success and so became, as it often has in the recent past, the reluctant tutor and unwilling evangelist of protest. The conflict is the product of confusion between television's sense of its duty to inform and its natural tendency and preference to entertain. Happily, some social upheavals permit the duty to inform and the preference to entertain to combine. The media then cheerfully use the technical proficiency at which they are masters and bring the upheaval to every home in the country.

Marshall McLuhan says the new electronic media have made the print-oriented conception of time irrelevant. The speed of information transmittal has increased to the point that rational decision-making is outmoded. For the frustrated and the impatient, the conventional decision-making process appears hopelessly slow. The consequence of the speed of information on television is "immediate involvement of the entire community." Thus, the student strike was announced on Saturday, May 2, 1970, by the President of the National Student Association. By the end of the week strikes had closed or crippled over four hundred colleges and universities across the country, in places with such tranquil reputations as the University of Idaho, the University of Kansas, and New Mexico State University.

What had happened to debate? The same thing that had happened to the political system itself. It did not respond. The President said that whether or not the war was popular he would continue it; the new left was encouraged to respond that whether or not a student strike (and they hoped a general strike) was popular, it had now become an indispensable and inevitable mode of protest.

In the long run broadcasters cannot shun controversy. Real

controversy lives too close to violence and the entertainment potential of violence is too great to be ignored indefinitely by a profit-oriented, privately-controlled medium. But can routine and fair and extensive coverage and access for the conflicts and the contentions in the nation ever be a reality in the media? Many years ago the free speech scholar and lawyer, Zechariah Chafee of Harvard, scoffed at the possibility of ever securing what he called "compulsory broadmindedness." Radio critic Charles Siepmann has observed that equal time for reply to personal attacks is insufficient: "One sentence of irresponsible abuse may require a hundred sentences to set the record straight."

Whether or not the usefulness of reply and debate on radio or television can be objectively demonstrated, the question remains, is broader access to the media necessary? Encouragement of access to the media responds to that which television itself has stimulated, the enormous need for all the components of our society to participate in it.

Portents for the Future

On June 9, 1971, the FCC turned its attention to a fundamental reappraisal of the fairness doctrine.[13] A flood of access petitions and unresolved questions about the adequacy of the fairness doctrine to meet access problems, had all served to generate the inquiry. The Commission proposed to review four general areas: (1) the fairness doctrine itself, (2) the problem of permitting access to the broadcast media to respond to product commercials, (3) the problem of access for discussion of public issues, and (4) the problem of application of the fairness doctrine to political broadcasting.

Announcement of the inquiry brought volleys of criticism from all sides. The establishment trade journal *Broadcasting* expressed a desperate wish that a concerted industry attack might finally persuade the FCC to kill off the hated fairness doctrine. FCC Commissioner Nicholas Johnson concurred in the decision to hold the inquiry, but hoped aloud that the prospect of an FCC hearing on fairness and access problems would not inhibit the courts from moving in new directions in the area of broadcasting.

Whether or not the fairness reappraisal was planned to halt the development of access law, it didn't work. The Federal Court of Appeals decision came anyway, opening up advertising time for ideas as a general proposition and not only in response to product commercials.

Speculation on the outcome of the FCC's review of the fairness doctrine is hazardous particularly since the Democratic National Committee decision imposes a new duty on the FCC to issue editorial advertising guidelines. But it is clear that if the FCC is reluctant, the courts are not.

The FCC in its notice of inquiry announced that it will propose rules which will be a "step in promoting access to the media." Judge Wright criticized the FCC's new proposals in the Democratic National Committee case because the desire of the FCC inquiry seemed to be the revival of the old fairness concept that it is the responsibility of the broadcaster to seek out opposing viewpoints and not to wait for someone to apply. Judge Wright quarrelled with this, saying that it was crucial that "noncommercial groups and individuals have the same rights of initiative as commercial advertisers." A difficulty with the Wright emphasis on letting the access initiative originate freely with the public in regard to advertising time is that initiative is no less important in nonadvertising time concerned with public issues. No overhaul of the fairness doctrine which fails to open up broadcasting to the initiative of the public and which leaves reply completely contingent upon attack or provocation will adequately resolve the need for access. Access must be provided for and the fairness doctrine strengthened by emphasizing its "seek out" aspect. But the fairness doctrine alone cannot provide access to the media.

Access to the broadcast media was given a future by the Supreme Court decision in Red Lion. Recent developments—opening up advertising time to editorial advertising, the movement to liberate part of prime time from the networks' grip—all flow from the impetus given by Red Lion.

The final perimeters of access to the media are difficult to predict. The Democratic National Committee case marks the actual arrival of the access idea in broadcasting, just as Red Lion heralded acceptance of the idea as a matter of legal theory.

In this book, discussion concerning implementation of legal rights of entry to the press has centered around the daily press, because of its immense importance as an opinion-maker. Radio and television, together with the daily press, comprise the most important components in the national opinion process. But if access is seen as beginning in the daily press, it must not end there.

If a community has only a single daily newspaper, many issues and topics excluded from it will not be sufficiently newsworthy for mention in print media elsewhere. This element of public dependence on the single community daily makes the case for compulsory entry a strong one. Sometimes, a similar necessity may exist even in a magazine. A very recent decision has produced the first American legal recognition of access to a magazine. A group called the Radical Lawyers Caucus sought to place an ad in the *Texas Bar Journal* to publicize its meeting during the Texas bar convention in San Antonio. The proposed ad announced that a hotel suite had been rented and that the lawyers were planning to discuss national problems and pass out literature about them.

The *Bar Journal* refused the ad on the ground that state bar rules prohibited accepting political advertisements. As is not unusual in these cases, the Radical Lawyers Caucus had no difficulty in showing that the *Bar Journal*'s definition of political was not so detached as it might have been. The *Bar Journal* editors had reprinted an editorial from the *Dallas Morning News* on the Chicago Seven, as well as a resolution by the state bar committee supporting the President's Vietnam policy and denouncing antiwar demonstrators. Counsel for the Bar said that permitting "political advertisements" would lead to ideological warfare and injure the State Bar's image of disinterestedness.

The federal court decided in favor of the Radical Lawyers Caucus.[14] The *Bar Journal*, as a state agency, could not accept commercial advertising to the exclusion of editorial advertising. Furthermore, since it had printed editorials and resolutions from bar committees, the *Bar Journal* was hardly in a position to maintain its claim to be politically neutral. The court said that it was "unquestioned" that the *Bar Journal* refused the ad because of its content rather than from any general advertisement policies. Censorship on the basis of content is clearly a violation of the equal protection and free speech guarantees of the Constitution.

Since the *Bar Journal* was a state agency, it was possible for the court to view the denial of access to it as invalid state action. But such situations occur where the journal is privately owned. It is here that Judge Wright's questions concerning the extent of First Amendment impact (How much of a forum is the medium in question? How much is it being used for communication in its field?) have real implications for the future. In the meantime, the Radical Lawyers Caucus case shows that the access principle is applicable to the print media beyond the daily press.

The print media cannot continue to evade legal responsibilities. The idea of access cannot stop with the electronic media.

335

The same wire services feed both broadcasters and newspapers. Often the same corporations and families own a television outlet and the only daily newspaper in a community. The broad meaning of Red Lion is clear: Legislation enforcing a right of access in the press as well as broadcasting would be constitutional. Daily newspapers are not scarce like broadcasters because of inherent technical limitations, but because of economics. The number of American daily newspapers of general circulation has steadily dwindled. Today there are less than 1800 in this country. The cost of establishing a daily newspaper is of such heroic dimensions that few are foolish enough to try.

Historians of journalism record that in revolutionary eighteenth century America, many printers operated on an open-to-all-comers basis.[15] Printers published little weeklies which reflected their own passionately felt views, but customarily allowed their rivals to hire out their facilities. Entry into the world of public and political debate is no longer so informal. The nineteenth and early twentieth centuries brought the rise of great mass circulation daily newspapers. But for fifty years, the steady pattern of the American press has been a decline in numbers. Famous journals of all political stripes have perished—the Republican New York *Herald-Tribune*, the Democratic Boston *Post*, the radical *PM*.

In 1909–10, 2202 daily newspapers were published, compared with 1761 in 1961.[16] But the decline in numbers has by no means led to a decline in influence. It is sometimes said that the loss of alternatives to American newspaper readers is not necessarily a matter for alarm since the rise of the electronic media, radio and television, provide an alternative forum. The American Newspaper Publishers Association contends, for example, that there is competition in news and advertising between the print and the broadcast media. But the reality is that often the print media compete with broadcast media, not in ownership or in content, but only in technology.

The Future of Access to the Media

In 1963, 153 of the 563 television stations were newspaper affiliated.[17] In 26 communities the only newspaper has an interest in the only television station. Daily newspaper circulation is over 60,000,000 but the number of cities possessing dailies with competing ownership has decreased from 117 to 58.

Twenty-eight of the 69 newspapers published in the country's top 25 television markets have ownership interests in television stations in the community where they publish. Moreover, in the few communities where one of two daily newspapers operates a television station, the nontelevision affiliated newspaper is at a competitive disadvantage. That does not augur well for the survival of the nonaffiliated competitor.

There is a temptation to seek vigorous enforcement of the antitrust laws in order to inhibit and perhaps to break up concentration of ownership and control in the media. It must always be remembered, however, that our objective is a multiplicity of ideas rather than a multiplicity of forums. Obviously, when media outlets have a common ownership, the existence and the exercise of independent editorial opinion in each is suspect. The chain newspaper is not only a monopoly voice in a community; very often, it is not even a community voice. The International Typographical Union has described the chain newspapers as follows:

> The chain paper, with wire services, "canned" features and editorials, and a modicum of local news, can be managed like a chain store or hotel.[18]

In 1962, 46.9 percent of the total daily circulation of American newspapers and 53.7 percent of the total circulation of Sunday newspapers was held by chains.[19] The big twelve newspaper chains are Hearst, Chicago Tribune, Scripps-Howard, Newhouse, Knight, Cowles, Ridder, Cox, Gannett, Chandler (*Times-Mirror*), Ochs Estate (*New York Times*) and Triangle. The cir-

337

culation of these twelve chains amounted to 20.4 million or 34.4 percent of the circulation of all daily newspapers. Sunday circulation of the Big Twelve totaled 21.8 million, or 45.2 percent of all Sunday circulation.[20]

From all these figures, the International Typographical Union concluded that "the free and independent press guaranteed by the First Amendment stands to be forfeited to monopolists and absentee owners unless remedial measures are taken." It is difficult to understate the monopolistic character of the American press. As of 1962 the following states were without any competitive dailies: Alabama, Delaware, Georgia, Idaho, Kansas, Louisiana, Maine, Minnesota, Montana, Nebraska, New Hampshire, New Mexico, North Carolina, North Dakota, Oklahoma, Rhode Island, South Carolina, Utah, Virginia, West Virginia, and Wyoming.

The possibility of new entrants into the daily newspaper business are probably more hypothetical than real. Concentration of ownership in the media generally, and a monopoly newspaper press specifically, are the reality now and in the foreseeable future. Take a single statistic: in 1968, out of more than 1500 cities with daily newspapers, only 45 had competitive newspapers.[21] Diversity must be accomplished within the existing outlets. How can that diversity be obtained? Direct entry into the press is what is necessary. But such entry is difficult. The pressure for access therefore manifests itself in and outside the media.

These facts are not lost on the Supreme Court. At the end of its opinion in Red Lion, the Court said that an issue it put aside for future resolution was the First Amendment significance of "legislation directly or indirectly multiplying the voices and views presented to the public through time sharing, fairness doctrines, or other devices which limit or dissipate the power of those who sit astride the channels of communication with the general public." Perhaps the way the court phrases the issue indi-

338

cates the answer the Court would give. Indeed, the Court followed up its remarks on this point by referring to newspaper cases where the invocation of antitrust principles was thought compatible with freedom of the press because antitrust enforcement inhibited concentration of ownership and concentration of opinion.

As the law presently stands, broadcasters face an obligation to provide an opportunity for reply and to some extent for debate, but they have no general duty to provide access to broadcasting. Newspapers are under no obligation to provide space for reply, debate, or access. Indeed in all but two American jurisdictions, publishers have no obligation to provide a right of reply even when they libel someone. The libel area highlights the contrast between the press situation and broadcasting. In 1964 the Supreme Court radically revised the law of libel.[22] The theory was that the freer newspapers were to criticize and discuss public men and public issues, the more "robust and wide-open" debate would be.

In even a primitive understanding of debate, there must be an assumption that if a newspaper says X, then someone must have an opportunity to say anti-X. Yet that is not what happens now when a newspaper libels a public person. The newspaper may attack public officials and private persons with public reputations with less fear of being subject to a heavy judgment than ever before. If any provision for reply is given by the newspapers to the victims of their attacks, it is entirely voluntary. Is that debate?

The paradox is that the Supreme Court in 1969[23] required debate and reply in broadcasting and in 1964[24] entrenched the prevailing lack of legal or social responsibility on the part of the press. The cases can be differentiated. In the broadcasting case, Congress by law had required fairness to include a right of reply to personal attacks. Therefore the Supreme Court had only to decide whether such an interpretation was consistent with freedom of the press. Their enormous contribution was that they did. In fact, they went further and indicated that legal mechanisms for dialogue implemented First Amendment values in a medium where access was limited economically and technologically. The newspaper libel case in 1964 between an Alabama public official and the *New York Times* did not present a direct question of the validity of right of access legislation. But neither was the Court presented with any statute which said that where public men are attacked by newspapers, the standard for recovery should be the heavy one of having to show that the particular libel was published in malice, i.e. with reckless disregard of the truth or falsity of what was said. Yet the Court carved out such a rule by interpreting the First Amendment as demanding the criticism of government and the encouragement of debate on public matters.

There is no objection to giving new perspectives to basic constitutional guarantees to give them continuing contemporary force and vitality, but the price of a new constitutional immunity ought to be some corresponding constitutional obligation. If libel law is to be softened to encourage newspapers to be more adventurous and daring on matters of public concern, then surely the same First Amendment which authorized the Court to change the law of libel should have been used to provide at least some new opportunities for participation in the press by the newspaper public. Where a public man as a result of the new rule has lost his right to a judgment for money damages against a newspaper, the newspaper should have to provide him with space for a right of reply. Such a rule is minimum decency.

On the access front, the Court in *New York Times v. Sullivan* missed a splendid opportunity to declare a constitutional duty to publish editorial advertisements. Just the announcement of such an obligation as a constitutional duty of publishers and a constitutional right of readers would have greatly enhanced the powers of communication of all groups in one-newspaper communities.

When the Supreme Court's broadcast access case and its newspaper libel case are put beside each other, is not the position of the press anomalous? Since there are far more broadcast outlets in the United States than daily newspapers, the argument is ludicrous that affirmative legal obligations must be imposed on broadcasting because it is a limited access medium. In the United States all the important media are limited access media.

There are now signs of change which suggest that the rights of the readership to the press which serves them will eventually be recognized. In June 1971 the Supreme Court, in a decision which extended the considerable immunity from libel which newspapers already enjoy to all situations where "the utterance involved concerns a matter of public or general interest," explicitly recognized for the first time the problem of access to the media.[25] Furthermore, the Court's remarks unquestionably revealed sympathy for the proposition that as a First Amendment matter there is a right of access to the press.

The context was a case involving a broadcaster who was sued for libel and who was given the benefit of the rule that to collect for libel a public figure must prove "actual malice," i.e. reckless disregard for the truth or falsity of what was said.

The argument was pressed at the Supreme Court bar by Ramsey Clark that the rule of relative libel immunity for the media in defamation cases would leave private individuals helpless. Those individuals having no access to the media could be pitilessly defamed and the newspapers would be immune to any legal responsibility to the subject of their attacks. Media publicity might destroy someone and then there would be no recourse. At this point, the Court for the first time saw the connection between relieving newspapers from fear of libel suits and the need for access to the press.

If the states were concerned about securing redress for private individuals wounded by media publicity, said the Court, a remedy should be sought in arming them "with the ability to respond, rather than in stifling public discussion of matters of public concern." Debate, not damages, was the answer. In a footnote Justice Brennan developed this idea. I quote it in full because it may well be a guide to the future of access to the press:

> One writer in arguing that the First Amendment itself should be read to guarantee a right of access to the media not limited to a right to respond to defamatory falsehoods, has suggested several ways the laws might encourage public discussion. Barron, Access to the Press—A New First Amendment Right, 80 Harv. L. Rev. 1641, 1666–1678 (1967). It is important to recognize that the private individual often desires press exposure either for himself, his ideas, or his causes. Constitutional adjudication must take into account the individual's interest in access to the press as well as the individual's interest in preserving his reputation, even though libel actions by their nature encourage a narrow view of the individual's interest since they focus only on situations where the individual has been harmed by undesired press attention. A constitutional rule that deters the press from covering the ideas or activities of the private individual thus conceives the individual's interests too narrowly.

A Supreme Court exhortation that judges should take into account the individual's interest in access to the press is encouraging for the future. If constitutional adjudication can provide for access to the press, then the Court must think that the state action problems which the lower federal courts and the newspaper industry have made so much of are not insurmountable. The

Court's remarks about access to the press appear at least to imply that a right of access to the press can be fashioned by the courts as a matter of First Amendment interpretation.

Attention is at last being given to the idea that the First Amendment grants protection to others in the opinion-making process besides those who own the media of communication.

NOTES

1. AP, *Washington Post*, October 3, 1971.
2. Florida Statutes 104.38, F.S.A.
3. Barron, "Access to the Press—A New First Amendment Right," 80 *Harvard Law Review* 1641 (1967).
4. *New York Times Co. v. Sullivan*, 376 U.S. 254 (1964).
5. *Rosenbloom v. Metromedia*, 403 U.S. 29 (1971).
6. *Valentine v. Chrestensen*, 316 U.S. 52 (1942).
7. *Business Executives' Move for Vietnam Peace v. FCC*, 450 F.2d 642 (D.C. Cir. 1971). But cf. *David Green v. FCC*, 447 F.2d 323 (D.C. Cir. 1971).
8. 47 U.S.C. §315.
9. *Farmers Educational and Cooperative Union v. WDAY, Inc.*, 360 U.S. 525 (1959).
10. 376 U.S. 254 (1964).

Chapter 2

1. *Chicago Joint Board, Amalgamated Clothing Workers v. Chicago Tribune Co.*, 307 F. Supp. 422 (N.D. Ill. 1969).
2. *Chicago Joint Board, Amalgamated Clothing Workers v. Chicago Tribune*, 435 F.2d 470 (2d Cir. 1970), *cert. den.* 402 U.S. 973 (1971).
3. *Id.*
4. Cf. *Rosenbloom v. Metromedia*, 403 U.S. 29 (1971).
5. Cranberg, "Is Right of Access Coming?" *Saturday Review*, August 8, 1970.
6. Newspaper Preservation Act, Public Law 91-353, 91st Congress 2d Sess., S. 1520, July 24, 1970.

7. See generally Barnett, "Cable Television and Media Concentration, Part I: Control of Cable Systems by Local Broadcasters," 22 *Stanford Law Review* 221 (1970).
8. *Washington Post,* July 13, 1970.
9. See the Newspaper Preservation Act, Public Law 91-353, 91st Cong., 2d Sess., S.1520, July 24, 1970.
10. *Lee v. Board of Regents,* 306 F. Supp. 1097 (W.D. Wis. 1969), *aff'd Lee v. Board of Regents,* 441 F. 2d 1257 (7th Cir. 1971).
11. 22 Ohio N.P. (n.s.) 225, 31 Ohio Dec. 54 (C.P. 1919).
12. *Bloss v. Federated Publications,* 380 Mich. 485, 157 N.W. 2d. 241 (1968).

Chapter 3

1. *Lee v. Board of Regents,* 306 F. Supp. 1097 (W.D. Wis. 1969).
2. *Lee v. Board of Regents,* 441 F.2d 1237 (7th Cir. 1971).
3. *Kissinger v. New York City Transit Authority,* 274 F. Supp. 438 (S.D.N.Y. 1967).
4. *Antonelli v. Hammond,* 308 F. Supp. 1329 (D. Mass. 1970).
5. *Zucker v. Panitz,* 299 F. Supp. 102 (S.D.N.Y. 1969).
6. *Wirta v. Alameda—Contra Costa Transit Dist.,* 68 Cal. 2d 51, 434 P. 2d 982, 64 Cal. Rptr. 430 (1967).
7. *Zucker v. Panitz,* 299 F. Supp. 102 at 105 fn. 4 (S.D.N.Y. 1969).

Chapter 4

1. *Schwartz v. Schuker,* 298 F. Supp. 238 at 242 (E.D.N.Y. 1969).
2. *Baker v. Downey City Board of Education,* 307 F. Supp. 517 (C.D. Calif. 1969).
3. *Tinker v. Des Moines Independent Community School District,* 393 U.S. 503 (1969).
4. *Antonelli v. Hammond,* 308 F. Supp. 1329 (D. Mass. 1970).
5. 42 U.S.C. §1983 (1964).

Chapter 5

1. D. L. Grey and T. R. Brown, "Letters to the Editor: Hazy Reflections of Public Opinion," 47 *Journalism Quarterly* 450 (1970).
2. *Wall v. World Publishing Co.*, 263 P. 2d 1010 (Okla. 1953).
3. *Id.*
4. Clifton Daniel, Address, Special Committee, Mass Media—Rights of Access and Reply, Section of Individual Rights and Responsibilities, Monograph No. 3, August 1969, edited proceedings, p. 7.
5. *Chicago Joint Board, Amalgamated Clothing Workers of America v. Chicago Tribune Co.*, 307 F. Supp. 422 (N.D. Ill. 1969).
6. *Rosenbloom v. Metromedia*, 403 U.S. 29 (1971).
7. A. Kent McDougall, *The Wall Street Journal*, Monday, August 31, 1970.
8. *New York Times*, Wednesday, July 29, 1970.
9. Transcript, *News In Perspective*—"The Right of Reply," National Educational Television, Wednesday, September 17, 1969 at 9:00 p.m. over WNDT/Channel 13, New York City.
10. *Lord v. Winchester*, 346 Mass. 764, 190 N.E. 2d 875 (1963). *Appeal dismissed and cert. denied*, 376 U.S. 221 (1964).

Chapter 6

1. Clifton Daniel, "Right of Access to Mass Media—Government Obligation to Enforce First Amendment?", 48 *Texas Law Review* 783 at 778 (1970).
2. Newspaper Preservation Act, Public Law 91-353, 91st Cong. 2d Sess., S. 1520, July 24, 1970.
3. AP, Chicago, November 7, 1970.
4. Memorandum of Leonard Iaquinta on Fourth of July ad in the *Kenosha News*, July 1, 1970.
5. A bill to amend section 4 of the Newspaper Preservation Act to require newspapers which are parties to joint operating arrangements

to provide a balanced and substantially complete presentation of issues of public importance, H.R. 18928, August 12, 1970.
6. A bill to require certain newspapers to provide a balanced and substantially complete presentation of issues of public importance, H.R. 18927, August 12, 1970.
7. See *Congressional Record*, August 12, 1970, H 8187. See also *Congressional Record*, July 30, 1970, H 7483 reprinting Straus Editor's Report, August 9, 1969.
8. *Congressional Record*, July 30, 1970, H.R. 7477.
9. *Roth v. United States*, 354 U.S. 476 at 497 (1957).

Chapter 7

1. Gilbert Granberg, "Is Right of Access Coming?" *Saturday Review*, August 8, 1970.
2. *Evans v. Newton*, 382 U.S. 296 (1966). Cf. *Evans v. Abney*, 396 U.S. 435 (1970).
3. *Chicago Joint Board, Amalgamated Clothing Workers v. Chicago Tribune Co.*, 307 F. Supp. 422 (N.D. Ill. 1969).
4. *Gitlow v. New York*, 268 U.S. 652 (1925).
5. *Katzenbach v. Morgan*, 384 U.S. 641 (1966).
6. *Ex Parte Virginia*, 100 U.S. 339 (1880).
7. Commissioner Cox, "Mass Media—Rights of Access and Reply," Section of Individual Rights and Responsibilities, American Bar Association, 3d Annual Meeting of the Section, August 1969, p. 6.
8. Reich, "Reflections: The Greening of America," *The New Yorker*, September 26, 1970.
9. Friedrich, *Transcendent Justice: The Religious Dimension of Constitutionalism*, 109 (1964).
10. Berle, "Constitutional Limitations on Corporate Activity—Protection of Personal Rights From Invasion Through Economic Power," 100 *University of Pennsylvania Law Review* 933 (1952).
11. See *Civil Rights Cases*, 109 U.S. 3 (1883).
12. R.H.S. Crossman, *The Politics of Socialism* 44 (1965).
13. I. Deutscher, *The Unfinished Revolution* (1967).

Chapter 8

1. Marcuse, "Repressive Tolerance" in Wolff, Moore, and Marcuse, *A Critique of Pure Tolerance* 110 (1965).
2. Mill, "Of Liberty of Thought and Discussion," in *Man and the State: The Political Philosophers* 150 (Commons and Linscott ed.) 1947.
3. 74 Stat. 554 (1960).
4. 395 U.S. 367 (1969).
5. Edith Efron has since tried to document this viewpoint. See Efron, *The News Twisters* (1971).
6. Speech, Des Moines, Iowa, prepared text reprinted in *Washington Post*, November 14, 1969, A23.
7. Speech, Houston, Texas, prepared text reprinted in *Washington Post*, May 23, 1970, A14.
8. Dr. Frank Stanton, "Problems of the Broadcast Journalist," International Conference, Radio-Television News Directors Association, September 24, 1969.
9. See Ellul, *Propaganda* 254 (1963).
10. J. Hohenberg, *The News Media: A Journalist Looks at His Profession* 106 (1968).
11. Barron, "Access—The Only Choice for the Media?" 48 *Texas Law Review* 766 (1970).
12. Clifton Daniel, "Right of Access to Mass Media—Government Obligation to Enforce First Amendment?" 48 *Texas Law Review* 783 (1970).

Chapter 9

1. Quoted in *Wolin v. Port of New York Authority*, 392 F 2d. 83 at 86 (2d Cir. 1968); *cert. den.* 393 U.S. 940 (1968).
2. *Wolin v. Port of New York Authority*, 268 F. Supp. 855 (S.D.N.Y. 1967).
3. *Wolin v. Port of New York Authority*, 392 F. 2d 83 at 90 (2d Cir. 1968).
4. *Marsh v. State of Alabama*, 326 U.S. 501 at 506 (1946).
5. *In re Hoffman*, 67 Cal. 2d 845, 64 Cal. Rptr. 97, 434 P. 353 at 359 (1967).

6. *Amalgamated Food Employees v. Logan Valley Plaza, Inc.*, 391 U.S. 308 (1968).
7. *Tanner v. Lloyd Corp.*, 308 F. Supp. 128 (D. Ore. 1970).
8. *Tanner v. Lloyd Corp.*, 446 F.2d 545 (9th Cir. 1971).
9. *Lloyd Corp. v. Tanner*, 92 S.Ct. 2219 (1972).
10. *Rowan v. United States Post Office Department*, 397 U.S. 728 (1970).
11. Address, Meeting on Mass Media, Trade Regulation Roundtable, American Association of Law Schools, San Francisco, December 29, 1969.
12. *Kissinger v. New York City Transit Authority*, 274 F. Supp. 438 (S.D.N.Y. 1967).
13. *Adderley v. Florida*, 385 U.S. 39 (1966).

Chapter 10

1. *United States v. O'Brien*, 391 U.S. 367 (1968).
2. These figures indicating the kind of media access Kiger's crime obtained are based on the appellate brief of Marvin Karpatkin and Alan H. Levine filed on behalf of Kiger. Brief for Defendant–Appellate, *United States v. Kiger*, 421 F. 2d 1396 (2d Cir. 1970).
3. *United States v. Kiger*, 297 F. Supp. 339 (S.D.N.Y. 1969).
4. *United States v. Kiger*, 421 F. 2d 1396 (2d Cir. 1970), *cert. den* 398 U.S. 904 (1970).
5. *Washington Post*, May 23, 1970.
6. *United States v. Spock*, 416 F. 2d. 165 (1st Cir. 1969).
7. *Whitney v. California*, 274 U.S. 357 at 375 (1927).

Chapter 11

1. *KFKB Broadcasting Association v. FRC*, 47 F 2d 670 (D.C. Cir. 1931).
2. 47 U.S.C. §315 (1964).
3. *McCarthy v. FCC*, 390 F. 2d 471 (D.C. Cir. 1968)
4. See *Report on Editorializing by Broadcast Licensees*, 13 F.C.C. 1246 (1949).
5. *Broadcasting*, November 16, 1970.

Chapter 12

1. *Mayflower Broadcasting Corp. v. The Yankee Network*, 8 FCC 333 (1940).
2. 13 FCC 1246 (1949).
3. *In the Matter of WHDH, Inc.*, 16 FCC 2d 1 (1969).
4. *WHDH v. FCC*, 444 F. 2d 841 (D.C. Cir. 1970), *cert. den.* 402 U.S. 1007 (1971).
5. Barron, "The Federal Communications Commission's Fairness Doctrine: An Evaluation," 30 *George Washington Law Review* 1 at 40 (1961).
6. "The Fairness Doctrine and Related Issues," Report of the Special Subcommittee on Investigations, 91st Cong., H.R. No. 91-257 p. 30, May 1969.
7. *Red Lion Broadcasting Co., Inc. v. FCC*, 395 U.S. 367 (1969).
8. *Broadcasting*, November 16, 1970.

Chapter 13

1. *Red Lion Broadcasting Co. v. FCC*, 381 F. 2d 908 (D.C. Cir. 1967).
2. *Radio Television News Directors Association v. United States*, 400 F. 2d 1002 (7th. Cir. 1968).
3. *Red Lion Broadcasting Co. Inc. v. Federal Communications Commission; United States v. Radio Television News Directors Association*, 395 U.S. 367 (1969).
4. See Barron, "The Meaning and Future of Red Lion," 3 *Educational Broadcasting Review* 9 (1969).
5. *National Broadcasting Co. v. United States*, 319 U.S. 190 (1943).

Chapter 14

1. *Sam Morris*, 11 FCC 197 (1946).
2. See *WCBS-TV*, 8 FCC 2d 381 (1967); aff'd *WCBS-TV, Applicability of the Fairness Doctrine to Cigarette Advertising*, 9 FCC 2d 921 (1967).
3. Public Law 91-222, 91st Cong., H.R. 6543.

4. *Banzhaf v. FCC*, 405 F. 2d 1082 at 1102–1103 (D.C. Cir. 1968), cert. den., *Sub. Nom. Tobacco Institute, Inc. v. FCC*, 396 U.S. 842 (1969).
5. *Retail Store Employees Union v. FCC*, 436 F. 2d 248 (D.C. Cir. 1970).
6. Richard W. Jencks, "Should the Press Have a Government Referee?," Proceedings, American Bar Association, Section of Individual Rights and Responsibilities, Monograph No. 3, 3d Annual Meeting of the Section, August 1969.
7. Proceedings, American Bar Association, Section of Individual Rights and Responsibilities, Monograph No. 3, 3d Annual Meeting of the Section, August 1969.
8. Commissioner Kenneth Cox, Proceedings, American Bar Association, Section of Individual Rights and Responsibilities, Monograph No. 3, 3d Annual Meeting of the Section, August 1969.
9. 13 FCC 1246 (1949).

Chapter 15

1. See *In re Complaints of the Committee for the Fair Broadcasting of Controversial Issues*, 25 FCC 2d 283 (1970).
2. *Id.*
3. Joint Resolution to Amend the Communications Act of 1934 in order to require licensees under such Act to provide time, as a public service, to authorized representatives of the Senate and the House of Representatives, S.J. Res. 209, 91st Cong., 2d Sess.
4. Statement by Senator J. W. Fulbright, Chairman, Committee on Foreign Relations, United States Senate, before the Communications Subcommittee of the Committee on Commerce, *Equal Time for Congress*, issued August 4, 1970.
5. *Id.*
6. *In re Democratic National Committee, Washington, D.C., Request for Declaratory Ruling Concerning Access to Time on Broadcast Stations*, 25 FCC 2d 216 (1970).
7. *Id.*
8. Pete Seeger, "The Air Belongs to Everyone," *Harvard Alumni Bulletin* 57, April 28, 1969.
9. *In re Democratic National Committee, Washington, D.C., Re-*

quest for Declaratory Ruling Concerning Access to Time on Broadcast Stations, 25 FCC 2d 216 (1970).

10. *Communications Control,* ed. Phelan, Ong, "The Polemic and the Word," 156 (1969).

11. *Business Executives' Move for Vietnam Peace v. Federal Communications Commission; Democratic National Committee v. Federal Communications Commission,* 450 F. 2d 642 (D.C. Cir. 1971). The Supreme Court has agreed to review the decision. *Cert. granted, Columbia Broadcasting System v. Democratic National Committee, Federal Communications Commission v. Business Executives' Move for Vietnam Peace et al.,* 405 U.S. 953 (1972).

12. *David Green v. FCC; G.I. Association, Stephen P. Pizzo v. FCC,* 447 F. 2d 323 (D.C. Cir. 1971). See also *Neckritz v. FCC,* 446 F. 2d 501 (9th Cir. 1971).

13. *In re Wilderness Society and Friends of the Earth,* 30 F.C.C. 2d 643 (1971).

14. *Friends of the Earth v. FCC,* 449 F. 2d 1164 (D.C. Cir. 1971).

15. *In the Matter of the Handling of Public Issues Under the Fairness Doctrine And the Public Interest Standards of the Communications Act,* 30 FCC 2d 26 (1971).

16. "TV Network Prime Time Program Ownership and Programming Restricted by FCC," FCC Press Release, Report No. 5979, May 7, 1970.

17. *Broadcasting,* November 30, 1970.

18. *Mt. Mansfield Television Inc. v. FCC,* 442 F. 2d 470 (2d Cir. 1971).

Chapter 16

1. *Office of Communication of the United Church of Christ v. FCC,* 359 F. 2d 994 (D.C. Cir. 1966).

Chapter 17

1. *Brandywine Main-Line Radio Company,* 24 FCC 2d 18 (1970). The station has appealed the FCC's decision. *Brandywine-Main Line Radio Inc. v. FCC,* Civil Action No. 71-1181, U.S. Court of Appeals for the District of Columbia.

Chapter 18

1. 52 F. Supp. 362 (S.D.N.Y. 1943).
2. *Associated Press v. U.S.*, 326 U.S. 1 (1945).
3. 16 FCC 2d 1(1969), *aff'd*, 444 F. 2d 841 (D.C. Cir. 1970).
4. *WHDH, Inc.*, 16 FCC 2d 1 (1969).
5. *WHDH v. FCC*, 444 F. 2d 841 (D.C. Cir. 1970).
6. Pastore Bill, S. 2004, 91st Cong., 1st Sess.
7. Dissent of Nicholas Johnson, *Policy Statement on Comparative Hearings Involving Regular Renewal Applicants, In re Petititions filed by BEST, CCC, and Others for Rule Making to Clarify Standards In All Comparative Broadcast Proceedings*, 24 FCC 2d 383 (1970).
8. *Policy Statement on Comparative Hearings Involving Regular Renewal Applicants*, 22 FCC 2d 424 (1970).
9. *Policy Statement on Comparative Hearings Involving Regular Renewal Applicants, In re Petitions filed by BEST, CCC, and Others For Rule Making to Clarify Standards In All Comparative Broadcast Proceedings*, 24 FCC 2d 383 (1970).
10. Goldin, "Spare the Golden Goose—The Aftermath of WHDH in FCC License Renewal Policy," 83 Harvard Law Review 1014 (1970).
11. See *Broadcasting*, February 8, 1971.
12. *Citizens Communication Center v. FCC*, 447 F. 2d 1201 (D.C. Cir. 1971).
13. *Ashbacker Radio Corporation v. FCC*, 326 U.S. 327 (1945).
14. 47 U.S.C. §309(e).
15. Federal Communications Act of 1934, 47 U.S.C. §307(d).
16. Cohn, "Should the FCC Reward Stations That Do A Good Job?", *Saturday Review*, August 14, 1971.
17. *In the Matter of Formulation of Policies Relating to the Broadcast Renewal Applicant, Stemming from the Comparative Hearing Process*, 27 FCC 2d 580 (1971).
18. Concurring Statement of Commissioner Nicholas Johnson, *In the Matter of Formulation of Policies Relating to the Broadcast Renewal Applicant, Stemming from the Comparative Hearing Process*, 27 FCC 2d 580 (1971).
19. *In the Matter of Formulation of Policies Relating to the Broadcast*

Renewal Applicant, Stemming from the Comparative Hearing Process, 27 FCC 2d 580 (1971).

20. Westen's Stern Community Law Firm helped in the preparation of the briefs for the co-plaintiff, Business Executives' Move for Vietnam Peace, in the Democratic National Committee case.

Chapter 19

1. *Hale v. FCC,* 425 F. 2d 556 (D.C. Cir. 1970).
2. *Applicability of the Fairness Doctrine in the Handling of Controversial Issues of Public Importance,* 29 Fed. Reg. 10415, 10416 (1964). Quoted in *Hale v. FCC,* 425 F. 2d 556 (D.C. Cir. 1970).
3. *Washington Post,* July 4, 1970.
4. *Broadcasting,* June 30, 1969.

Chapter 20

1. *Broadcasting,* January 25, 1971.
2. *Broadcasting,* January 11, 1971.
3. "A Progress Report," Citizens Communications Center, p. 4, March 15, 1970.
4. "A Progress Report," Citizens Communications Center, p. 7, March 15, 1970.
5. *Broadcasting,* November 2, 1970.
6. *Washington Post,* February 16, 1971.
7. *Washington Post,* October 31, 1970.
8. *Ibid.*
9. *The Citizens Committee to Preserve the Present Programming of the 'Voice of The Arts' in Atlanta on WGKA-FM and AM v. FCC,* 436 F. 2d 263 (D.C. Cir. 1970).
10. *Washington Post,* November 13, 1970.
11. *Washington Post,* July 4, 1970.
12. Letter to *New York Times,* Sunday, May 24, 1970.
13. *In re Application of The Evening Star Broadcasting Company,* 27 FCC 2d 316 (1971), *aff'd subnom. Stone v. FCC,* Action No. 71-1166, U.S. Court of Appeals for the District of Columbia, June 30, 1972, *reh. den.* September 1, 1972.

14. *Broadcasting*, February 8, 1971.
15. *Ashbacker Radio Corp. v. FCC*, 326 U.S. 327 (1945).
16. *Citizens Communications Center v. FCC, Hampton Roads Television Corporation v. FCC*, 447 F. 2d 1201 (D.C. Cir. 1971).
17. *In the Matter of Summary Decision Procedures*, 27 FCC 2d 426 (1971).
18. Gellhorn and Robinson, "Summary Judgment In Administrative Adjudication," 84 *Harvard Law Review* 612 (1971).

Chapter 21

1. Nicholas Johnson, "The Careening of America or How to Talk Back to Your Corporate State," Poynter Fellow Lecture, Yale University, March 8, 1971, FCC Public Notice 64807.
2. *Broadcasting*, April 12, 1971.
3. *First Report and Order*, 20 FCC 2d 201 (October 24, 1969).
4. *Fortnightly Corporation v. United Artists Television, Inc.*, 392 U.S. 390 (1968).
5. Letter to Senator Pastore from Clay T. Whitehead, Office of Telecommunications Policy, Executive Office of the President, November 15, 1971.
6. FCC, *Letter of Intent*, 31 FCC 2d 115 (1971).
7. *Broadcasting*, November 2, 1970.
8. *Memorandum and Order, Petitions for Reconsideration of First Report and Order on CATV*, 23 FCC 2d 825 (1970).
9. See *Petitions For Reconsideration*, 23 FCC 2d 825 (1970).
10. D. L. Maggin, "Cable TV for Middle-Size Cities?" *Christian Science Monitor*, February 5, 1971.
11. FCC, *Letter of Intent*, 31 FCC 2d 115 (1971).
12. Remarks of Theodora Sklover, "Cable Rap," Symposium on Cable, *Woodwind*, Vol. 2, No. 9.
13. *Farmers Educational and Co-operative Union of America, North Dakota Division v. WDAY, Inc.*, 360 U.S. 525 (1959).
14. *U.S. v. Southwestern Cable Co.*, 392 U.S. 157 (1968).
15. Public Notice, FCC 71–205, March 5, 1971.
16. *Broadcasting*, February 22, 1971, p. 33.
17. Bagdikian, *The Information Machines: Their Impact on Men and Media* (1971).

18. Remarks of Theodora Sklover, "Cable Rap," Symposium on Cable, *Woodwind*, Vol. 2, No. 9.
19. Roger Starr, "Consciousness III," *Commentary*, December 1970.
20. FCC, *Letter of Intent*, 31 FCC 22115 (1971).
21. *Midwest Video Corp. v. FCC*, 441 F. 2d 1322 (8th Cir. 1971). This decision was reversed. U.S. v. Midwest Video Corp., 92 S. Ct. 1860 (1972).
22. 20 FCC 2d 201 (1969).
23. See Thomas, "The Listener's Right to Hear In Broadcasting," 22 *Stanford Law Review* 863 (1970).
24. Second Report and Order in Docket 18397, 23 FCC 2d 816 (1970).
25. See Barnett, "Cable Television and Media Concentration, Part I: Control of Cable Systems by Local Broadcasters," 22 *Stanford Law Review* 221 (1970).
26. *Second Further Notice of Proposed Rule Making in Docket 18397-A*, 24 FCC 2d 580 (1970).
27. See *New York Times*, April 18, 1971.
28. FCC, *Letter of Intent*, 31 FCC 2d 115 (1971).

Chapter 22

1. 395 U.S. 367 (1969).
2. *In re WUHY-FM*, 24 F.C.C. 2d 408 (1970).
3. *Jack Straw Memorial Foundation*, 21 FCC 2d 833 (1970).
4. *In the Matter of the Renewal of Station KRAB-FM*, Dissenting statement of Commissioner Nicholas Johnson, 21 F.C.C. 2d 833 (1970).
5. *In re Application of the Jack Straw Memorial Foundation For Renewal of the license of KRAB-FM*, Initial Decision of the Hearing Examiner, 29 F.C.C. 2d 334 (1971).
6. 47 U.S.C. §326.
7. 18 U.S.C. §1464.
8. 354 U.S. 476 (1957).
9. *A Book Named 'John Cleland's Memoirs of a Woman of Pleasure' v. Attorney General of Massachusetts*, 383 U.S. 413 (1966).
10. *In re Application of the Jack Straw Memorial Foundation for Renewal of the license of KRAB-FM*, Initial Decision of the Hearing Examiner, 29 F.C.C. 2d 334 (1971).

11. *In re WUHY-FM*, 24 F.C.C. 2d 408 (1970).
12. See *Report of the Commission on Obscenity and Pornography* (1970).
13. Johnson, book review, 68 *Michigan Law Review* 1456 (1970).
14. *Rowan v. United States Post Office Department*, 397 U.S. 728 (1970).
15. *Ginsberg v. New York*, 390 U.S. 629 (1968).
16. Lockhart and McClure, "Censorship of Obscenity: The Developing Constitutional Standards," 45 Minn. L. Rev. 5 (1960) quoted in *Ginsberg v. New York*, 390 U.S. 629 (1968).
17. *Regina v. Hicklin*, (1868) L.R.3 Q.B. 360. Cf. *Roth v. United States*, 354 U.S. 476 (1957).
18. *Broadcasting*, April 26, 1971.
19. *In re Applications of Pacifica Foundation for Renewal*, 36 FCC 147 (1964).
20. *Palmetto Broadcasting Co.*, 33 FCC 250 (1962).
21. *Robinson v. FCC*, 334 F. 2d 534 (D.C. Cir. 1964).
22. R. W. Jencks, Should The Press Have a Government Referee?, Section of Individual Rights and Responsibilities. American Bar Association, Edited Proceedings, Monograph No. 3, August 1969.
23. Clifton Daniel, "Right of Access and Reply," Section of Individual Rights and Responsibilities, American Bar Association, Edited Proceedings, Monograph No. 3, August 1969.
24. *Roth v. United States*, 354 U.S. 476 (1957).
25. *Beauharnais v. Illinois*, 343 U.S. 250 (1952).
26. Pemberton, "Can the Law Provide a Remedy for Race Defamation in the United States?", 14 *New York Law Forum* 33 (1968).
27. *In re Complaint of United Federation of Teachers, New York, N.Y.*, 17 FCC 2d. 204 (1969).
28. *Anti-Defamation League of B'nai B'rith, Pacific Southwest Regional Office v. FCC*, 403 F. 2d. 169 (D. C. Cir. 1968).
29. Justice Brandeis, concurring, in *Whitney v. California*, 274 U.S. 357 (1927).
30. Justice Douglas for the Supreme Court in *Terminiello v. Chicago*, 337 U.S. 1 (1949).

Chapter 23

1. Bagdikian, "Right of Access: A Modest Proposal," 8 *Columbia Journalism Review*, 10 (1969).
2. *Editor & Publisher*, December 16, 1967.
3. Freedom of Information Center Report No. 005, School of Journalism, University of Missouri at Columbia, October 1967.
4. Aronson, *The Press and the Cold War* (1970).
5. Reston, *The Artillery of the Press* (1967).
6. *Saturday Review*, September 27, 1969.

Chapter 24

1. *Gitlow v. New York*, 268 U.S. 652 (1925).
2. *Abrams v. United States*, 250 U.S. 616 (1919).
3. *Wall Street Journal*, December 10, 1970.
4. *Cook v. The Advertiser Company*, 323 F. Supp. 1212 (M.D. Ala. 1970).
5. *Chicago Joint Board, Amalgamated Clothing Workers v. Chicago Tribune*, 435 F. 2d 470 (2d Cir. 1970).
6. Newspaper Preservation Act of 1970, Public Law 91-353, 91st Cong. 2d Sess., S. 1520, July 24, 1970.
7. See *Business Executives' Move For Vietnam Peace v. FCC, Democratic National Committee v. FCC*, 450 F. 2d 642 (D.C. Cir. 1971) *Cert. granted, Columbia Broadcasting System, Inc. v. Democratic National Committee; FCC v. Business Executives' Move For Vietnam Peace*, 405 U.S. 953 (1972).
8. *Associates & Aldrich Co., Inc. v. Times Mirror Co.*, 440 F. 2d 133 (9th Cir. 1971).
9. *Chicago Joint Board, Amalgamated Clothing Workers v. Chicago Tribune Co.*, 435 F. 2d 470 (2d Cir. 1970).
10. *Shelley v. Kraemer*, 334 U.S. 1 (1948).
11. *Broadcasting*, August 9, 1971.
12. Ellul, *Propaganda* (1966).
13. *In the Matter of the Handling of Public Issues Under the Fairness Doctrine and the Public Interest Standards of the Communications Act*, 30 F.C.C. 2d 26 (1971).

14. *Radical Lawyers Caucus v. Pool,* 324 F. Supp. 268 (W.D. Tex. 1970)
15. Bleyer, *Main Currents in American Journalism* (1926)
16. Nixon and Ward, "Trends in Newspaper Ownership and Inter-Media Competition," 38 *Journalism Quarterly,* 5 (1961).
17. The following figures were obtained from Chairman Newton Minow's statement and testimony before the House Subcommittee on Antitrust and Monopoly, Excerpts from Concentration of Ownership in the News Media, S.1312, The Failing Newspaper Act, Part V, April, 1963.
18. ITU, *Federal Responsibility for a Free and Competitive Press* (1963).
19. Raymond B. Nixon, "118 Owner Groups; 4.9 Average Holds," *Editor & Publisher,* April 21, 1962.
20. ITU, *Federal Responsibility for a Free and Competitive Press* (1963).
21. Nixon, *"Trends in U.S. Newspaper Ownership: Concentration with Competition,"* 14 *Gazette* 181 (1968).
22. *New York Times v. Sullivan,* 376 U.S. 254 (1964).
23. *Red Lion Broadcasting Co. v. FCC,* 395 U.S. 367 (1969).
24. *New York Times v. Sullivan,* 376 U.S. 254 (1964).
25. *Rosenbloom v. Metromedia,* 403 U.S. 29 (1971).

INDEX

ABC, 170
ACLU, 66, 204, 214, 321–24
Adams, Elsie B., 28–29
Adams, Justice (Mich.), 23
Administrative Conference of the
United States, 245
advertisements: Chicago unions de-
nied right to buy, 13–20, 62–64;
editorial, 7–12; judicial creation
of right of access to, 22–25;
movie theatre refused, 23–24; on
television, 150–59, 185
Agnew, Spiro, 77, 78, 85–93, 131,
168, 307
Alabama State College, 7–8
Alaska pipeline case, 183
Albee, Edward, 283
Aldrich, Bailey, 123
Altoona, Pa., Logan Valley Mall,
101–4
Amalgamated Clothing Workers of
America, 13–17, 48
American Bar Association, 66, 157
American Cancer Society, 152
American Civil Liberties Union, 66,
204, 214, 321–24
American Jewish Community, 205
American Jewish Congress, 205
American Newspaper Publishers As-
sociation, 18, 55, 260, 336
American Society of Newspaper
Editors, 66
Anti-Defamation League of B'nai
B'rith, 298–99
anti-Semitism, 293–97
Aronson, James, 312–13
Arthur D. Little Report, 192
Ashbacker case, 218, 244
Ashtabula, Ohio, case, 155–56

Atlanta, Ga., broadcasting stations,
234, 237–38
Atlanta Journal, 49
audience, search for a, 94–116

Bagdikian, Ben, 258, 304–6
Bahran, Thea, 293–94
Banzhaf case, 151–54, 184, 186
Barnett, Stephen, 18, 266–67
Barron, Jerome A.: agreement with
Agnew on media power, 92–93;
Brennan's comment on, 342;
Cranberg's comment on, 66; and
draft of access statute, 53–54;
News in Perspective debate with
media representatives, 309–14;
suggests press be subject to over-
sight, 89
Bartley, Robert T., 272
Battle Creek, Mich., *Enquirer and
News*, 23–24
Battle Creek, Mich. theatre case,
23–24, 60
Bazelon, David, 153–56, 186
Beauharnais, Joseph, 289–91
Berle, Adolph, 70
Berrigan brothers, 124
Beverly Hills, Cal., high school, 37,
39
Bill of Rights, 70, 73; *see also* First
Amendment
Black, Hugo, 209, 291
black: challenges to TV stations,
194–98; citizen group's attack on
Pastore bill, 214–18; negotiations
with stations, 231; social an-
nouncements in Montgomery,
Ala., papers, 323–24